In praise of *The 7 S...*

I work in a people business. The ... ter and confidence of our people ... every single day is what makes us s... nurture character and confidence ... bedrock you can do amazing feat... the authors, being a mix of a serving Army officer, who has wide operational experience, and a highly qualified and experienced chartered psychologist, have also captured the essential components of strategy execution and leadership in a way that is clear, concise and usable. For those wanting to learn ways to improve morale, the character of their leaders, the focus of their capability – for those who want to win – I'd say this is essential reading.

General Sir Mike Jackson, former Chief of the General Staff, the British Army GCB, CBE, DSO, ADC

The military has always watched carefully the development of management techniques in the world of business, with an eye to adapting them to their own particular needs where this makes sense. But the reverse has been much less common. And yet the military routinely operates in the most complex and dynamic situations, and has had perforce to develop effective ways of dealing with them. Business and the military are different, but neither has a monopoly on wisdom or best practice, and both can and should learn from the other. This excellent book goes a long way to redressing what has up until now been an unfortunate imbalance in the flow of ideas.

Sir Jock Stirrup, Chief of the Defence Staff ACM, GCB, AFC, ADC, Dsc, FRAeS, FCMI, RAF

British military leaders have been and still are celebrated as 'best in class'. This book brings alive the secrets of their success, capturing modern day 'Mission Analysis' in an easy-to-read and eminently transferable way. This book allows business leaders to tap into the thinking and methodologies of successful military leadership and transform the way they lead their companies.

Paul Musson, Head of Capability & Leadership Development, BAE Systems plc

The British Army is arguably one of the most enduringly successful organisations of all times. It's about time that one of its leaders teamed with an occupational psychologist to produce an informative guide on how war-winning techniques can be turned to win for us in the commercial world. There is so much in this book and there is something that everyone can think about and learn from. I recommend it to all managers and leaders who want to win in today's business world.

Steven Bird, Group HR Director for Trinity Mirror plc

We were introduced to the principles of military leadership several years ago and for the past three years our organisation has been reaping financially measurable benefits from a management development programme run at the Royal Military Academy Sandhurst that incorporates many of the operationally pragmatic secrets that armies have been honing for centuries. This highly accessible handbook links those secrets together in a coherent and cohesive way and shows how they can be applied in the complex commercial world of the twenty-first century. It should be essential reading for all those corporate business generals who are seeking to inspire their people to raise the performance bar and extract more value from their enterprises in increasingly competitive marketplaces.

Roger Nichols, former Head of HR, Group Operations, Lloyds TSB

[*The 7 Secrets of Leadership Success*] sheds light on the many myths and legends of military leadership. If you think that military leaders preside over an autocratic and inflexible culture in which personal charisma is recognised above team interests then it really is time to think again. In this book, the reader learns that military leadership is based on sound concepts and principles that, when deployed coherently, are a very potent and effective approach to delivering sustained success. The reader is guided through the key concepts and given practical examples of their deployment in a military context together with comparison examples from the business world.

Simple guidance points and questions – both aimed as a key aid to reflection – deliver the information business leaders need to challenge their own leadership approach. This makes the book an excellent text for business leaders interested in learning what a leader can do to build and deliver a successful organisation and, importantly, how they can do it.

Nic Anderson, Managing Director, CAE plc

There are Business books. There are Military books about strategy or tactics. But an easy-to-read book combining the two? This is new; this is different; this asked questions of me; this answered questions before I thought of them. If only part of it is relevant to your business and only some of the advice fits your situation (and perhaps you should then be thinking if you're in the right dimension), it is still an excellent road map through the turbulence of today's business seas.

Lord Digby Jones, former Director-General of the Confederation of British Industry and Minister of State for UK Trade & Investment

THE
7 SECRETS OF
LEADERSHIP
SUCCESS

Deborah Tom and

Major General Richard Barrons

Vermilion
LONDON

1 3 5 7 9 10 8 6 4 2

Published in 2009 by Vermilion, an imprint of Ebury Publishing
First published by Vermilion in 2006 as *The Business General*

Ebury Publishing is a Random House Group company

Copyright © Deborah Tom and Major General Richard Barrons 2006

Deborah Tom and Major General Richard Barrons have asserted their
right to be identified as the authors of this work in accordance
with the Copyright, Designs and Patents Act 1988.

The Random House Group Limited Reg. No. 954009

Addresses for companies within the Random House Group
can be found at www.rbooks.co.uk

A CIP catalogue record for this book is available from the British Library

The Random House Group Limited supports The Forest Stewardship
Council (FSC), the leading international forest certification organisation.
All our titles that are printed on Greenpeace approved FSC certified paper
carry the FSC logo. Our paper procurement policy can be found at
www.rbooks.co.uk/environment

Designed and typeset by seagulls.net

Printed in the UK by CPI Cox & Wyman, Reading, RG1 8EX

ISBN 9780091906931

Copies are available at special rates for bulk orders. Contact the sales
development team on 020 7840 8487 for more information.

To buy books by your favourite authors and register for offers, visit
www.rbooks.co.uk

If you are keenly interested in leadership and work at being a great leader, building a great organisation and developing other great leaders, we wrote this book for you.

Contents

Part One

Part Two

Acknowledgements

We would like to record our appreciation for all of those who have added to our understanding of leadership: bosses who have been good role-models; clients who do the right thing; subordinates who have had the courage to show us the way; authors who have fired us into new thinking; comedians who have given us fresh perspective; and all the many poets, musicians and artists who keep us going along the way.

Our thanks are also due to Julia Kellaway, whose careful editing helped make the book a much easier read; to Fiona MacIntyre and Robert Kirby, for believing in the concept and our ability to deliver; and to family and friends, for their unquestioning expectation that we could pull it off.

Foreword

Trafalgar, the greatest sea battle under sail was the culmination of a series of victories won by Nelson. It established the Royal Navy 'brand' as the world leader for over 100 years. The Royal Navy of that time was a devastating instrument of power leading the world in logistic supply, chart-making and survey, procurement on a vast scale (making blocks on the first ever production line), training and gunnery (better metal, better casting etc). In Deborah Tom and Richard Barrons's analysis this is the 'right team, right stuff' of their Power Pyramid. Good management by a cadre of highly experienced commanders and bureaucrats ensured this.

The magic 'Nelson touch', where management became leadership that enabled the instrument of power to win annihilating victories, formed the other two sides of Deborah and Richard's Power Pyramid. Nelson inspired in all his men the desire to emulate him whether in bravery or professional competence. He realised that 'soul matters'. He set and articulated core values. Nelson was also aware of the need for everyone in his fleet to throw their abilities behind his aim. The 'Band of Brothers' who met regularly around his dining table harnessed the thinking power of his organisation – the 'synchronised thinking'. It enabled him to fight with the minimum of orders, exercising 'mission command'. The result was total and annihilating victory.

In *The 7 Secrets of Leadership Success*, Deborah Tom and Richard Barrons have distilled the key aspects of military leadership and in a step-by-step format identify 'seven secrets' that can transform a business, whether it is a multi-national or a small family enterprise. They highlight how important, as a leader, your character, integrity, commitment, self-discipline and resilience are to the success of your enterprise. Management-speak and adherence to business principles are not enough on their own in this fiercely competitive world. People matter and all of us want to feel we are taking part in something special.

This book is full of sound guidance and allows opportunities for self-analysis as well as rigorous assessment of your organisation. It is *not* a book to skip through lightly; some of the ideas are complex and require concentration. I can see it becoming a textbook in due course.

There is no absolute formula that is guaranteed to turn you into a great leader and take your company to the top of the league. But the guidance in this book is a superb starting point.

Admiral The Lord West of Spithead GCB DSC DUniv

Preface
How This Book Came to be Written

You may wonder how this book came to be written. After all, most businesses and other organisations would not necessarily think of turning to the Armed Forces for advice on how to succeed. For one thing, most people have very little first-hand knowledge of how the Armed Forces operate and the impressions they have are often formed by exposure to war films and the stereotypical lampoonery of some television programmes. Some really dumb impressions of Armed Forces as inherently autocractic, inflexible and slow-witted persist in the public mind, even though Armed Forces in places such as the United Kingdom score consistently highly as respected institutions. The average person has no real idea about what warfare really entails, beyond the narrow snapshots television, newspapers and magazines provide. This is perhaps a mark of a relatively peaceful world. The real complexity, the risks, the scale and the human challenge of modern military operations, from warfighting to peacekeeping and nation building, remain screened from civilian life – less so perhaps for those few who have made a point of dipping into military history.

On their part, the Armed Forces are generally content to get on with their business out of the public eye and pride themselves on getting a difficult job done well with minimum fuss when the need arises and society calls. They know that what they must do necessarily makes them different from most other walks of life. The people who choose to serve must accept the restrictions as well as the advantages of *la vie militaire*. There is sometimes a public debate about why Armed Forces need to be different in some respects from the societies that maintain them; most of the time it passes unnoticed. Similarly, from behind their fences the Armed Forces sometimes wonder how their civilian counterparts achieve so much – or indeed anything at all – without a common ethos, joined-up ways of thinking and a high common standard of training, but they rightly do not feel the need to point this out. Usually military and civilian life proceed alongside each other in a state of more or less blissful mutual ignorance, until fate and history force them to collude – such as in the Second World War and now, to a lesser extent, in the conflicts in Iraq, Afghanistan, the Middle East and Africa.

This was pretty much the conversation that took place between Deborah and Richard at a school sports day in 2003. From the widely different perspectives of a Chartered Occupational Psychologist/Certified Management Consultant, providing leadership and management training to several FTSE 100 companies, and a serving Army officer just back from Afghanistan and heading for Iraq, it appeared that there was actually a great deal of common ground once you pulled back the veils and dispensed with the caricatures. Better than that, it appeared to open up a rich seam of thinking that could make a huge difference to how leaders achieve success outside the Armed Forces, if it could be put across in the right way.

So this book is the result: an attempt to examine how contemporary Armed Forces work and transfer those ideas to the widest setting possible, aimed at leaders of every kind. We don't expect every reader to either agree with all we say or find it all equally valid for them, but we would be amazed if every reader didn't find something here that made them think and something that gave them the means of doing whatever they do better in some way.

You may not like the military but that shouldn't stop you from learning from their mistakes and what they have learned to do right. They do sometimes kill but let us not forget that some of their work is about preventing genocide, training people in ethical and disciplined military tactics and creating safety for humanitarian aid workers to do their work. They have had some wonderful success at this, and some infamous failures and in the '90s were dragged through the painful process of self-examination by visionary and determined Chiefs. That reinvention makes them the most respected force in the world. As you learn about their standards, we think you will admire them; you may still not like them, but you will admire them.

Introduction

This book has been written to give leaders in many types of organisation the opportunity to draw from the experience and knowledge of the Armed Forces. You will find comprehensive thinking and methods, many of which seem innovative and yet are well proven. That they come from the Armed Forces may initially come as a surprise. We might expect contemporary businesses to have come up with successful methods because they are the ones who have to turn a profit.

In fact, if you look at what the Armed Forces of modern countries are required to do the parallels with the challenges found in business and the public sector are striking. Armed Forces are required to deliver results in war in conditions which can be filled with uncertainty, complexity and risk. The general planning his or her attack on an area infested by a fast-moving, hostile and unpredictable opposition has to deal with many of the same issues as the business person planning his or her next move in a difficult market. The Armed Forces, like business, now usually operate in an international setting, working alongside other nations' forces with similar capabilities and intentions on the basis of carefully constructed agreements. The Armed Forces have to make hard decisions about organisation, design, technology and strategy, as well as have the means to adjust complex plans even once they are under way. There must be enough resilience and confidence in the organisation to manage pressure and adversity well, making consistently good decisions in all circumsatnces. Perhaps above all, the Armed Forces have to recruit, train and keep enough high-quality people to win. So, aside from the Armed Forces' requirement to be successful in all the specific stresses and strains of battle, including inflicting and taking casualties, comparisons with business are easier to draw than may at first be apparent.

There is more to it than that. What if the way the Armed Forces achieve success amidst all the perils of the battlefield on land, sea and in the air could be applied in a probable winning formula to commercial activity? Can the insight into military methods be transferred over to business and not-for-profit organisations to lead to greater, and lasting, success?

The theme of *The 7 Secrets of Leadership Success* is that there is much to be learned from modern Armed Forces in how they deliver success and we detail how some of those ways can be applied to give new and highly effective solutions to common problems. This has not been attempted in this format before, so many of these ideas will be reaching the business arena and beyond for the first time. There is no other published information about contemporary military leadership and management in the way it can be customised to help managers and leaders in business.

The book divides into two parts, making Seven Secrets in all. The first part tackles how to take a coherent approach to assessing organisational assets and in organisational design. Each of the first three Secrets in Part One stands alone as an indispensable part of any strong organisation. But it is important to analyse them together to assess the capability in an organisation. We call it **The Power Pyramid**. It answers some tricky questions and fuzzy dilemmas that organisational leaders face:

Does everyone in your firm have clarity around the firm's purpose, objectives and how you want to behave? Have you got a common way of approaching challenges and situations in your organisation? Or does your organisation clash and rattle along on the basis of ad hoc slogans and the latest buzz words of a few? *Secret Number One – Synchronised Thinking* is about how to harness all the thinking power in your organisation. It is this common intellectual framework that will give you the solid foundation from which to question and to innovate.

Has your organisation got commitment, high morale, moral courage and strong integrity? Or does your organisation suffer from the selfish ambition and egocentricity of some of its leaders? Are your employees demoralised, disengaged? Do they trust the leaders? *Secret Number Two – Soul Matters* is about building the spirit, values and character that enable people to thrive in any organisation. Far from being soft and fluffy, the military know that the soul of an organisation is what makes it win or lose battles. Building soul is about getting the best from people at all levels of your organisation because the firm and its purpose matter to them.

Does your organisation have the right balance of structure, technology, skills and training? Or is it inefficient and uncompetitive because of lack of equipment, inadequately trained people and the wrong mix of roles and skills? *Secret Number Three – Right Team, Right Stuff* shows the importance of getting the physical aspects of an organisation in balance and stresses how all leaders must involve themselves in this and drive it, even if they are not specialists in technology, training or logistics.

Do you have a coherent strategic approach to building your organisation? Or do functions and units run pretty independently? *Part Two – Into Action* concentrates on applying capability in a hard and fast-moving world. Every leader knows that assembling the best team possible is just the beginning; the bigger test is likely to come in making this team deliver the results it is capable of.

Are you smart about knowing where to spend your energies and knowing which opportunities to go after? Or are opportunities grasped at random and doggedly pursued at almost any cost? *Secret Number Four – Dynamic Manoeuvre* transfers the highly successful military philosophy of 'manoeuvre warfare' to business. It means finding the smartest, fastest way to win at least cost. It means focusing on opportunities and finding unorthodox ways of exploiting them. It is about being flexible and creative, not just battering your organisation to a standstill against the toughest face of your competition.

How well is delegation and empowerment done in your organisation? Is it second nature, used to the full to maximise talent at all levels – or is everything done without much thought or by detailed instruction from the top, with too much of the initiative and autonomy held by centralised control? *Secret Number Five – Mission Management* applies the military technique of Mission Command, offering a comprehensive and tested way of creating wise delegation and genuine empowerment. Used in conjunction with Dynamic Manoeuvre the results can be spectacular.

How well is the activity of your organisation orchestrated? Are the different parts in tune and in time? Is there a well-thought-through strategy and plan that drives all actions and decisions, or is life more or less taken on the chin? *Secret Number Six – Command the Campaign* debunks strategy and shows how the Armed Forces run campaigns that synchronises complex activities – and how this can be used in your business. It is about finding that mix of art and science that successful leadership in a dynamic environment requires.

How good are you at thinking through what needs to be done when under pressure, at reacting to the unexpected and at seizing fleeting opportunities? The final section, *Secret Number Seven – Ride the Tiger* shows how a structured and intuitive approach can co-exist. It is used by the Armed Forces to examine a problem and has been translated to be used successfully in any setting. It concludes by looking at the specific aspects of leadership that make a 'Business General'.

This book contains a wealth of information that will be useful to leaders in any organisation, illustrated where appropriate with both examples from military history (including the present day) and business. It has been written with leadership practitioners in mind, rather than as a contribution to purely academic or historical debate. To make the content easier to apply in a practical setting, three devices have been used to guide your thoughts about your own circumstances:

- In Part One, there are '**Traffic Light Assessment**' tick lists to guide your analysis of where your organisation now stands.

- Throughout the book there are 'pauses' entitled **'Commander's Comfy Chair'** (the metaphor is of a military commander taking time out in the heat of battle to take stock and make decisions). You are invited to stop and think about the material using the questions offered and consider how the issues and methods presented square with you.
- In addition throughout the book there are sections called **'Build Your Armoury'**, which are sets of 'tools' to help you apply the content of the book. There are, for example, structured check-lists that will guide the introduction of Business General ideas into your own field.

To make application easier, the content of the Commander's Comfy Chair and Build Your Armoury sections can be downloaded from our website: www.thebusinessgeneral.com

Whether you are the leader of a few or of thousands, you will find *The 7 Secrets of Leadership Success* gives you new ways of thinking and new ways of delivering success. The book is designed to be read as one piece, with all the Secrets related to each other and in a logical order, although readers who choose to dip into parts that particularly attract them will not find this unsatisfactory. However, we do certainly believe that understanding the synergy between all Seven Secrets is what makes a real Business General and that this insight will offer many businesses a new and powerful route to success.

Part One

Secret One
Synchronised Thinking

Harness all the thinking power
of the organisation

The most powerful secret in creating a great organisation is having every single person think in a common way about the meaning of success and how it is delivered. People join an organisation for a wide range of reasons and bring to it very different experiences and expectations. Left to their own devices they will form individual views on what is important and how things should be done. Everybody has their own sorry tale of the sharp-suited manager marching with total conviction over the backs of others, inflicting wholesale disaster on a situation without a hint of self-realisation that he or she is the business equivalent of a rogue missile. Building a great organisation is more than getting the right people and equipment: without a common frame of reference for success you don't have a chance. Secret Number One is about how to align thinking and so harness the thinking power of your firm, in other words: Synchronised Thinking.

This is the first of the three sides of what is known as the 'Power Pyramid' and is about getting every level of talent, creativity and effort focused and synchronised. This is achieved through doctrine. Doctrine is not about how Armed Forces impose rigid dogma in an authoritarian way – that is the antithesis of the contemporary Armed Forces approach. Modern commanders appreciate that they need empowered soldiers exercising dynamism and creativity in order to win on the modern battlefield.

UNDERSTANDING SYNCHRONISED THINKING

Synchronised Thinking is about pointing people in the same direction, working with all the skill and energy they have to fulfil their part in collective success, knowing how they fit into the overall scheme and working with as much independence as possible to find the most brilliant solutions. It is absolutely not about everyone having exactly the same, limited thoughts at exactly the same time. That would be like breeding a herd of cattle that are pliant, docile and heading for extinction. A common framework is partly the 'vision thing': a simple statement that explains what and where your company is striving to be. But it is more to do with having your own body of coherent thought that helps to map out in detail what needs to be done. It all needs to be genuinely understood and intelligently, intuitively applied. Mouthing the current chief executive's (CEO's) favourite slogan is not enough. Even if you are the owner of a small business, the same thing applies. Your assistant and your associates need to understand fully and adapt to the way you plan to do business. Getting this firmly understood and intelligently applied takes concerted focus that is both systematic and 'systemic' (that is, concerning the whole body). If you haven't applied your common view of success, if you haven't ensured constant, aligned focus on that and you suspect that you are not getting the best out of your team or organisation – then maybe it's time to get back to basics. Establish what you want to achieve and how, and ensure everyone else shares the vision.

Advantages of a Common Framework

A common framework is one that stimulates innovative, coherent, dynamic thinking at all levels in an organisation. It means the most junior secretary knows how to add to the success of a thriving team just as much as the finance director. This is because they both have a clear idea of what constitutes success and a shared set of well-articulated references for getting there. You might be thinking 'Okay, I'll buy that. But how do I create a process that stimulates innovative thinking, that is geared to a coherent picture and that leads to joined-up actions? What is this theory? Where do I find it and how am I going to get my associates to go along with it?'

Training helps, but it is only a piece of the jigsaw. The investment in training needs to be designed for systemic fit and systemically reinforced or your time and money will be wasted. You may have been here before … a manager is sent on a course for a few days and comes back with a head full of energising phrases that will invariably contain terms like 'empower', 'collaborate', 'embrace diversity' and 'intrapreneurialism' yet their enthusiasm dwindles if they get drawn back into the old systems and old culture and find that their cry is that of the lone wolf. Training nearly always has good intent behind it, but it is rarely thought about systemically and evaluated well. Nor is it always transferred in a robust way to those places where it will have the greatest impact. Good training is no good if it remains no more than notes in a desk drawer. The same applies to training in Sychronised Thinking. It needs to be systemically designed and reinforced – one without the other leads to limp results. We will show you how to do this via the Secrets in this book, which are designed to lead to a coherent and cohesive intervention.

The 'Right' Theory

Finding the 'right' theory in the first place is the other part of the problem. The Armed Forces face the same dilemma. For centuries there has been a ceaseless, global search for the military theory that will deliver guaranteed victory at least cost in blood and financial outlay. Armies that have been on the receiving end of a total thrashing are inclined to look hard for a way of thinking that will avoid a repeat performance. Armies that have won a crushing victory tend to cling to what went well when they embark on their next encounter. No wonder then that the military have really thought through these issues and come up with some useful ideas: they've had to, lives are at stake. But things are often different in the business world. When a business goes bust, people disband, apportion blame, and do not usually learn from the experience. There is not the same collective dogged determination to understand what happened, perhaps because they are more interested in looking for their next job. The Armed Forces stay together after their mistakes. They have had to find a way of learning from them and move on, continuing to work alongside each other again. Not easy to do. Through thousands of such discussions, a system has been worked out that is considered fair, thorough and constructive. We can share it with you here so that you can put it into practice at your firm.

Such thinking is not new – it goes back to the fifth century BC! Sun Tzu is still the most widely consulted writer on war because he managed to set down enduring truths that still hold good today, even though technology, culture and learning have evolved so much.

*'For just as flowing water avoids the heights
and hastens to the lowlands, so an army
avoids strength and strikes weakness.'*
SUN TZU, THE ART OF WAR

However, while Sun Tzu's advice may be useful, students of military thinking, whether soldiers, sailors, airmen or historians, have devoted years of effort looking for the perfect scientific theory of war. It doesn't exist. The good news is that centuries of slaughter and mayhem have led to some general conclusions about what works and what doesn't, and these have been embedded in a comprehensive theory that can be taught and applied uniformly throughout the Armed Forces.

Doctrine Not Dogma

Making war is a blend of art and science and subject to an unlimited set of variables such as the weather, morale, equipment, and just plain luck – any one of which one may prove decisive on the day. This has come as a huge disappointment to generals over the ages who have tried to resolve the outcome of their battles by geometry or astrology. Business is the same: the basic tenets of real success can be picked out across the years and these nuggets are often part of the intellectual capital of those who have been in business a long time. Accessing this thinking is a vital component of future success – a body of coherent, well-articulated thought that can be used to inform future decisions, but never to the point of dogma. Dogma is inert, it can't be challenged. Doctrine is dynamic and evolves. Soldiers need to avoid preparing 'to fight their last battle again' just as much as businesses must not focus on selling last year's product or service.

Train People to Think

Give people *time* to think and train them *how* to think. Too many businesses tell people *what* to think and don't give them time or space to think things through, to question, or come up with a creative alternative. Not enough are training people *how* to think. Look at the courses your firm offers – how many are on thinking? Quite contrary to the popular view of 'command and control', military leaders encourage their teams to think and to challenge – a much more healthy approach than we see in businesses today.

Time to Think

Do you regularly take 'time out' to think and reflect? This can mean stopping the rush, stepping back from a situation and seeing it from a different light. It can mean a change from giving directions to asking questions. It can mean taking time to play, to connect, to do something completely different. It can mean rest. All these things, psychologists have found, allow the 'incubation' of ideas and allow for lateral, creative thinking and responses. Most of the very successful people we have interviewed make time at the start of every day for vision and at the end of the day for reflection. How often you do this depends on your circumstances, but it becomes more necessary, not less, when the heat is on. As you direct the work of others, do allow them time out too. Don't drive yourself without these pauses and different activities, and don't keep your people flat out in action – it is a sure way to restrict the creative flow. After personal reflection, encourage dialogue to tap into what others are thinking.

Successful leadership means being clear and honest about what is achievable, how things are really going and what must be done. It is not about how you would like things to be going in a perfect world. We can deceive ourselves only too easily. Humans have imperfect perceptions, judgement and memory, and these can all affect the way the facts are recorded for future reference. This aspect of human performance is so common it has a name: cognitive dissonance – literally 'mental disharmony'.

Cognitive Dissonance

The state of cognitive dissonance is the discomfort people feel as new information contradicts their beliefs or intended actions. This discomfort is often subconscious, so even if they feel they are being open and grown up about hearing unwanted information, they may still be experiencing cognitive dissonance. The natural drive in all of us is to have consistency within our opinions, which means one of the pieces of the puzzle has to go when the 'fit' is wrong.

Sometimes we change our attitudes and beliefs to match the new information. So if, for instance, someone we liked at interview turns out to underperform in their post, we will either admit we were wrong (rare) or convince ourselves that we weren't that sure about them in the first place – 'hindsight bias' (the more common response). Because the brain cannot process a mass of information each time it makes a decision, we cluster information, make rules – and these are usually based on the recent past. The difficulty in learning from experiences lies here. A typical approach is to recognise some similarity in the current situation and transport those assumptions to the new situation – often far too widely – thus making incorrect generalisations. This is obviously not the same as analysing the new situation rigorously to see how it is related to the previous one.

Hindsight Analysis

The Armed Forces recognise this and accept that planning to fight tomorrow's battle with yesterday's plan is not usually a good idea. Only by honest hindsight analysis can we look forward and optimise how we tackle problems in the future. The military process of 'Lessons Identified' systematically analyses what worked and what didn't and this helps to prevent people making false assumptions, or making decisions based on the past rather than what is likely to confront them in the future. Many global businesses are becoming trained to use this process, with good results.

BUILDING A LEARNING CULTURE THROUGH THE LESSONS IDENTIFIED PROCESS

The military have become master practitioners of the art and science of building a 'learning culture'. This is where every operation is an opportunity for learning, for thinking about something in a better way and doing something better in the future. We can train ourselves and our colleagues to be better at decision-making by being aware of all aspects of cognitive dissonance – including rationalisation and hindsight bias – and calling into question what we now think about a situation, given all the new information. It is a vital discipline – as a Business General you will need this discipline and the moral courage to confront the facts honestly and completely.

Most businesses carry out some sort of review of major projects – 'some sort' being the operative words. Usually these take the form of closure meetings, 'proforma' exercises or postmortem discussions of what went wrong or right. They are communicated (usually once, and often passively on the Intranet) and then expected to be acted upon and maybe added to best practice/standards. If they are followed at all it is usually by the few close to the original action. Not enough effort is made to ensure that the lessons learned previously are used on the current project. Things that have gone right are often not analysed at all. The result? Investment is not analysed properly to see where the maximum gain could be made. Safety measures that failed are repeated. Both the waste of brilliance and the potential for disaster gone unnoted are avoidable.

The big deal about Lessons Identified is that they are part of the design of any campaign project. First the commander briefs the mission and purpose. It might seem a lot of bother but the benefit is that everyone has a clear understanding of what, why and how their group is to achieve its goals. They will have expectations about what will happen, identified challenges, named assumptions and generated a testable hypothesis in the form of a plan. Evidence is then found to decide whether to discard the plan or to continue. The discipline required to do this is going to be tough for busy business people but the payoff is worth it.

The Lessons Identified process continues throughout the campaign and at the end of it. The before-action planning sets the agenda for the after-action evaluation. It builds a climate of honest, candid, critical appreciation of the task involved that sets the tone for the frankness of the evaluation. Everyone involved takes note, making explicit links between the lessons identified and future actions. These feed back into the strategy/execution cycle. They are not intended to 'give closure', they are not to be 'filed in the knowledge bank', they are to be used by the people who:

- Generated the learning.
- Will need it the next time.

During the Lessons Identified process, hierarchy, positioning, political playing has no place. Through candour and focus, constructive dialogue and opinion is achieved. This is, in part, how the doctrine stays alive, dynamic, shaped by the hands of those who play it. This calls for the intellectual rigour and self-discipline that the military teach officers from the beginning of their training. Many people think that the UK's Army officer training establishment, The Royal Military Academy Sandhurst (RMAS), is mostly about running up hills with a rucksack full of sand, whilst being shouted at in uncongenial terms by a Sergeant. There is an element of truth in this – officers need to be as fit and robust as the men and women they lead – but more importantly the training helps build the qualities, skills and character needed to lead in battle. It is probably the most demanding mental and physical leadership training in the country – a full year of well-structured and challenging instruction.

It is also not just an 'attendance' course: students have to meet the standards required or try again, and if they fail, they leave. The young leaders who pass the course have both presence and humility, they are able to plan thoroughly and improvise intelligently when the plan goes astray, and they must remain disciplined, clear headed, unflappable and focused in times of unpredictability, chaos and danger. The soldiers they lead in battle, and the taxpayers who put their faith in them, expect nothing less. And this is just the start of their training.

Learning the Lessons

As a Business General, you need to have a process, consistently applied, to learn the lessons of successes and failures. Do you have such a debriefing process? Is it totally candid? Are the lessons applied to other groups and used in present and future situations? Think of the last big success you were involved with. What information can you extract from that situation that will provide vital lessons that others could learn from? Is that information available and are people accessing it? How can it be represented in a way that ensures it is accessed and utilised for the next project?

You need to find out what works in your organisation and use that as the basis of your own theory, your common framework of success. Identify what approach, what way of thinking is working. Tease out what constitutes that success (who, how, when) and then create your own leadership ethos around it. Train people in that ethos and agree how to recognise when people are getting it right and when they are not. Do not allow that ethos to keep changing with every guru-of-the-year's new idea or with each alteration in senior management. Simple to say, but so often not done rigorously well. Reward good performance and penalise a lack of professional discipline. Make sure that what is important in your leadership doctrine is adhered to. Then brand it in some way – keep your internal branding/messaging/way of working consistent with your external branding. This will build authenticity – keep it focused, simple, standardised and galvanised. Educate your entire workforce in the clear rights and wrongs of their professional life. Engage their minds and dialogue in the 'fuzzy' dilemmas of what it means to show integrity, honesty and respect. Continue to educate until there is one common approach to thinking about old problems and hypothetical or new problems, so that when things change there is a reference point. This does not mean stifling creativity: it means having a common starting point for a vigorous debate.

This is one easy way of building trust. If you want followers to trust their leader's judgements (and vice versa), to be more able to share information, to get decisions made more quickly and have solidarity behind those decisions, then train them to use common problem-solving and decision-making skills. Instil them, check they are used and be sure that the senior leaders use them all the time. A by-product of this is that you will alleviate stress and gain clarity and shared perspective. Communicating directives will be swifter and win greater acceptance because there will be more trust in the way the decision was made.

Every organisation has a different set of requirements determined by service, product, size, constituents, market, location, and degree of competition – so there is no detailed, one-size-fits-all template that works uniformly well. As a Business General you need to know how to create a common platform of understanding among your workforce that covers how to go about a problem, treat people, delegate and report back. If you do this well, the potential for focus, pace and momentum in taking decisions that are in harmony with the goals of the organisation is vastly increased. You will avoid dangers such as inactivity through lack of direction, hesitation under pressure and mistaking unfocused activity for progress.

Practical Ideas – Not Pointless Theories

You can have too much of a good thing, of course. Your staff need theories that will be genuinely useful in their daily working lives. They do not need to be overwhelmed with detailed advice about issues that are way beyond their sphere of interest or influence. Armed Forces' staff colleges and business schools produce some people bursting with the pressure of storing up so much theory. They are able to talk for days without drawing breath in a language tangentially related to English, and are as much use in practice as a chocolate fireguard. They need to be restricted to the areas where they actually add value. Nonetheless, there is a role in any organisation for those who set the pace in driving the way people think in a common way, and this is the role of the leaders. Leaders at all levels need to be able to galvanise the organisation, drawing on shared theory and understanding to ensure that all parts of the enterprise work in harmony to the greatest effect. This is what we mean by Synchronised Thinking.

Synchronised Thinking – the Military Experience

The military organisation most often cited as having achieved synchronisation was the Prussian General Staff. With the arrival of universal conscription (from 1793 onwards, shortly after the French Revolution) armies grew enormously in size and it was no longer possible for a general to command on the basis of direct line of sight across the entire battlefield without chaos ensuing. To go with the challenge of supplying and moving armies of perhaps 500,000 men, new technology brought greater complexity in weapons, ammunition and equipment as well as – vitally – the potential for rapid mobilisation and movement offered by the growth of railways across Europe. In short, generals needed a professional staff to organise, supply and direct their forces. Prussia established a General War Academy in 1810, training carefully selected officers in a common way of warfare, bound together by carefully instilled ideas of service, loyalty, discipline and honour. Once trained, these officers were placed in key appointments throughout the Army, providing a mechanism for distributing common understanding about how to plan and conduct the warfare of the day.

There are many examples of the effectiveness of building this sort of staff system with high levels of common purpose and understanding, but one of the most vivid was the success of the Prussian Army in the war against France in 1870. France declared war on Prussia on 19 July 1870, using the Spanish Succession as a pretext, and then made a shambles of mobilising and deploying their forces. Soldiers found they were short of vital supplies;

indeed some had no weapons or uniforms. Under the Prussian General Staff, however, German mobilisation worked as smoothly as the train timetables they were based upon, with three armies totalling some 430,000 men put swiftly into the field. This efficiency went further than just getting to the battle. By early September the Germans had turned the threat of French invasion into the encirclement and surrender of French forces of 124,000 at Sedan, and the abdication of Napoleon III. The model of a 'General Staff' has since been adopted by all modern Armed Forces with many differences of style and content, but all founded on the advantages of having key people trained in a robust, common way for the conduct of a complicated and bloody business.

Synchronised Thinking in Business

Are there – should there be – parallels with a 'general staff' outside the Armed Forces? In fact, many organisations do lean towards a similar approach already, as seen in the recruitment and placing of the best MBA graduates and the fruits of impressive in-house development schemes such as those run by Mars and BP. Carefully chosen, carefully placed leaders are intended to have a catalytic effect on their businesses, initially as the creative spark and driving energy at business unit level and latterly as seasoned board members. In many ways the galvanising effect of the Prussian General Staff is emulated in a few top-class firms like these.

In the Armed Forces, all leaders are trained in the basics of a unifying philosophy, common method of command, and universal approach to particular problems. There are clearly advantages in having this degree of organisational capability more widely, and with the leadership problems inherent in the business and public sector of today the advantages are becoming clearer and clearer. So, in addition to MBAs, it is essential that a degree of training and expertise exists at all levels: otherwise the Jedi Knights will lead and no one else has will have a clue how to follow. Every leader in your organisation needs training in elements of business theory, ethics, decision-making, the lessons of past successes and failures, and how to live the values of that organisation. This is part of 'being in command' and inextricably part of getting accountability and empowerment right. We return to this theme in Part Two.

Synchronised Thinking Under Pressure

Chairs, CEOs, MDs and all directors have to get a grip on staff training and the adoption of some core unified ways of thinking, otherwise the team will be without a common approach to problem solving. Without this, when the going gets tough and people in power start vying for their own way of doing things, the going just gets tougher. Differences in ways of thinking and approaches to problem solving open up like a fissure when the team is placed under pressure. If key people act in wildly different ways, hurtling off in different conceptual or practical directions, the troops will soon get confused, fed up and cynical. This is not about a rigid, immovable, set of rules here. New texts, new doctrine should be introduced. In fact, this is essential to keep people's creative instincts sharp and for the team to be assertive about improving itself. What it does mean is that new ideas about how to do business need careful discussion and review, and then are either incorporated into the way that a team does its business or discarded. The time to debate these issues is not during a crisis.

For example, if the commander of all US forces in Afghanistan wants to know how a major commanding a company of 100 men high up in the Hindu Kush is approaching his mission, they will have that discussion using commonly understood terms with well-defined meaning. Were the same company commander to offer his views in an entirely new lexicon, the conversation would break down, with a consequent lack of understanding, confidence and trust. In fact, the US commander could confidently have the conversation with a company commander from UK or Germany – or indeed any NATO member – as common doctrine is rigorously agreed and taught across the Alliance. It's not a perfect process, but it is a major contributor to building efficiency and effectiveness in multinational operations.

MCKINSEY & COMPANY

A firm that exemplifies good Synchronised Thinking is the management consultancy McKinsey & Company. It started in 1926 and now has annual revenues of around £2 billion from around 7,000 employees in 40 countries. The leaders have developed a working environment where people work to the same high standards, synchronised to be effective and without the loss of personal autonomy and freedom of execution. Members of 'The Firm', as it is affectionately known, are said to use similar language, ethical ethos and choice of processes. This is doctrine being used well. It doesn't constrain, but liberates the talented to be dynamic. That doctrine embodies a set of choices about whom they recruit (people of high intellect, character, accountability, ownership, initiative and imagination) and how they keep them. In fact, they still have a ruthless policy of 'up or out' – if one doesn't rise up the ladder, one is asked to leave. Remarkably such a process doesn't chuck out resentful ex-employees; rather, they become part of the argot of 'alumni' who are proud of their time there and of the club to which they belonged.

Doctrine – Bet It Ain't What You Think!

'Doctrine is indispensable to an army...
Doctrine provides a military organisation
with a common philosophy, a common language,
a common purpose, and a unit of effort.'
GENERAL GEORGE DECKER

The Armed Forces have adopted the term 'doctrine' for their body of theory. 'Doctrine' sounds like the formula for rather dated, autocratic and hierarchical command and control. It isn't that. Doctrine is also often hugely misunderstood as simply rigid dogma applied by rote, handed down in tablets of stone, left unquestioned. In fact, doctrine is reviewed constantly as the vehicle for drawing in new thinking. It is the body of theory employed by the Armed Forces to sharpen analysis and promote efficiency by establishing performance standards for the kind of situations and actions the units face. It does draw on the experience of the past, because it is possible to draw some general conclusions about what works in warfare and what does not, but without binding the future to them. There is a subtle distinction here that it is very important to understand: a Business General is informed, assisted, released by doctrine, not tied down by it.

Believe It or Not, You Want Dilemmas

Dilemmas are bound to occur in the minds of those who think. If you are not discussing dilemmas it could be because people are not thinking deeply enough, merely complying, and with compliance comes lack of dynamic momentum. The Armed Forces question 'the-tried-and-tested' traditional aspects of military ethos and practice with fresh ideas (sometimes too fresh for some old generals!) This isn't unhealthy. What is impressive about the

Armed Forces is that these dilemmas are made explicit and dialogue is encouraged. Is that true of your organisation? How open is the dialogue about the best thinking from the past leader or method and how intelligently is this kept and fused with the opportunities presented by new technology, ideas and methods? To do this takes courage, intellectual honesty and firm leadership. The idea of having a comprehensive doctrine in business makes sense. Many of the problems in business exist because leadership theory from one boss to the next in the commercial world is inconsistent and more often than not leads to internal conflict and discontinuity. The Armed Forces' experience shows the value of rigorous open dialogue about competing approaches, with intelligent respect for the past, leading to the adoption of theory that has the best fit for future organisational success.

How You Can Synchronise Thinking

The Armed Forces have been working on theories of winning to the extent that these have been honed and tried-and-tested in war to the point where there is now a coherent and comprehensive body of doctrine to draw on. How strong is your organisation in this area? Do you have a method of Synchronising Thinking? You can start with an assessment of your current position.

THE 'TRAFFIC LIGHT' ASSESSMENT

How Well Do You Use Synchronised Thinking Now?

We have devised a quick way you can check how your organisation fares in relation to Synchronised Thinking; to reflect on where you are as an organisation. Use the Traffic Light assessment to show where you are, by and large, getting it right (tick the lower traffic light), where you are some way there or where there are pockets of good work (tick the middle traffic light) and where you are not doing well (tick the top traffic light). Do that for all three of the levels of assessment – where you are now, where you are against your preferred standard and how you would perform if suddenly faced with maximum pressure, given the capability you have now.

SYNCHRONISED THINKING TRAFFIC LIGHT

Ask yourself:

A) How are we doing now?

B) How are we performing against best-practice and best-in-class?

C) How would we perform if we were put under maximum pressure with the resources we have right now?

Doctrine

A B C
○ ○ ○
○ ○ ○   We have a body of theory about our business that
○ ○ ○   guides analysis and decisions.

A B C
○ ○ ○
○ ○ ○   We draw on the past to understand the present
○ ○ ○

A B C
○ ○ ○
○ ○ ○   We are honest about the dilemmas we face and have
○ ○ ○   bold dialogues.

A B C
○ ○ ○
○ ○ ○   Our thinking on leadership is aligned.
○ ○ ○

A B C
○ ○ ○
○ ○ ○   The strategy is known and accepted by all.
○ ○ ○

A B C
○ ○ ○
○ ○ ○   We know how we contribute to the aim and how our
○ ○ ○   boss/subordinate does too.

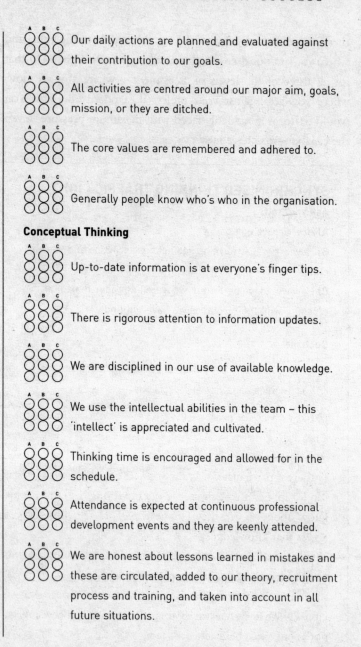

Our daily actions are planned and evaluated against their contribution to our goals.

All activities are centred around our major aim, goals, mission, or they are ditched.

The core values are remembered and adhered to.

Generally people know who's who in the organisation.

Conceptual Thinking

Up-to-date information is at everyone's finger tips.

There is rigorous attention to information updates.

We are disciplined in our use of available knowledge.

We use the intellectual abilities in the team – this 'intellect' is appreciated and cultivated.

Thinking time is encouraged and allowed for in the schedule.

Attendance is expected at continuous professional development events and they are keenly attended.

We are honest about lessons learned in mistakes and these are circulated, added to our theory, recruitment process and training, and taken into account in all future situations.

A B C
◯◯◯ We have a process for encouraging good decision
◯◯◯ making.

A B C
◯◯◯ The ethics of our profession are well known and
◯◯◯ abided by.

A B C
◯◯◯ We use systemic processes to tap into our creativity.
◯◯◯ We appreciate and use each other's strengths.

Create a Doctrine that Differentiates You

Having established where you are now, you are well positioned to work out the 'doctrine' of your organisation. The details of this will vary widely from organisation to organisation and will evolve as time passes and circumstances change. The essential features you need to decide on are:

- Clarity in the philosophy and purpose that drives your organisation. For example, do you want to make a profit for shareholders or for private owners, deliver a leading-edge public service, or provide charity where none existed before? This will govern the culture and operational style of the organisation.

- Is there a particular commercial or technical knowledge that can be applied throughout the organisation? If so, do people know about it, are they competent in it? Do most people access that knowledge?

- Vitally, what sort of leadership style and substance do you want to have? Again, are people aware of what is expected of them and what to expect in return? What are you doing to cultivate that leadership style in successors or those with potential?

- What other key aspects of your organisational life do you need to get agreement on and what are you doing to instil these throughout your organisation? Some of this may be governed by laws, on diversity or regulation, and some of this is a matter of choice: faith, politics and attitudes to factors such as social events and flexible benefits.

BUILD YOUR ARMOURY
Establish a Doctrine

Here is a list of tools and tips giving specific advice on how to establish a doctrine as part of your 'business armoury'.

▷ Set up a working party to collate views on what works as a leadership and management style in your organisation. You might want to look at theories, practices and philosophies from academics and expert practitioners.

▷ Take the next step that is probably not taken by your competitor: collate case studies of success and failure in your organisation and link the theories, practices and philosophies to those case studies as a way of helping you understand them and find the language for them.

▷ Invite a wide selection of stakeholders to debate which philosophy and approach to adopt in the organisation. Then create your own doctrine around what works for you and set this up to become a body of your corporate thought-leadership.

▷ Market the doctrine and train people to use it as a guide to analysis and decision-making. Embed the behaviours that support it with recognition and reward and discourage those behaviours that undermine it.

▷ Find out the level of alignment to your strategy in the minds of the major players – who is on side, who is giving you lip service, who categorically disagrees with it. Consider independent consultants for this task. They might be given more honest information than internal staff and these consultants would facilitate the discussions thereafter.

▷ If you think you have a strategy and stated way of doing things – test it. Go and ask a few people to see if the answer is the same. You might want to do this properly by running a stratified random sampling survey to test how well the strategy and values are known within a diagonal slice of the organisation. (You might want to contact your local university for a Masters business or occupational psychology student to do this for you, for the cost of their course. If you build a good relationship with the lecturers you can offer the paid project only to the best candidates.)

▷ Be ruthless about people who exhibit selfish motivation and actions – there is no place for them in your firm; they will destroy real team work. We really mean that. Selfish and over-ambitious people keep back information that will harm their reputation and they rarely share information that could be useful to others.

▷ Create a process that asks each person to think about how well their activities that day are going to contribute to the aim and then share that information with boss, subordinate and peer. Check back and evaluate at the end of the day. Through such monitoring and dialogue you will soon have your people focused on the very things that are important and that lead to your strategy.

▷ Introduce a system that allows people to talk about whether people are living or defaulting on the ethics and values. Some of our clients choose to use a yellow card or red card system based on football – they show a red card to those who default on one of the values, say in a meeting or behind-the-scenes discussion. Others prefer a system of congratulations, which are offered on the spot to those doing things right or, conversely, pointing out to them quickly that their behaviour did not match the standard required. The congratulations can be a pat on the back, a 'high five', or a chitty towards some prize.

THE PRINCIPLES OF WAR

There is one critically important source of thought-leadership in the military: the Principles of War. Military doctrine is now a large, comprehensive and international body of thought. It ranges from very detailed, technical advice on the tactics that apply to small groups, to thinking that drives the solutions to major challenges such as warfare on a grand scale. We do not intend to go too far into all this, but at the root of most military doctrine is a set of principles, known as the Principles of War, which we believe are easily and usefully transferable to other organisations and walks of life. In military circles, opinion varies still about how many Principles of War there should be, but there is very little disagreement about the key maxims. They have been arrived at over centuries and provide a general guide to success. Observing them will never guarantee victory – battles are too complex and fickle for that – but wilfully failing to abide by them is very likely to be a precursor to defeat. They offer well-researched wisdom, not a magic recipe, but they're a whole lot better than starting afresh every time conflict breaks out. You need to get your head around these: they will underpin your doctrine. It might feel a bit dense in places but we can't turn important principles into sound-bites – your leadership, career and organisation are at stake.

Like all good rules, if the Principles of War are applied with good judgement they can be a decisive aid to success. They are useful both in thinking about what to do and in testing a plan for strengths and weaknesses. These principles could have very significant value when transplanted into the commercial arena. They provide an easily understood, simple and proven menu for building Synchronised Thinking in any organisation. There are 10 military principles that reflect a broad consensus and that if ignored can be expected to jeopardise success:

- Selection and maintenance of the aim (the master principle)
- Maintenance of morale
- Security
- Surprise
- Offensive action
- Concentration of force
- Economy of effort
- Flexibility
- Co-operation
- Sustainability

THE PRINCIPLES OF WINNING

To transfer the Principles of War to business and not-for-profit organisations, we need to explain each principle and recast it in a way that you can relate to your own field. For the Business General, these can be used as a rough guide or a template for doctrine in the business world. We think they are more easily understood and employed outside the military context if renamed the 'Principles of Winning', but the logic and the force behind each remains unchanged.

Selection and Maintenance of the Aim

The selection and maintenance of the Aim takes top place – with all the other principles behind in no particular ranking. The benefits are that:

- Everyone sings from the same hymn sheet
- You won't be bothered by silly annoying questions
- You and your team won't waste time
- Key strengths are exploited to achieve the Aim
- There is a greater sense of purpose

By selection we mean make clear to subordinates exactly what is to be achieved so that all activity can be focused on it and co-ordinated effectively. Every business needs to know where it is going – 'the Aim' – or it has nothing against which to judge success. Selecting the Aim must reconcile the competing views of investors, directors and employees: each stakeholder needs to believe that the enterprise recognises and advances their needs and expectations.

The Business General will also apply this principle to the goals of individual jobs. All employees need to be clear about their aims and what success looks like when they achieve it. Surprisingly, many are not so do a test. The selection and the maintenance of the Aim is the master principle: all action must be reviewed against the Aim, and tested for the contribution it will make to it.

COMMANDER'S COMFY CHAIR
Selection and Maintenance of the Aim

Take some time now to review last week's actions against the overall Aim of the business and your own definition of success in your role. You might decide that it needs further work – over days/weeks.

Can you confidently state the main Aim of your organisation?

How sure are you that everyone would give the same answer?

Do you know what other top three things the organisation is focusing on?

Would others agree with you or would they have different ideas?

Does the rhetoric match the actions?

Do you know and appreciate why that is the Aim?

Does everyone 'get' it?

Are your actions, on a daily basis, measured against the effectiveness towards that Aim?

How do you communicate the aim of the organisation daily in your actions and behaviours and attitudes?

Did you do that well yesterday?

What could you have done more of, less of?

What do you need to start doing?

What do you need to stop doing?

How much did you use your key strengths to contribute to the Aim – and those of your team?

How much did each day, half-day, hour contribute to that Aim?

How much of your team's time was spent using their key strengths in the pursuit of a goal that directly contributed to the Aim?

What would it be like to discard all that did not contribute to the
   Aim?
How could you go about dropping what doesn't contribute
   directly?
What is this telling you about the focus in your business and
   what is the potential if focused were increased?

Learn from the military: they are ruthless about this – anything
that does not help to achieve the Aim is discarded. This kind of
focus is what enables missions to be accomplished. The Aim has
to be understood and accepted fully. This is achieved by understanding the underlying purpose – the *why* behind the *what*.
People need to ask themselves: What am I being asked to do?
Why am I being asked to do it? How does that relate to the overall Aim? Leaders need to make sure they cover all of those
questions in any request from their team.

Can the Aim change? Of course. Key factors and interests
may change so that it is entirely right that a company should
decide it needs to do something different. Like the captain of a
battleship, it is a key task for busy leaders not to get their heads
so stuck into piles of detail that they lose sight of the horizon,
ignore warnings and fail to spot the gathering storm clouds until
it is too late to take avoiding action.

A lot depends on how the Aim is defined in the first place. If
the Aim is set as 'maximise the return to shareholders', for example, then it doesn't matter whether the company sells full-fat ice
cream or water sorbets so long as the returns are the best achievable. If the intent is to maximise returns and the ice cream market
collapses it is time to think about organic sorbet. That is hard to
say to someone who has spent their whole working life working

in a dairy, but it is through resolute 'selection and maintenance of the Aim' that the right, difficult decisions can be made, even if they are hard to bear.

By knowing the intent behind the Aim, junior leaders are able to act independently and intelligently without constantly referring to superiors for detailed guidance. This avoids being badgered by juniors asking questions that interrupt your thought-flow and steal your time. This understanding allows the organisation to be more flexible, pragmatic and adaptable, seizing fleeting opportunities with confidence and avoiding spurious effort. In business, the trend over the last 20 years has been to articulate a vision, identify objectives that direct corporate strategy and settle on the goals of individual business units – even down to the goals of each employee – but how often is this structure focused on *why* as much as on *what*?

Too often, the top-to-bottom link is neither taut nor consistent, leaving the organisation and its effectiveness fractured and under-performing. There is no point having a clearly identified Aim unless the workforce not only knows what it is, but is also properly led and motivated to achieve it. There is a lot more to this than having a great slogan. The aim should be consistently articulated through the hierarchy of the boss's statement of his or her vision, the objectives at the heart of corporate strategy that will deliver it and the more limited targets of individual business units.

BUILD YOUR ARMOURY

Selection and Maintenance of the Aim

Here is a list of tools and tips giving specific advice on how to use the principle of Selection and Maintenance of the Aim.

▷ Ask a random sample of people in the business if they know *what* the business aim is. Then dig deeper – do they know the '*why*'.

▷ Run a time-management check to find out how much activity is focused directly on the Aim by having all staff record what they do in half-hour slots of a day, a week, a month, and then analyse the efficiency and focus.

▷ How do you want your stakeholders to understand your Aim? How are you managing their perceptions?

▷ Evaluate and record the expected benefits of possible actions such as a new product, a training intervention, extra coaching, an acquisition or new hire. Analyse the benefit in relation to the Aim.

▷ Discard all that does not add value to the Aim.

▷ Find out more about your teams. What do they do in their spare time? What have they achieved in the past? How might that help the Aim?

▷ Train your top team leaders in how to talk about the strategy to their staff. They have to inspire others as they talk it through; keep coaching the leaders until it does.

▷ Make sure all newcomers know 'who is who' and where they can access information.

Morale Really Matters

Morale is really important. Improving your company's morale will bring the following benefits:

- People will 'get on' better; there will be no 'atmosphere'
- Work will be more fun and this positive attitude will lead to inspiration
- There will be more freedom because there will be more trust
- Stress will be more easily managed and resilience increased

The newest weapon technology, with the best supply of ammunition and spare parts, will count for little if the soldiers operating it are inert, depressed and entirely lacking in motivation and engagement. Conversely, highly motivated and well-led soldiers armed with only basic equipment can have a devastating effect on a much larger and better-equipped force. The morale of the people involved can often make the difference between a poor organisation and a great one, and between failure and success. For soldiers, high morale comes with the skill and confidence imbued by good training, from close professional relationships with their immediate companions based on friendship, trust and integrity, and reserves of courage, energy, determination and will. High morale in soldiers means knowing what you have to do, why you have to do it, that it matters and that you have the character and expertise to do it successfully – accepting too that there will be a cost, however much we try to minimise it. Without high morale, soldiers will struggle to endure the mental and physical pressures of the battlefield, to resist attacks with the resilience and ferocity required, and to maintain the offensive spirit needed to attack and to win.

The parallels with business are obvious. Everyone has encountered the miserable, untrained, disaffected, unknowledgeable and unhelpful shop assistant. Compare them with a Gap assistant who greets you at the door, offers to run around the shop finding stock for you, liaises with their associates by earpiece and then wraps up your purchase carefully in a box. What's the difference? Training and connection to the main aim via *daily* motivational calls to the shop floor team prior to the store opening. There may be many reasons why this assistant is so negative: clearly low morale is fundamental to it. In bigger firms and organisations the role of morale is just as significant.

COST CUTTING AND THE IMPACT ON MORALE

There is a fine and important balance to be calibrated when managing a business by squeezing its costs; for every action there are untold consequences. Judicious cost cutting balanced with investment in the right place usually allows most people to feel part of an efficient team. However, many managers cut costs time and time again, relentlessly, all over the place and this usually results in lowering morale as well as its costs. When cost cutting hits training / conferences / bonuses and leads to downsizing, the leader's relationship with his or her employees is a critical factor in whether people keep focused, performing and committed through the changes.

Some businesses we have known have coped with redundancies and even closures in an atmosphere akin to a boom – C&A was one such closure: it hired motivational experts to help the staff understand, and look after themselves and each other, and helped them move on.

In other cases we have seen leaders make grand cost cuts, with grave warnings of commercial imperatives, and where it has all gone horribly wrong. The leader of one of those businesses was not liked, or admired, nor did he have a great relationship with his employees, and when he imposed change, they revolted, went on strike and brought the business to a halt.

The right strategy might be to cut costs, but you need a climate of trust and commitment so that people stay with you through the tough times, fully focused on your aim (and not aiming for one foot in the headhunting agency).

BUILD YOUR ARMOURY
Morale Matters

Here is a list of tools and tips giving specific advice on how to improve the morale of your organisation.

▷ Measure the level of morale in your business with a proper survey. If it is low, do not pass 'Go'! You must rebuild confidence, commitment and morale before you do anything else.

▷ Find out the reasons for the high/low levels of engagement and address them. Preferably use a third-party consultant for this as people will readily talk more freely. But if costs do not permit this, use the person with the best facilitation skills.

▷ Ask if you can track those who leave. Arrange to contact them every week during the first month after they leave, then once a month thereafter for six months. Have a third party do face-to-face interviews with them. See if their impressions change after time. You will pick up a lot of market information that way as they go about their job search and settle into other firms – you may even entice talent back.

▷ Educate people in building rapport and relationships – have the best people shadowed and give feedback and advice to those less able.

▷ Make sure the leadership is visible and providing good role models for the organisation's values. We know that people show better leadership qualities if they have previously seen them modelled – as opposed to merely being encouraged. A case of 'do as I do, not just what I say'.

▷ Make sure people who live the organisation's values are recognised. Build confidence – you can do this by taking the time to thank properly, eyeball to eyeball. Recognising when people get things right has a tremendous effect – people can focus on their strengths (not their weaknesses) and do more of it.

▷ Emphasise self-discipline around the highest standards of conduct.

▷ Do not allow anyone to get away with showing disrespect, no matter how senior. Find out from subordinates who makes them feel valued and go out of your way to praise them. Find out who doesn't and make sure it is coached out of them or remove them – they are costing you too much.

Get Ahead Without Getting Hurt

By security, what we are talking about is taking the risks needed to achieve success whilst not exposing weaknesses that present an opportunity to the opponent to strike a telling blow. The benefits are that you:

- Make bold moves but not foolhardy ones.
- Protect your 'silver'.
- Separate the fakes from the diamonds.

In the Second World War, winning the Battle of Britain, from the UK's perspective, primarily meant keeping RAF airfields open so that the aircraft based there could attack German bombers, and also threaten any German invasion fleet from the air. The protection of the key assets, the airfields, is what gave Britain the capacity for offensive action to defeat an assault mounted from France before it even arrived on shore. Successful military operations need a balance of offensive action to attack the enemy directly, and security to protect the vital assets that enable such freedom of action.

In business terms, the application of the principle of security is equally important. Businesses need factories that are protected from theft, as safe from fire risks as practical, and where the work-force can safely and efficiently maximise production. Health and safety legislation is a security measure. Businesses also need to protect against the effects of too much debt, cash shortfalls, exchange rate fluctuations and many other potential risks. Business leaders will know how such risks will limit their ability to increase investment, expand market share and contemplate acquisitions. The public and not-for-profit sectors need to ensure that their stakeholders' money is well spent, costs are kept tight and yet an optimum level of service is given.

HOW DO YOU BALANCE RISK MANAGEMENT WITH ENTREPRENEURIALISM?

The UK is a nation of small businesses. The government's own small business website reckons that there are 4.5 million small businesses (defined as businesses with a turnover under £5m and with less than 50 employees) employing half the workforce in the UK and accounting for half the turnover. Yet over half of those businesses fail within the first three years. So, thinking about and learning how to balance entrepreneurialism with risk-management is vital to anyone wanting to be a success in business.

BUILD YOUR ARMOURY

Balance the Risks

Here is a list of tools and tips giving specific advice on how to reduce risk in your organisation.

▷ Identify your high-value assets – and protect them above all else. Give recognition to those who achieve in the right way.

▷ Invite everyone to focus on the returns that are measured – the profit, the share price, market share – get every level involved in understanding and suggesting.

▷ Guard your intellectual property, otherwise competitors can copy your ideas and associates leave and replicate them elsewhere. There are two approaches. The first is to have a watertight contract with associates and suppliers. The second is to heed the advice in this book and ensure that your firm has such a strong way of doing things that others will not be able to emulate your style and your staff will be loyal to you. Never, of course, take on anyone, no matter how much you need their skills, if their integrity is questionable.

▷ Take risks but avoid hopeless gambles. Arrange forums to discuss the risks you face: such as the threats, the weaknesses. Encourage an openness about those risks, is there a current plan to manage the consequences, or worst case scenario?

▷ Reward whistle-blowers, punish those who play company politics with information.

▷ Introduce a way of making sure the organisation's culture is open and honest and not secretive or suppressing unpalatable information. Go and meet the juniors – ask them questions.

▷ Make sure that Lessons Identified from successes and failures are circulated, understood and used by recruiters, trainers and suppliers.

▷ Don't leave your people under-resourced; make it a priority to obtain the right equipment for them to do their job properly.

▷ You are only as strong as your weakest link. Offer close, visible support to new people, to those in training, to 'problem children'. Don't let the dysfunctional minority upset the better majority.

Think Ahead of The Crowd

Surprises keep your competitors on the defensive and your own people inspired. Surprise is an attitude of mind, a way of thinking, and a key aspect in battle and in business. The benefits are that you can:

- Have a laugh at your competitor's expense.
- Gain success (always the best revenge).
- Gather and use intelligence on your enemy.
- Create a compelling aura – a mystique that allures.

In the military sense, surprise means doing everything possible to catch the enemy off-guard, at a time and place of your own choosing, where the enemy is least able to resist effectively. In the commercial sense, surprise means thinking ahead of the crowd, doing what others might scoff at because it seems so ridiculous or requires too much work. Instead of asking 'why?', asking 'why not?'

Successful surprise requires creativity, the courage to take measured risks, and the confidence to ensure speed of execution so that an opponent can't keep up. It is reinforced by a high standard of information security and good communication. Bear in mind, though, there are rarely any plaudits if you give nasty surprises to your own staff!

Surprise also means thinking carefully about how the enemy could do the same to you. By enemy, we mean any aggressive competitor or colleague, unreliable supplier and unethical customer. Surprise applies at all levels of the organisation. It should be part of the top-level strategy. (Deciding to do something significantly different rather than just the same old thing better.) It applies in areas such as sales and marketing in particular; and it works at an individual level for the manager or salesman who sees how to secure advantage in new and unexpected ways.

Astute research and development, well-sourced production, clever advertising, good control of market-sensitive information and many other activities contribute to surprise. You don't want newness for novelty's sake: the boundary between genius and crackpot is a fine one. People are happy to fork out for the latest fashions and innovations in mobile phones, sunglasses and hair-cuts – but surprises that shock the customer aren't always positive (for example, the Sinclair C5 and 'New Coke' recipe).

Surprise in the business world means treading a fine line between openness and secrecy. For example, telling your competitor's customers who you are and why they should come to you while also concealing your intentions from your competitors. There is often a need to keep the full purpose behind your actions concealed so that the competitor is not able to act in time to thwart you or prepare a counter-attack.

BUSINESSES IN INCUBATION

When some serial entrepreneurs open a new venture it is often unveiled in a big launch. Behind the scenes, many well-known entrepreneurs 'have a go' at creating a new business. The business is hot-housed and trailed by staff who are often locked away in shabby, low-key, low-cost, crowded offices working on very low wages, having signed strict confidentiality clauses – all for the promise of capital shares and rewards of a high-profile job in a firm launched with massive PR. We don't get to hear about all of them – around half collapse and the story is never told. Only after tests confirm a business's chance of success do we hear the fanfare as the new brand is launched. Striking imagery, bold symbolism, novel marketing ploys can then surprise the competition and create an aura of power, all done with seeming effortlessness.

BUILD YOUR ARMOURY

Principle of Surprise

Here is a list of tools and tips giving specific advice on how to make use of the principle of surprise.

▷ Encourage your staff to surprise their colleagues and other parts of the business. Let staff ask the questions that take them outside their customary restraints. What would we do if? How can we delight our customers further? What can we think of that will put us ahead of the wave – ideas that others haven't thoughts of or articulated yet? Ask the people who think up the best ideas to take them further, test the water, experiment and report back. Give them the resources to do it well.

▷ Try at least one completely new thing every year.

▷ Gather intelligence on the competition from their websites, their conference notes, network with their people, ask mutual clients, and their clients, find out what you can from interviewees who have worked with them, from the press, the web. Collate it and circulate it. Make sure it is available to everyone in your business and that they make use of it.

▷ Make sure you keep on top of quality.

▷ Don't tell all and sundry about your plans. Keep some mystery about what you do, create some myths and mystique.

▷ Draw a crowd – people like to deal with brands that have style and do something different.

▷ Review what you have been doing. If it worked, build on it. If it didn't, let it go.

Offensive Action – Attack to Win

You can't expect to win by being exclusively defensive. Sometimes encouraging an opponent to batter himself to a standstill against a strong defence may be the best route to victory, but even then subsequent offensive action will be required to clear the remnants from in front of the ramparts and to seize back lost ground. The benefits are that you can:

- Stand firm against fierce opposition.
- Make alliances with strong people.
- Shut up the naysayers decisively.

It is sometimes necessary to trade space (territory) for time, to draw an enemy over a piece of ground whilst he dissipates his strength and thereby creates the optimum moment for you to strike back. This was the disadvantage that both Napoleon in 1812 and Hitler in 1941 encountered in Russia. The huge land mass and harsh climate provided the opportunity to weaken the attacker as he was drawn deeper and deeper into the country, over-extending supply lines and providing countless opportunities for the defenders to harry them from the flanks and the rear, while all the time falling back towards their bases and preparing to counter-attack.

In the commercial arena, there are many equivalents to the principle of offensive action. A company with the necessary financial muscle can dominate a particular market by acquiring the competition and winning over customers and suppliers alike. The march of Microsoft across the globe in the 1980s–90s shows what great products, determinedly led by a revered leader and powerfully marketed, can achieve. Equally, a company that sees its current markets shrinking could elect to downsize, take stock and then move aggressively into new areas. And every now and again the market is stormed by a company with such a new and innovative product that it changes the way of life of millions of people: the Model T Ford, the 747, the iPod and Viagra. Success is not easy to guarantee and any entrepreneur would tell you that it is half hunch (built up of keenness, sensitivity and passion) and half luck.

In the world of hostile acquisitions, a small company can grab a much bigger rival by striking when investors see that the target is suffering from poor leadership, outmoded products and an unsustainable debt, but with the potential for greatness to be restored. Just as important as practical activity, offensive action should be an attitude of mind at all levels in an organisation, military or commercial. This sense of disciplined aggression ensures that opportunities are made, not waited for, that small successes are quickly exploited and failures rapidly bypassed. Offensive action exemplifies the entrepreneurial mindset, the propensity to fast action, seizing a window of opportunity to make a daring calculated move.

EASYJET

The innovative style of low-cost carriers such as easyJet has fundamentally reshaped the aviation industry in the face of bigger, well-established rivals – a strong example of commercial offensive action led from the top. Stelios' genius was in daring to think differently, catching out everyone who thought the idea too preposterous to take seriously. His main offensive was his 'price elasticity' and 'yield management' – lower the price to increase demand and then manage the price according to demand. He made sure his staff were fully behind his mission (they were equally enthusiastic about efficiency and the importance of not wasting resources – even to the extent of sharing Biros).

BUILD YOUR ARMOURY
Offensive Action

Here is a list of tools and tips giving specific advice on how to take offensive action effectively.

▷ Ask yourself what you don't like about the status quo. Ask others what they think. Do something different – set yourself apart from your competitors.

▷ Get everyone involved in the conversation. What would be a better way? Where's the gap? How and where can you seize the initiative?

▷ Often the people at the sharp end are those who feel most frustrated, upset, fired up – use that passion to get them to see through the new idea.

▷ It doesn't matter what you do, sell, provide – how can you make your customers pleased and proud to use you? What can you do differently to get a great reaction, make you look special and your end user feel valued?

▷ Who could you form an alliance with or take over, a support business, a competitor, allied businesses abroad? No matter how small your business, who could enhance what you do? For instance, if you do presentations, who is out there that knows how to add music and voices to your PowerPoint? If you make handbags, who is out there painting on silk that would make great linings? If you are a not-for-profit organisation, why are you in competition with other charities? How could you work together?

▷ What do you do better than anyone else? How can you capitalise on that in offensive actions? Pluck up courage, ask your clients why they chose you. What do they think you do better? Find out and enhance it.

▷ Don't think your customers always know best. Henry Ford said if he'd asked his customers what they wanted, they'd have said, 'a faster horse'. Think ahead of your customers, well ahead. Do some 'What If' thinking. You'd be surprised how many people can contribute; they do not even have to be in your line of business at all!

▷ You don't get lucky sitting watching television or bemoaning your fortunes in office corridors. If you want an apple to land on your head it helps to stand in an orchard – so get out and about. Get yourself and your people involved, connected, engaged with other people and their problems and then all sorts of opportunities may pop up.

▷ Know what you do well and shout it from the rooftops, or whatever your chosen marketing medium. It is no use being brilliant if only two clients know about you. You have to market yourself intelligently and continually ask, where else, how else?

▷ Ask the team, what would really light their fire? Listen and watch carefully – use their passion.

Concentration of Force

In business as in war, it is very rare to be strong everywhere, so you need to focus the pressure you bring to bear through the concentration of force. The benefits of concentration of force are that you:

● Enjoy least effort for maximum gain.
● Exploit your strengths.
● Reap success through focus-focus-focus.

Even the US, the world's only Superpower, does not have the troops, ships and aircraft to strike everywhere it may wish to in its global war against terrorism at the same tine as it protects its forces abroad and looks after the US homeland. Hurricane Katrina in 2005 showed this in grim detail as we watched the response to that disaster. Adequate resources must be set aside to meet each challenge, and this will generally mean contingency planning that takes into account all the possible outcomes. (For example, the planning for the eventuality of serious hurricanes around New Orleans had a contingency for the levees running over, not for the levees collapsing.)

Concentration of force in a military sense means applying decisive effort at the most decisive point. It may mean staging battles in a planned order rather than trying to have them all on the same day. Concentration of force is accomplished at the right time and at the right place. Napoleon understood this well, dividing his forces into corps (each effectively an independent mini-army), which marched on separate routes to converge on the enemy commander in overwhelming force at the decisive time and place. This did not always mean having more forces overall than his enemies, it meant having enough in the right place so that he could defeat even larger forces in increments. It is not about chivalry: if crushing an enemy can be achieved by concentrating vastly more powerful forces so that victory is delivered more quickly, with fewer own casualties and with such great effect that the enemy's will to continue the war collapses, that is a good result.

The principle of concentration of force applies equally well in business, the public sector and the voluntary sector in the way resources are applied. The timing and direction of investment to maximise return, the timing and location of shop openings and the plans required to launch new products into a market all require decisions about concentration of force in which 'force' is manpower and money. To make an impact it is usually necessary to create the right effect at the best time: a big launch to sell holidays will not prosper as well in September, when people are just home from their annual trip away, as just after Christmas when the sky is grey and summer is a long way off. Small packets of manpower and money scattered across the market place, with none enough by itself to make any inroads, are less likely to bring success than a major concerted effort at a single, high-profile location.

APPLE

Apple computers are a good illustration of the value of concentrated force exploiting what it knew it was good at. Steve Jobs and Steve Wozniak were a couple of 20-something college dropouts who started Apple Computers in the family garage in 1976. They built a circuit board they named Apple 1 and had 200 sales within a few months. A young millionaire then invested in them and by the end of 1980 they had become the industry leader, selling more than 100,000 Apple 11s. Of course, when IBM entered the market things changed. IBM's PCs relied on Microsoft's DOS operating system and Intel's microprocessors. While this might not have been as exciting as Apple's machine the PCs could be cloned by other manufacturers wishing to make compatibles and resulted in Apple becoming marginalised. In effect the concentration of force behind the IBM revolution swamped Apple.

By the 1990s plenty of companies, including Dell and Compaq, were selling PCs with Microsoft software and Intel microprocessors. After Apple had tried and ousted a few CEOs, they brought Steve Jobs back. His greatest coup was the iMac – Apple's stylish entry into the low-priced consumer market, with plug and play peripherals. Apple now has 10,000 employees and annual sales of up to $6 billion but that is still only around 3 per cent of the home market, with Dell, HP and Microsoft as its main competitors. However, with miniMac and iPod as icons of cool, superb customer service, additional products such as iTunes – and now iWork and iLife – and 'genius bars' at its Apple stores, the company is really shaking its arse at its competitors. Apple has focused the pressure it can apply to the market through innovation and differentiation.

BUILD YOUR ARMOURY
Focus the Pressure

Here is a list of tools and tips giving specific advice on how to use the principle of concentration of force to best effect.

▷ Identify where you are needed in the market place – this will be easier the wider you read. Read the specialist press and trade journals, and access the Internet to gain a wider variety of views on the same subject. Get to events that yield information on how others see you. Go to lectures, conferences, symposiums as well as informal networking lunches with people in and around your field so that you will be able to gauge your likely impact on the marketplace.

▷ Look at the costs of investment realistically. It is much better to spend your money on one solid project, and get it right, than launch two weak projects that buckle through lack of funding.

▷ Build teams that bring all the necessary skills together, and keep the teams intact and focused until the job is done. Do not allow people to flit between teams unless you are prepared to invest in the training necessary to ensure that their replacement will pick up from where they left off and do just as good a job (as is the case in the military). In the absence of such training, it is a dissipation of forces to replace team members every couple of years.

▷ Monitor and regulate cash flow rigorously, so that resources are spent on what is identified as core activity.

▷ Ensure that training is well planned and focused on where it is needed most. Then evaluate how effective it has been in four phases: immediately, at three months (what can be remembered?), at six months (what are the effects on the people around them?), one year (what have been the effects on the business?).

▷ Pay more than the going rate for top skills and then talk money no more – concentrate minds on the work and on recognition, not reward. Do not hire someone on the cheap – second-class pay means second-class results. Likewise, hire for talent not just because the candidate is easy going (such people often peak at mediocrity). Be brave enough to hire brilliant but difficult candidates, who speak their mind and rock the status quo – then hone your management skills to ensure you can cope with them.

▷ Identify each of your teams' strengths and ask yourself how well you are exploiting that talent? Can others in the business readily name their teams' strengths? How well do your peers/bosses manage the talents of their teams? How well do they really know each other and their potential?

▷ Can everyone in the business recognise the critical moments that you need to grab and execute perfectly? Have the dialogue – make everyone clear and establish a process where people can identify and speak up and get those 'critical moments' right.

THE 7 SECRETS OF LEADERSHIP SUCCESS

▷ Have a success check-point (SCP) – a quick dialogue to check that what you have just done or are about to do is the most effective way to achieve your aim. Is your workforce totally focused on effectiveness? Look around you, watch for a while, or spend a half day evaluating those around you. Is there a better way they could do things? Or are they doing the wrong thing altogether?

▷ Review where you are spending money and allocating resources. If the needs are not there, the market turns sour. Do not throw cash after lost causes, no matter how strong the emotional attachment. Concentrate resources for the future, not the past.

▷ Are you keeping costs under control? Do your managers have at their fingertips the cost/yield ratios of the equipment/activities you are involved in? Don't leave it to the finance department – look closely at the figures yourself and use your common sense and your intuition to work out what they are telling you.

Economy of Effort

It is very rare indeed that commanders will have all the resources they need to be powerful everywhere, so as well as using concentration of force you need to make shrewd moves. The benefits of economy of effort are that you:

- Make cute moves.
- Know your game.
- Are clear about the effect you want to produce.

The best effects are achieved by concentrating power at the right moment and in the right place – the 'Decisive Point'. Even then, it is important not to throw everything at it, but to keep something back for the next battle. This is particularly important at senior levels of command: more junior leaders will rightly be primarily concerned with winning the current battle, and give less thought to what might follow. It is the task of the Business General to think more broadly, applying resources to a sequence of encounters that will bring the campaign as a whole to a successful conclusion. This means not burning up all creative energy or equipment on the first day.

Economy of effort means making shrewd choices. It means thinking carefully and intelligently and gathering the knowledge you need wherever you can find it. All military leaders have a habit of reading a variety of papers and watching the news. They do this to keep abreast of the wider political and social situations they may find themselves in. You need to do the same. If you are ignorant about current or business affairs you cannot make intelligent moves! For example, an army moving forward through hostile territory may focus its power at the front as it pushes on, but it will need to protect its flanks and its rear as it does so. That doesn't necessarily mean keeping a host of troops to do the job – it might be that there is a large natural feature, such as a river to do the job, perhaps local militia can be persuaded to help, or airborne surveillance could provide the necessary protection. The point is that economy of force can involve creative thinking about how to minimise risk and maximise resources for the main event. It involves thinking about the effects you want to achieve and working back from there, brainstorming and using lateral thinking techniques to explore options on how that could be achieved.

Economy of force applies equally well to both offensive and defensive actions. For example, the minimum power necessary should be expended to beat off the enemy, saving resources for a counter-attack to be launched just as the opposition is running out of steam and at his most extended in terms of supplies, energy, and willpower. Economy of force also means good support systems. For example, rather than replacing damaged equipment it might be better to have an effective repair system deployed on the battlefield so that equipment can remain effective for longer, without the need to bring in costly new items.

BEF

A good example of economy of force in military operations is provided by the conduct of the withdrawal of the British Expeditionary Force (BEF) from Dunkirk in 1940. A small force was maintained to hold the perimeter of the port and surrounding area against German attacks. This bought time for as much as possible of the BEF to be evacuated to continue the campaign in the future, at the cost of those left behind to fight a losing battle (the French forces still fighting elsewhere were not enthused by the news of the British evacuation). The alternative, to commit the whole of the BEF to fight to the last, might have inflicted more short-term damage on the German forces, but at the expense of saving enough combat power to rebuild to fight another day. This approach involved making some tough choices. For example, the wounded were evacuated after fit men in order of priority, such was the premium on saving usable resources. Manpower was far more important than equipment. Factories could replace equipment far faster than a population could make up for high levels of casualties. As a result, 218,000 British and 120,000 French soldiers were successfully withdrawn, an irreplaceable core of trained, experienced manpower from which to build a new invasion force, which was to return to France on D Day four years later.

In business, the logic of economy of force is equally applicable as a Principle of Winning. Investment must be managed by careful timing, perhaps focusing expenditure on hiring new creative talent one year and on replacing equipment the next. Every business will be faced with its own unique set of decisions, so it is up to senior managers to decide where economy of force can be best applied. This can be achieved by introducing better systems and processes, for example, by reducing waste, ending unnecessary activities, returning to the core business, outsourcing, and freeing up underused capital and so on.

It is important not only to maximise resources for key activities, but also to protect the business from financial and other threats at least cost. It is sometimes the case that a business has a successful core process, upon which management is completely focused, as well extremely inefficient supporting activities, which are going unnoticed to the detriment of the concern as a whole. For example, there is no point in being brilliant at making and selling a product if the profits made are swallowed up by the costs of administration or recruitment. Similarly, is a marble foyer an essential attribute for a thriving business, or just an expensive way of expressing the self-esteem of the CEO of the day? The leadership must take the wider view that the principle of economy of force demands.

BUILD YOUR ARMOURY
Shrewd Moves
Here is a list of tools and tips giving specific advice on how to use economy of effort in your organisation.

▷ What effect do you want to achieve? Be clear. Challenge your assumptions about the best ways to achieve that.

▷ Where do you need to increase or slow the pace for a while?

▷ Do an old-fashioned time-and-motion study to test efficiency. For example, mark down how long it takes different activities to be completed, note what someone is doing over the course of a week – in 15-minute increments. It is boring and tedious to complete, but adding up at the end of the week exactly how the time is being spent can provide the insight that enables you to improve efficiency.

▷ Get people into the habit of asking, 'I can but should I?' Coach people to delegate to the level that stretches and motivates, leaving only those tasks that they and they alone can best do for themselves. Anything else is waste. Getting people to let go of what they can do but shouldn't is a constant challenge that requires concerted effort and support. But the rewards for clarity of role in terms of stress levels and well-being are huge.

▷ Check where you are investing – look at the payoffs in the cold light of day. Have you been over-investing in one area at the expense of somewhere else?

▷ Think about outsourcing work that could be managed more easily by others if it frees up your team's key strengths and resources for more useful areas.

▷ Pace activities in your organisation around key events. There is no point urging people to work on your best idea on the week before Christmas. Get the rhythm right, up the pace to a high tempo only when the situation calls for it and let people ease off at other times. A languid pace, with time out, is good for reflecting and being creative. Too many businesses operate at a pace that is either too moderate or too frenetic all the time.

▷ Maintain a proper work-life balance. Leaders who thrash themselves seven days a week will lose perspective and judgement and will lack the reserves needed to show patience, resolve, assertiveness and humility for the really big events. Get a life. It is up to you to find the balance.

▷　Relax and get perspective. Do not treat every task as top priority. In part, business success means identifying those jobs that need maximum effort from top down, and those that should be left to more junior staff to cut their teeth on.

▷　Pace tasks sensibly and do not attempt to do everything concurrently. The military know about pacing. If necessary, they will concentrate on one vital task at a time, generally giving it sufficient time to complete. Don't rush, don't flit and don't panic.

Flexibility – In People and Plans

Flexibility is as much about character as it is an aspect of project management. The benefits are that you will:

- Be able to regroup in the midst of chaos.
- Keep cohesion in times of rapid change.
- Give people enough time to do a good job.

Flexibility is about being able to stretch without breaking. It is about bending only as much as is necessary (without bending over backwards), and moving back when required. Flexibility begins with mental robustness – the ability of senior leaders to see clearly in the heat of the moment that change is required and to find the creative spark, the energy and the resilience to make it happen. Likewise, flexibility means changing course when it is right to do so, owning up to a plan that hasn't taken all considerations into account, accepting that a decision was taken without the right information. It is a tough call to have to communicate a change of direction knowing the reaction it will have – but those who fail to make that call (perhaps for fear of being disliked) fail in their duty as keeper of the vision and mission.

Leaders need to be trusted and respected if they are to ensure that dramatic changes to plans are followed through faithfully by the staff. A workforce will often worry about change, particularly in ambiguous or chaotic circumstances. Sadly, levels of trust and respect, in much of business today, are low. These qualities have to be earned by having a history of competence, and that means handling themselves well in all situations and the ability to make the right decisions under pressure. This is how good leaders establish their reputation. Leaders who are technically competent but get hot under the collar when under pressure, who show others little respect and who are not loyal to their teams are in turn not respected or trusted. Their mood will affect that of their staff, and that hinders constructive and clear thinking. Leaders whose style cracks in adversity cannot expect to be promoted.

The Principle of Winning is about having the flexibility of character and behaviour needed to do something different in the face of failure. As Einstein said, doing the same thing and expecting a different result is madness. A great plan, one that has considered the challenge from every angle and produced the optimum solution – with well-identified and managed risks – is often only 10 per cent of the route to success. Warfare, like business, is not set in an inert environment where key factors oblige by staying the same throughout the conception and execution of the plan. In fact, military plans – at all levels – usually have to evolve even as they are being written to keep pace with the situation as it really is, not as it was. This requires leadership and planning skills of the highest quality. It is highly tempting for a leader to resist new information that conflicts with the plan that has been laboured over in conditions of great stress – the more so when tired and battle is about to start.

Once a large-scale plan has been put into action there can be so many moving parts that it is impossible to isolate one failing cog in the machine. For example, the plan as a whole may succeed, but at the cost of unnecessary casualties. So flexibility as a Principle of War means having both the attitude of mind and the organisational strength and training to meet the demands of changing, unexpected situations in order to beat a freethinking, agile opponent.

A vital component of senior leadership is the ability to introduce a change of plans, even fundamental changes, to a tired and perhaps demoralised or angry staff. This is much easier if senior commanders routinely avoid becoming immersed in too much detail and retain an eye on the horizon. It also helps if they have the freedom to think carefully and honestly about the relevant information they ask for and issue instructions in sufficient time. In the era of the digitised battlefield it is possible for the general to direct the movement of individual vehicles. But this is hopeless if it means he is fighting the corporal's battles for him and is not looking at the battle as a whole. So flexibility means finding the vision and the strength of will to keep the organisation fighting the battle they are actually faced with, rather than the one they planned for.

Organisational flexibility is just as important as flexibility in terms of an attitude of mind and an attribute of character. One of the features that distinguishes a large but badly organised army from a great one is that the former will be slow to change direction once committed to battle. Long columns of armoured vehicles with miles of support traffic behind it, all communicating indifferently by radio, will quickly dissolve into chaos when asked to turn in a new direction. A great army has the training, practised drills and good communications to manage such a change on the move without losing momentum and cohesion.

It takes time to develop this degree of organisational capability. It involves good teamwork: people who know each well and have developed common practices to enable them to move quickly as a cohesive unit. This requires good training, confidence, trust and the tools necessary to move information around swiftly and accurately. Flexibility also applies to equipment and organisation. In the Armed Forces this means designing equipment that can operate in a wide range of climates and terrain, and is easy to transport by sea and air. One of the legacies of the Cold War in Europe was that so much equipment had been specified for use only in temperate north-western Europe that it struggled to work when deployed at short notice to the Gulf in 1991. This had not been foreseen at the time of acquisition, and the cost and industrial effort to overcome this lack of foresight did not come cheap. Similarly, organisations that had settled into a routine along the Inner German border for 40 years had to make a major readjustment when pitched into the Balkans and the Gulf for the first time. In many cases, it is flexibility of mind that is decisive, overcoming the limitations of the relative inflexibility of equipment and organisation in the short term. This is a key leadership role.

Flexibility is required at all levels of an organisation. It is not enough that the corporate headquarters is positively throbbing with energy, if the departments below it are ill equipped to keep pace. It is imperative that leaders imbue flexibility into all parts of their organisation so that change is made in a coherent and synergistic manner. This involves culture and corporate spirit as well as systems and processes, and is a two-way flow: just as head office must require lower-levels to be responsive, so the lower-levels need the room to execute decisions independently without having their own flexibility inhibited by the need to report back, defer decisions and consult in detail. This is generally harder to achieve in Government-led institutions such as the Armed Forces, where the hierarchical nature of the organisation can breed friction.

One-Third/Two-Thirds Rule

A major irritation for bosses is that they issue new instructions and then wonder if their words have simply vanished into the ether because no one has reported back. It is equally infuriating for employees when the boss burdens them with a heavy work-load without notice. The following technique avoids annoying your subordinates or having them annoy you. This technique creates the optimum flow of information so that people can make changes effectively. It is a great way to galvanise and programme your subordinates to ensure an optimal flow of information.

The one-third/two-thirds rule works like this: the commander receives instructions about what to do next. He or she then estimates the total time that is left until the change must be implemented. One-third of this time is set aside to plan and issue the commander's own instructions. The remaining two-thirds of the time is made available to subordinate leaders so that they can make and issue their own plans. This avoids creating a rush of orders that are issued and have to be carried out in a hurry. It is called Battle Procedure.

Here is an example of battle procedure being applied to the business world. The scene is the managing director's office in a small business making and selling leather goods. A big order comes in for bespoke folders for a new corporate client. The client wants the order delivered in 30 days. It is no good the designer and head of sales hogging most of this time and then suddenly letting the machinists know what is required with only a week to go. Using the one-third/two-thirds rule, the MD issues a warning notice as soon as he or she receives the order – Day 1. This notice goes out to everyone who will be involved in filling the order – in this case the leather supplier, the machinist supervisor, the packing manager and the logistics head. The notice states that full instructions will be given on Day 10 (that is, one-third of the 30 days until the order must be filled). The design must be finished by Day 10, with a full set of instructions ready to be sent to all those next in command. This gives the rest of the team two-thirds of the time to fill the order. On Day 1 the MD also chooses a date for 'rock drill'. This is the final briefing meeting when the team explain their plans so that the MD can sign them off and might be set for, say, Day 22. (The name 'rock drill' comes from the days when generals made a model of the battle using rocks!) From Day 2, the team would have been thinking about what they need from any supplier or junior staff member and would have issued their own warning notices. Their full instructions would be sent to the team on Day 11.

Let Us Take Another Example ...

A department has been asked to provide training for another department in four months' time. The boss of that department lets his team know on Day 1 and issues a warning notice. Then he might get the design team together and on Day 10 issues a full set of instructions to the trainers and administrators. They in turn issue a warning notice to their teams and suppliers. They then go off and design the sections they are training around the objectives, prepare the slides, plan exercises, arrange the music and venue, produce manuals, including getting any outside help they need. The rock drill is set for Day 20 when all the trainers explain what they are going to do to achieve the objectives of their section of the course, either by phone or face to face. The slides are sent to the boss and the admin team report back on the venue booked. The plan is signed off and the last prelims (preliminary execution activities) are carried out. There is a final prelim face-to-face meeting to make sure all the pieces are in place.

Flexibility requires good information, but it is of no use if the information is found and analysed too late to do anything with it. It is essential that individuals do not act selfishly here. They need to consider the time of others as well as their own. For example, the fact that the Allies were able to read the German 'Ultra' codes during the Second World War made a decisive difference to the 'Battle of the Atlantic' between allied shipping and German submarines. The information that was received about the intentions of the German submarines made it possible to re-route shipping and get anti-submarine defences in place. The outcome of this vital campaign would have been completely different if the Allies, having received the information in time, had been unable to move quickly enough to act on it.

Facing Facts

Business leaders are as liable as military commanders to be overwhelmed by circumstances and the very human reaction of denying the existence of unpalatable facts rather than dealing with them. The requirement for flexibility of mind, founded on intellectual and emotional robustness, is the same. How many businesses have gone to the wall because for too long they continued producing a tired product or service, and lacked the will, vision and energy to break away from the well-trodden path? How many companies provide what they can offer easily, rather than what the customer really wants?

The organisational challenge is as high. The merit of investing in production capacity, stock, training and so forth hangs on making the intended return. If market conditions change – so must the firm. Making or providing too much of something when the market has moved on is the road to ruin, even if it can be delayed for a time by consuming reserves or implementing price cuts. The most successful commercial organisations constantly assess what they are doing now and intend to do next against their operating environment. They need the mental and physical agility to make the 'fit' as close as possible for as long as possible. If this is not possible, perhaps because new legislation suddenly closes an existing market, then a flexible business leader has the vision to negotiate the best possible exit terms – not fight on until the shareholders' last pound is spent.

BUILD YOUR ARMOURY

Flexibility in People and Plans

Here is a list of tools and tips giving specific advice on how to make your organisation more flexible.

▷ Use the one-third/two-thirds rule on your current project.

▷ Introduce the one-third/two-thirds rule as part of every piece of delegated work, with warning notices on 'Day W' (as soon as possible); full instructions on 'Day X' (one-third of the time available to delivery); rock drill 'Day Y' (a date that allows people to have accomplished their tasks and be ready to report back, while still allowing time for last-minute changes); and prelim day 'Day Z' (just before event).

▷ Recognise that a perfect plan is only 10 per cent of the route to success, and 90 per cent of the route involves reacting with appropriate degrees of resolve and flexibility. You can't have a leader who is only great at planning. He or she needs to be flexible – and great at getting staff to accept the changes as well.

▷ Encourage people to see pragmatism and flexibility as a strength, not a lack of character or will. Show where such behaviours have led to success.

▷ Create the climate where it is acceptable to acknowledge when you are off course and to identify quickly where change is required. Create the culture where junior members of staff, people from other departments and customers can all be heard if they think that a course of action is unwise. Discourage staff from sticking to a course of action when all the evidence points another way.

▷ Show your character and develop potential by your response when things do not go as planned – admit the situation has changed and learn from it. Encourage those around you to do the same and make sure that 'the system' doesn't make them scapegoats. Celebrate their honesty and generosity in sharing Lessons Identified so that others might learn from them. These are qualities that need to be recognised and rewarded.

▷ Create resilience and mental robustness by making sure leaders believe in the plan, but also recognise and resolve problems by creating a new plan when the time is right. Have the courage to let go of what is no longer needed and re-equip yourself with vital and relevant skills/products/services.

The Value of Co-operation

Many companies underestimate the value of co-operation. They applaud toughness and independent thinking, but too much of it results in unco-ordinated independent action and unnecessary confrontation. The benefits of co-operation are that you:

- Use the diversity of beliefs, skills and attitudes available.
- Don't confuse leadership with independence.

Co-operation is seen as the soft option, a compromise, whereas finding 'a third way' is the hard option, the creative response. There is a game called 'prisoner's dilemma' played in numerous management development courses where the most obvious way to win is to play selfishly in order to win points and avoid penalties. Yet the game cannot be won by selfish endeavour alone; people have to co-operate to win. As that is not obvious, so few of those taking part do co-operate. This attitude is played out in meeting rooms across the land.

The principle of co-operation covers people, units, organisations, even international coalition partners. For the Armed Forces, this means co-operation within and between the Navy, Army and Air Force to combine their capabilities to greatest operational effect. For the Army, the challenge of 'combined arms' warfare presents a huge training task. A tank crew must learn to operate a very complex machine to its full potential on its own, and then alongside other tanks, and then as part of a grouping of tanks, artillery, engineers, helicopters and infantry numbering from a few hundred to a few thousand soldiers.

Increasingly this co-operation is being extended to include the Armed Forces of other countries (with different tactics, equipment, training and language), where divisions or misunderstandings could expose fatal Coalition weaknesses. The same occurs in modern peace support operations such as in Bosnia and Kosovo, where different operating methods between national contingents can be exposed and manipulated by opposition elements – for example by relocating criminal activities from areas that are patrolled by what are perceived as 'hard' contingents to 'softer' ones. UK forces now work closely with the Government

Department for International Development (DfID) in many theatres, each retaining considerable independence under overall Cabinet Office direction. The UN and its agencies dealing with human rights, refugees, food distribution and employment, and other global non-governmental organisations, are all part of the co-operation patchwork: no single person or organisation is able to exercise full control.

Co-operation in business also operates at two key levels: between the individuals working in teams within an organisation, and between separate organisations required to work closely for common goals.

BAE SYSTEMS

BAE Systems has managed a successful joint MoD/Industry partnership set up to explore network-enabled warfare. The aim is to develop an integrated network – NITEworks – that transmits relevant, timely and accurate information to commanders and decision makers. NITEworks uses BAE Systems' own state-of-the-art Battlespace Management Evaluation Centre as a key tool for integrating systems, visualising concepts and as a hub for experimentation. It has required a subtle change in culture to make this work. BAE Systems needed to find a different process and style, and to achieve this they have invested in building a collaborative culture of shared attitudes, perspectives and behaviours. They have been successful in creating trusting and open relationships with former competitors, clients (the Defence Procurement Agency) and the end users (the military). The desired outcome is to engage in pre-concept dialogue rather than the more traditional model – 'accept the tender/brief, respond, and then negotiate more after the contract is signed' – that the industry had previously found to have a negative effect on creating innovative solutions.

BUILD YOUR ARMOURY
The Principle of Co-operation

Here is a list of tools and tips giving specific advice on how to use the principle of co-operation well.

▷ Write, present and coach others on the way you want to co-operate with suppliers, departments and stakeholders.

▷ Introduce more shadowing and secondments. These are good ways to improve awareness and consideration, develop empathy, uncover hidden potential and improve working relationships.

▷ Introduce 'collective training' – which everyone goes to – covering subjects including your code of leadership, the aim of the organisation, who is who, and how you all fit together.

▷ Devote time and resources to helping people get to know each other and relate to one another.

▷ Appreciate each other's customs, preferences, values, goals and procedures as a way of building respect. Ask, share, disclose and publish the results.

▷ Uphold previous commitments, however large or small, as a way of showing respect and building trust.

▷ Encourage more women to reach management positions. A Henley management college study entitled 'Leadership in the Twenty-first Century' concluded that a mix of men and women was vital to achieve optimum leadership. A gender balance enables companies to benefit from the different qualities that men and women bring to the workplace. The forces could do more here. The relationship skills that women in leadership posts contribute will be a vital element in winning the support and trust of communities needed for the global war on terrorism.

▷ Look for signs of unhealthy internal competition and strife and tackle it at source. Ensure people listen to and accommodate others. Seek out those who persist with selfish agendas and get them to change – or ask them to go.

Sustainability

Sustainability is about logistics and we advocate all leaders getting involved in that supply chain. The benefits are that you:

- Complete tasks to everyone's satisfaction.
- Engage everyone in the end process of the work.

For the Armed Forces, sustainability means providing the logistical support needed to enable an operation to succeed. Logistics defines the art of the possible: even the finest Army will fail if it lacks food. Sustainability is a commander's business, and not the exclusive preserve of specialists – even if such expertise is truly indispensable. The commander will know how far he can move his forces, how long they can last with existing stocks, how many casualties can be handled at any one time, and what medical threats, such as malaria, the soldiers may face. He needs to know this if his plans are going to be realistic. He can then spot where he is vulnerable to enemy action and decide quickly how to act when changes become needed. He will not, for example, keep all his ammunition in a single depot where it presents a golden opportunity to his opponent to end the battle with a single strike. He will also judge how to pace limited, high-value stocks such as cruise missiles throughout his plan of campaign. It can then be left to the specialists to ensure that the commander's intent is met, to provide advice on options and to keep the commander fully informed as critical capabilities change. A key component of sustainability is simplicity: logistical and support plans may define the commander's level of operational flexibility. A plan that is so complex that it is inadequately understood and too slow to change is a significant handicap for a commander. Warfare demands an excess of stock over requirements so that the effects of losses and the unpredictable turn of events can be managed.

The principle of sustainability in business obviously has very wide application. Just as on the battlefield, a business needs the freedom of action that good logistics and administration provide – this is a key element of a company's power. The Business General must ensure resources are sufficient to meet his or her objectives and are applied with the necessary military precision, timing and effect. There are a great many launches in business that turn out to be false starts – a cost cut might call off an initiative, a new leader might redirect resources, people might go back to old systems that don't support new plans. Sustainability requires dedication, resolve, detailed analysis, the capacity to finish the job – qualities that many people lack. It takes dedication and perseverance to think through all the details necessary to make everything mesh together. It is often quiet, back-office work – not the flashy, high-profile stuff that seems to get people noticed for promotion. Yet it is indispensable and vital. Leaders need to put sustainability right in the spotlight. Without it, they may fall flat on their faces.

BUILD YOUR ARMOURY
Keep Going to the End

Here is a list of tools and tips giving specific advice on how to use the principle of sustainability.

▷ Make sure all department heads are fully aware and involved in the logistics – from start to end. Check that logistics, support, admin, back of house, back office staff have a status equal to those, like marketing, in the forefront of the business. All have an equally important part to play.

▷ Stamp out attitudes or activities that disadvantage any element of the workforce. Recognise that enabling functions such as buildings management are as important as accountants and lawyers.

▷ Let everyone know that you think this way and make sure no one gets away with treating others badly – no matter what their position or value to the business.

▷ Make everyone feel important. The PA to the head of one of UK's Armed Forces said recently: 'He makes me feel important, as if my job is important, too. I therefore think it is important and behave as if it is. I feel proud to do a good job.' If heads of department are making their staff feel undervalued, unimportant – do something about it or ask them to go. They are causing harm to your business.

▷ Use good project management techniques to direct resources and support to the right place at the right time. There is no justification for delays due to a shortage of basic items such as envelopes and bolts.

▷ Review the way key supporting equipment, such as transport and information technology, is provided. Are they bought in the right mix of quality, quantity and supportability?

Too little, and the business is at risk, too much and the costs go through the roof – and maybe the competition will forge ahead.

▷ Are staffing requirements being met? The firm should not be reliant on the health of one or two key individuals. Train reserves and deputies. Make sure you have your successor ready, too!

▷ Make sure people take holidays and weekends – this conserves their energy, creativity and goodwill for the longer haul.

THE 'TRAFFIC LIGHT' ASSESSMENT

How Well Do You Use the Principles of Winning Now?

Use the following 'traffic light' assessment to show where you are, by and large, getting it right (tick the lower traffic light), where you are some way there or where there are pockets of good work (tick the middle traffic light) and where you are not doing well (tick the top traffic light). Do that for all three of the levels of assessment – where you are now, where you are against your preferred standard and how you would perform if suddenly faced with maximum pressure, given the capability you have now.

PRINCIPLES OF WINNING TRAFFIC LIGHT

Ask yourself:

A) How are we doing now?

B) How are we performing against best-practice and best-in-class?

C) How would we perform if we were put under maximum pressure with the resources we have right now?

Selection and maintenance of the Aim

A B C
We are absolutely clear about the Aim.

A B C
Everyone in the organisation is also absolutely clear.

A B C
All of our time is spent directly contributing to the aim.

Maintenance of morale

A B C
We are forging ahead and morale – commitment, engagement, optimism – is high.

Security

A B C
We have identified our highest-value assets and are protecting them securely.

Surprise

A B C
We are using intelligence to steal a march on competitors.

Offensive action

A B C
We are exciting our and our competitors' customers.

A B C
We have new plans that will create a storm.

Concentration of force

A B C
We are focusing our efforts and the team's efforts on all the right things.

A B C
There are no shortfalls in terms of input, force, insistence, time.

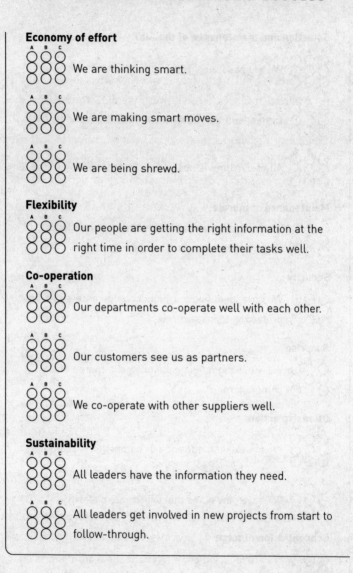

Economy of effort

A B C

We are thinking smart.

We are making smart moves.

We are being shrewd.

Flexibility

A B C

Our people are getting the right information at the right time in order to complete their tasks well.

Co-operation

A B C

Our departments co-operate well with each other.

Our customers see us as partners.

We co-operate with other suppliers well.

Sustainability

A B C

All leaders have the information they need.

All leaders get involved in new projects from start to follow-through.

Summary of Secret Number One: Synchronised Thinking

- This Secret deals with the power of ideas and is the first of the three sides that make up the Power Pyramid, which forms the basis of a coherent and effective organisation.

- Harnessing the thinking power of your organisation ensures that everyone has a common understanding of the goal they are striving for and a common understanding of the best way to achieve it.

- As a Business General, Secret Number One can help you shape your team, department or organisation via a common 'doctrine' or frame of language, reference points and processes.

- A well-constructed doctrine can provide you with a decisive competitive advantage. You can develop a doctrine for your own firm to create a cohesiveness such as never before.

- Synchronised Thinking helps your group to really focus their efforts – invaluable if you've ever been concerned about people being pulled in different directions, ultimately leading to wasted effort.

- The Principles of Winning are a well-proven and robust set of maxims. You can use them as the root of good decision-making and planning and change management in your area of work.

Implementing Secret Number One thoroughly into your organisation will make significant improvements – do keep us informed how you are doing via our website: www.thebusinessgeneral.com

Next Secret...

In the next section, Secret Number Two: Soul Matters, we go on to look at the second side of the Power Pyramid, which explains the importance of establishing an organisation's core values.

Secret Two
Soul Matters
Build the spirit, values and character that enable people to thrive

'In war, morale is to material as three to one.'
NAPOLEON BONAPARTE

Whatever it is that makes a soldier pick himself up from the relative safety of his trench and hurl himself at an enemy that is doing his best to kill him, it is not the money. Yet when all logic and every instinct for self-preservation scream at him to stay at the bottom of his hole, soldiers around the globe have got up and taken the fight to the enemy – often paying a terrible price for glory or defeat. Just occasionally these people seem to have been born to be heroes, with characters that are the stuff of legend and a sense of destiny about them. More often than not they are men and women who just happened to be there when the situation demanded something extraordinary – and they did it.

Heroism in any context is bound to raise the question, why? Why did he do that? What drove him on when he could just as well have stayed put and dramatically improved the prospects of seeing another day? Few of us have been in circumstances where the risks were overwhelming, where blood may be spilled and yet the motivation to succeed was so powerful that medals were won. However, all of us have encountered the opposite situation, where people are so complacent, dull and selfish that opportunities are wasted. The difference is in the soul of the individual, as well as the organisation. This soul can be found and developed in everyone. Soul is as fundamental as intellect, technology and physical strength in achieving success. The second side of the Power Pyramid is the essential contribution that soul makes to an organisation. You need this, whatever else you do.

'On 23 August 1914 during the First World War Battle of Mons in France, Private Sidney Frank took over a machine gun defending a bridge after his officer had been fatally wounded. He kept the German enemy at bay for two hours, and in so doing covered the retreat of his comrades. Despite being wounded twice, he managed to dismantle the gun and throw it into the water before eventually being taken prisoner.'

TAKEN FROM THE CITATION FOR SIDNEY FRANK'S VICTORIA CROSS, THE UK'S HIGHEST AWARD FOR GALLANTRY.

The Importance of Commitment

In a recent study of 500 senior managers, over half had changed jobs within the last two years. They said they had left their previous employment because the work wasn't fun; they had no sense of accomplishment and little fulfilment. Throwing money at them would not have been the solution, as it could easily have been matched by the competition. Anyway, you can't substitute care and attention with money. Their employers failed to get their commitment, and commitment is chiefly an emotional attachment. It is felt through the right overall mix of incentives:

values, attitudes, sense of community, terms of reference, and flexible and customisable benefits.

APPLE

Four years after Apple was founded it become the biggest manufacturer of desktop computers in the world. Steve Jobs was definitely the leader, pushing the team to work faster and to perfection. The way he would issue unreasonable edicts or veto something out of hand has entered business folklore, yet he did so without being arrogant, and on occasion he relented when he realised he was wrong. Apple staff are quoted as saying, 'He wanted you to be great and wanted you to create great things (good was not enough) and he was going to make you do that. We felt like we had the chance to do something extraordinary.' Another colleague said, 'The values, the attitudes, the personalities of our designers are reflected in thousands of subtle choices coalescing into a spirit or feeling imparted to users.' The message is that if you concentrate on the quality of the work, the money will follow. Focus on morale, emotion and passion – and the extraordinary will happen.

VIETNAM

In the military sphere, it is certainly easy to see the difference between those who have got the soul right and those who have not. In the Vietnam war, the scale and intensity of North Vietnam's 1968 'Tet' offensive caught the US off guard. Despite the fact that the US and South Vietnamese forces had emphatically beaten the attackers back, this offensive came to play a significant part in President Lyndon B. Johnson's decision to leave the Oval Office and instigate a US withdrawal. At the time, US domestic support for the war was ebbing fast, a situation not improved by the death of four students at Kent State University during an anti-war protest. US forces were filled largely by conscripts, many of whom questioned the point of continuing the war and the manner in which it was being conducted. As it became clear that the politicians were now looking for a way to get US forces out, the enthusiasm among soldiers for pressing on and possibly joining the already long list of casualties understandably declined. Discipline and effectiveness were seriously affected. Occurrences of insubordination, attacks on 'gung ho' officers with fragmentation grenades (known as 'fragging') and drug abuse (7,000 soldiers – 3 per cent of the total force – were charged with heroin-related offences) were all features of an Army in crisis. The histories of many other Armed Forces, including those of the UK, France and Russia, contain similar examples of campaigns that went off the rails following a collapse in morale.

There are many more accounts of battles being won against dramatic odds, because the victors had the courage, spirit and inspirational leadership to win through under unrelenting pressure. Any conversation with a US Army company commander in the heat of battle in Iraq in 2003/4 showed how far that organisation had travelled since Tet days, back to the roots of the organisation in the US Civil War.

'STONEWALL' JACKSON

General 'Stonewall' Jackson earned his nickname in 1861 at the Battle of Bull Run during the American Civil War. Not far from

Washington DC, Jackson and his brigade stood firm on Henry House Hill under intense artillery fire, even though 2,000 other soldiers of the Confederate Army nearby broke ranks and started to flee in confusion in the face of advancing Union infantry. His unswerving example was followed by his soldiers and gave fresh heart to others, not least a fellow commander, Bee, who then rallied his men and led them in a charge against the Union advance. Had Jackson and his brigade broken as well, and joined in the general panic, the day would have been lost for the South. By responding to the news that the Confederates were being beaten back with, 'Then we will give them the bayonet,' Jackson's sheer force of personality, courage and example saved the day. He could not have done so if his soldiers had not placed their trust in their commander and chosen to stay, even when their ranks were being thinned by relentless fire (Jackson's brigade lost 488 of its 3,000 men). The result of this strength of spirit in the face of huge pressure played a vital part in the Confederate victory that day. Standing firm like a wall against the elements, Jackson became 'Stonewall' Jackson, and his brigade the 'Stonewall Brigade'.

To use organised, industrial-scale violence to take life, and to be faced with an opponent who will be doing everything within his power to do the same, creates a climate of extreme fear, stress and uncertainty. To stand up to these pressures demands courage and integrity at individual level and teamwork of the highest order. It also requires the discipline and moral authority to abide by the laws of armed conflict and national law. In short, you need 'soul'.

WHAT IS SOUL?

Defining 'soul' is like examining a great painting: everyone can sense that it is good, even if for most people it is hard to articulate precisely why. You can see it in all walks of life from time to time, such as the hospital medical team that really gels and works seamlessly, the pit crew in a Formula One team that shaves hundredths of a second off each tyre change and the winning spirit found in a victorious sports team. It is about how individuals feel and how they come together as a team. It's something of a paradox. Many in commerce are nervous about talking of soul and morale for fear of being labelled as limp, whereas in the Armed Forces even the toughest cookie knows the vital role that spirit plays in battle. This is the thrust of Secret Number Two: Soul Matters – to see the importance of the soul of an organisation in achieving greatness. The same can be seen in all walks of life. There are many factors that combine to create the conditions that cause people to feel good about their work, to commit to it and to put every ounce of their intellectual, physical and emotional capital into producing the best performance they are capable of. There are as many other factors that cause people to operate at the minimum threshold of commitment and skill, and still get paid. On the battlefield, courage, self-discipline, determination and integrity contribute to the high morale that enables ordinary people in uniform to do extraordinary things. Yet the vital part that morale plays in enabling an organisation to fulfil its potential is often given only cursory, begrudging regard in business.

Components of Soul – Character and High Morale

Character and morale are the two essential components of 'soul'. Both need to be developed to the degree required to get people fully committed and aligned with the organisation – and both are made up of many variables. It can be hard to separate character from morale, but for our purposes here, the two attributes of Character and Morale include the following aspects:

Character:
- Moral courage
- Conviction
- Work-life balance
- Resilience
- Emotional intelligence
- Self-discipline
- Integrity
- Team spirit

Morale:
- Trust
- Commitment
- Inspiration

Character Is Vital – and Can Be Developed

A strong organisation needs people with the character to put the greater needs of the whole before their own. Some people are born naturally considerate and altruistic, while others have to be educated, encouraged, coached and even coerced into matching their needs with those of others. This does not mean that you should subjugate your own interests entirely – that nearly always leads to resentment, jealousy, envy and revenge. People with the right character find a way to see how their objectives can be achieved by working *with* others, rather than by going it alone. There is a fine balance to be struck – the tricky part is to avoid watering everything down to a common denominator so that the mission is fatally compromised. The trick is not simply to find a compromise, but a 'third way'. McKinsey, the management consultancy, is a good example of how very bright, able (and therefore independent) thinkers manage to come together to form a cohesive group yet maintain their individual freedom. In another example of 'one's place in the system', McKinsey charges high rates to corporate clients and does pro bono work for charities and governments unable to afford their standard fees.

Moral Courage – Doing What's Right

Having moral courage means putting oneself in a position where one might be admired but not liked. As most people like to be liked, moral courage is not easily summoned up at the critical moment. Making people redundant, closing down unprofitable businesses, retiring those no longer fit for work, disciplining others for poor, inefficient or illegal conduct, and sending employees into life-threatening situations – all these and many other situations demand a degree of moral courage.

Moral courage is about fulfilling the responsibilities that come with being a member of a community or an organisation, whether at the bottom or the top. Without it, a spiral of indifference, fear and selfishness takes hold on the shop floor and in the boardroom. When we look at the moral courage modern troops are asked to find, it is awesome. They are sent in to stabilise communities after ethnic cleansing, anarchy, genocide. Such a brief tests their moral courage to the limit.

Moral courage must not be confused with self-justification. Faith in oneself without a degree of healthy scepticism may lead to moral arrogance, driving actions that actually undermine the very values we believe we claim to espouse. So while we need leaders and managers with the moral courage to take difficult decisions, we also need to guard against any sense of 'moral mission' that fails to doubt itself with sufficient intellectual rigour. No one has all the answers to every question.

COMMANDER'S COMFY CHAIR

Moral Courage

Take a few hours to think about 'moral courage' in relation to yourself and your organisation. You might decide that the issue needs further work – over days/weeks.

If you had 20 per cent more courage what would you do?

What could you open up to more?

What do you need to let go of?

Who do you need to stand up to?

On what do you need to find your voice?

Will you be happy with the way you've been living your life, say, in ten years' time?

How many managers wholeheartedly put their team above all else?

What are the consequences of that?

How well does your business spot the quiet heroes?

Do those with the biggest mouth, who talk themselves up, who sing their own praises get noticed most?

Are people with humility, perspective, honesty and calm determination, who are widely liked and trusted and act as role models of high standards, getting passed over as leaders?

What needs addressing?

Are you avoiding having 'difficult conversations'?

Who do you need to have a dialogue with?

What is your relationship with conflict?

Do you give in or do you always like to have your way?

What are the consequences of that – for you and for others?

Conviction – the Foundation of Your Team

Conviction in a team – the strength of belief that they are all equally committed to a worthwhile activity – is the foundation of their energy and power. It springs from the belief that those setting the aim of the mission have values similar to the rest of the group and that everyone has a shared interest in achieving success. Conviction helps to build the confidence, creativity, loyalty and tough-mindedness to overcome disappointments or resistance. On the battlefield, lack of conviction makes soldiers hesitant, averse to taking risks and poor team members – perhaps hoping that someone else will do the difficult parts of an operation. In business, lack of conviction has the same deleterious effects.

Maintaining Work–Life Balance

The UK has the most stressed culture of working long hours in Europe. US job satisfaction has fallen since the seventies and their work-life balance is the worst in the industrialised world. Striking a work-life balance is a personal business, potentially achieved in many ways. However it is done, it needs to be done well. Achieving work-life balance is a key part in sustaining absolute conviction. Artists and other creative people often immerse themselves in their art for long periods without sleep, food or social niceties; surgeons can't stop to watch the football on the television in the middle of a heart by-pass operation; and soldiers in action have to complete their mission whatever the conditions. However, every human being benefits from a respite somewhere along the line and we need rest and play alongside work in order to come back at full efficiency for another day.

No matter how dynamic, energetic, enthused by their work, every single person needs to get away from it and to experience what else life has to offer if they are to excel again and again.

Sometimes people overwork and over-focus on their work because they have a dysfunctional need to achieve, to prove, to feel valued. This need is much better addressed by building relationships we value, gaining recognition from people we value, spending time doing other things we value – and not simply by climbing the greasy pole of corporate promotion. People who are too tied up in their own careers can become pretentious and full of their own importance – they lose the essential quality of being people others want to hang out with. Sure there is power in having qualifications, a title, knowledge, but real leadership power comes from the capacity to inspire and influence, and the people who are better at this are those with a full and rounded life.

If someone in your team has established a pattern of unrelenting attachment to their work, help them to reassess their priorities and what they can delegate or drop. It is time to stop, to step back, to re-examine what is important, and to look at their needs and how else they can be satisfied. Sadly, even though they might have the best of intentions, if people are relentlessly overworking they may well be sowing the seeds of their own destruction. Leaders not only need to watch out for this in themselves and also in those for whom they have responsibility, and take the necessary steps to put it right. You have to have fun in your job or what is it all for?

COMMANDER'S COMFY CHAIR
Work–Life Balance

Review the following questions in the context of 'work–life balance'. You might decide that the issue needs further work – over days/weeks.

Are you and your peers overworked and stressed?

What are you doing to stop those trends and insist that your people take and then see the benefits of balance?

Where and when can you stop colluding with unnecessarily long working hours?

Is the importance of a balance of work and home life recognised throughout your organisation?

Do leaders set an example?

Do leaders encourage, and ensure that their staff strike an appropriate balance?

Is extra, unavoidable effort recognised and adequately compensated?

Resilience – the Strength to Keep Going

There will be bad days in any difficult, complex project (and many apparently simple ones too) and teams need spiritual strength to get back on track. Setbacks can come from many sources: new competitors, ill health, the vagaries of the stock-market, fragile suppliers and dilettante customers, among many others. Leaders and followers should assume that there will be bad days from time to time and pride themselves on counter-attacking to restore progress. Resilient companies get their hands on the right information at the right time and pass it on to the right people in good time to do something about it. They don't waste time waiting for 90 per cent or 100 per cent of information because they know that with around 50 per cent of information, coupled with intuition, they can go with it. Such attitudes are found in the military and in entrepreneurial businesses and that ability to go with what they've got, full stride, head on, is a kind of optimism and cheerfulness that gets things done. Weak companies are filled with more passivity, lip service, compliance, hiding behind rules and status – they use the protocols to avoid putting themselves on the line. That behaviour leads to a smugness and complacency but when hard times hit, they are the least able to recover.

At an individual level, the military pride themselves on being so dedicated, confident and well trained that they are able to recover from setbacks quickly. Setbacks can arise from countless sources, such as a technical difficulty, a breakdown in intelligence or the supply of essential items during a battle.

Setbacks can be deeply personal: the loss in battle of a close friend is always a traumatic personal tragedy. But it cannot be allowed to deflect from the efforts needed to get the job done. Business leaders who let setbacks get them down to the extent that the whole office is affected, are not serving anyone. He or she may recover tomorrow, but others may not recover so quickly and the effect on their morale affects performance negatively.

A person's stock of resilience is run down when events overtake the best-laid plans, when luck runs out, people are tired, and what were apparently good ideas fail in practice. It is important that people, especially leaders, see in advance that every day will not be filled with sunshine and roses, and that it is necessary to learn from and overcome setbacks. A resilient team redoubles its efforts, surging creative energy, when confronted with a setback, rather than slumping off home for a groan.

This mental and emotional toughness is vital to pressing ahead of the pack and to overcoming setbacks. It has been established as *the* vital differentiator in Olympic competitors, particularly gold medal winners. Resilience can be created through knowing one's values and living according to them. Those who have thought about their values and aligned them with their work, those who can name them and live by them, those whose behaviour is congruent with their values – these are the people with the highest self-esteem and lowest inner personal conflict.

In the military sphere, the demands on resilience are often immense, as one would expect. The risks in battle are acute, and nothing short of absolute belief that what must be done is necessary and appropriate will underpin success. Lack of resilience means that the will to fight erodes rapidly in the face of extreme pressure and setbacks. A battle can be lost because a small number buckle under pressure and a ripple of panic then sweeps through the force, causing it to break. It requires a certain mental and physical toughness to withstand the pressures of harsh terrain, difficult climate, fatigue and constant fear, even before a soldier is told to go forward and close with the enemy.

Ruthlessness is sometimes necessary – just don't confuse it with callousness. It is true that many in the military are ruthless, they are necessarily tough minded and can do 'what needs to be done'. But this is not without thinking or caring about the consequences and especially the effect on others. The Armed Forces are required to do what they are told to do by civil governments democratically elected by the societies from whom they draw their people and other resources. Their actions are held to account by those governments, and by media and public opinion – so they do care and certainly think very carefully about how, for example, to create minimal collateral damage as they set about achieving their objectives in battle. Commanders need to be ruthless to execute a job that must be done without deferring to personal sentiment, to their own need to be liked, or to tradition. It is this kind of ruthlessness that achieves dynamic results, moves mountains and cuts through 'politics'.

Emotional Intelligence – Managing Mood

Good leaders must know what effect they have on other people's resilience. It is part of the 'emotional intelligence' that is vital to the whole 'package' of leadership skills. Leaders need to know themselves, recognise their moods and be vitally aware of how they affect others. They need to be able to manage those moods, be good at reading others' moods, relate well to others and have the courage to raise difficult topics. If you show your irritability and frustration at work you are blackening the waters around you. If the boss or senior person has poor emotional intelligence it has a deleterious effect on all the talent in the firm. The reason many people leave a firm is that they want to get away from their boss. In 'exit interviews' people say that their boss killed their enthusiasm, made them feel uncomfortable because they felt he or she didn't trust them, micromanaged them, kept moving the goal posts, was fickle, made decisions depending on whatever mood he or she was in at the time, was often a misery and didn't stand up for them. But the employee never told the boss that directly. They usually gave the excuse that they were leaving because 'a better opportunity has come up' or 'they want to move out of the area'. Their boss would never know how they had not only failed to inspire the employee but had actually diminished them.

A leader who neglects or merely pays lip service to improving their emotional intelligence is unlikely to survive for long in a senior position in today's world. Many male managers notice the mood in their team, but do not say anything until and unless they are unbuttoned by alcohol or crisis. They tend to 'tough it out' and hope for a change. The military, still predominantly male organisations across the globe, are no different here and if there are two things that the military could learn to do a lot better –

one is coaching/mentoring and the other is paying more attention to developing emotional intelligence. Of course, the military capacity to 'tough things out' is important: it is not possible to halt the battle for a group hug and discussion about who has a sad face that day, but the tough aspect of military culture can be overplayed. Where entire units operate in a climate of depression and mutual loathing, held together by formal discipline rather than real respect and affection, they are likely to be brittle and inflexible under pressure.

COMMANDER'S COMFY CHAIR
Emotional Intelligence

Take a few hours to think about 'emotional intelligence' in relation to yourself and your organisation. You might decide that it needs further work – over days/weeks:

How often do your leaders help your people visualise a better future? Does this create an emotional and passionate response?

Does this engage their sense of purpose and connectivity with each other?

Do people refuse to turn a blind eye to poor personal and professional behaviour?

Do you really know the 'personal agendas' of those around you?

How will you ask them?

How much loyalty is there around you?

Have you clearly communicated your needs, wants, goals, values?

Can your team say them back to you accurately?

What are you annoyed about?

What irks you?

What opportunities do you see?

What plans are not being seen through?

What are you doing about that?

Is it okay to own up to a mistake where you are?

Is that experience used to add to the learning of the organisation?

After disappointments, do you pick yourselves up quickly and move on?

Charisma Comes In Many Forms

Charisma is the gift of being able to inspire and influence. To be charismatic you don't have to be a larger-than-life, loud, colourful, extrovert personality; you don't have to be outrageous or set out deliberately to inspire others. Humble, quiet, clever, unassuming, ingenious people have plenty of followers too; theirs is a quiet charisma. Humble folk show others more respect – and therefore gain their co-operation and find others more willing to collaborate. However, by 'charismatic' we don't mean those managers who are more skilled at playing up to an image of themselves rather than managing and developing the talent in the organisation.

If you want to be more charismatic do what charismatic leaders do: they frame messages with care, are selfless and connect with others through their similarity and their shared values. They refer to higher purpose, they tell stories and use metaphor well, they are expressive and they manage impressions. People like charismatic leaders, they respond to them in many useful ways: they feel more motivated, inspired, free to be innovative; they have greater group cohesiveness; are more adaptable to change –

all this produces performances in staff that exceed the original expectations and goals.

Self-discipline – the Bedrock of Soul

Many people outside the Armed Forces think that military discipline is exercised and maintained exclusively top-down, reliant on the individual being disciplined by others set above him. In fact, the emphasis has to be on developing self-discipline. Soldiers, sailors and airmen need to do the right thing at the right time, regardless of risk or whether or not they are being observed by anyone senior to them. Of course, there is an element of compulsion required – the urge to stay tucked up in bed rather than turn out into the field of battle can be compelling in all but the most keen and enthusiastic soldiers, but then the same principle applies in any organisation where tough and unattractive work has to be done from time to time. Self-discipline is not something reserved for people in uniform or positions of authority, we all need degrees of it just to live in a modern, crowded world – whether it is regulating our behaviour at work or giving up a seat on the bus to someone who needs it more. Self-discipline is a complex issue. In part it is about ideas and motivation: the selfless commitment to others and to a set of ideas or an organisation. In part it is about behaviour: having the will-power and internal strength to do what must be done in circumstances of great adversity, perhaps even at some personal cost.

One of the less-attractive features of the contemporary western world is a drift towards an emphasis on the needs of the individual at the expense of a sense of the wider needs of the community. It is the 'me first' syndrome, and inevitably this is an attitude that many people bring to their employment. The first thought is 'What am I going to get out of this', rather than 'How can I contribute?' Of course, it is bound to be harder to foster a climate of common endeavour and purpose in a team if this is the prevailing attitude. In the Armed Forces, the need to subordinate individual wishes to the requirements of the team does not require much elaboration. But it does require considerable training, beginning on the first day of training, just as it has for hundreds of years. Today, young men and women who join up are put into shared accommodation, given identical clothes to wear and subjected to a rigorous and challenging regime that stretches their mental and physical capacity. It is often their first time away from home, the first time sharing a room and the first time they have been made to do something when they really would rather not do. This demands self-discipline.

There is also the matter of foot drill: marching in unison with others through a range of unfamiliar routines that have their roots in the drills and tactics of wars fought across the ages. This is not done for want of more imaginative things to do before breakfast. It is a means of instilling disciplined teamwork and pride into the group. Anyone who doesn't believe this should make a point of seeing a squad of recruits on parade pass out of basic training in front of their families. The transformation is so great that mothers may fail to recognise their own sons and daughters.

In former times, when the Armed Forces were built on conscription and compulsion, and effectiveness was maintained by the fear of the lash and the promise of rum and plunder, this drill was the only means of delivering cohesion and operational effectiveness. This is not what underpins the Armed Forces of countries such as the UK and the USA today – discipline is founded on self-discipline. Part of this self-discipline is the understanding that it may be necessary to do hard things, even fatally hard things, to ensure the success of the group. In fact, not many soldiers have willingly gone to the grave for their country, but many have died for their comrades and because they felt that fighting, even far away from home, protected their families.

The best organisations in any field rely heavily on the self-discipline of their staff, not only to do the simple things well, like turn up on time, but also to apply their time and their talents to the full in order to add to collective success. Self-discipline includes seeing that individual well-being and advancement will be secured primarily by working as a fully integrated part of a team.

COMMANDER'S COMFY CHAIR
Self-discipline

Take a few hours to think about 'self-discipline'. You might decide that it needs further work – over days/weeks.

Is performance in line with the code of ethics and aims rewarded and praised?

Is poor performance and political behaviour dealt with and penalised?

Do your leaders set the example by their personal and professional conduct?

Integrity – Doing the Right Thing

Self-discipline is seamlessly joined to the idea of integrity, doing the right thing because it is right, even when easier alternatives may be on offer or nobody is looking. This can be in small things, like not taking stationery, and it can be in major issues like insider dealing or turning a blind eye to bullying and theft. We all know when colleagues act with integrity: we respect and value them for it, and as a result we trust them and place confidence in them. Similarly, where that integrity is missing, the results are obvious too. Not only does everybody keep one hand on their favourite mug, they also guard their careers, reputations and workload with equal fervour. A team without integrity cannot deal with massive difficulties. Only a team enjoying the commitment, trust and co-operation that a strong bond of mutual integrity engenders has the bedrock necessary for successfully working through difficulties.

At its simplest, integrity is about recognising what constitutes acceptable and unacceptable behaviour and abiding by that, even if it poses some uncomfortable dilemmas. For example, when a soldier steals from comrades in the closely confined and Spartan living environment in the field, it is not only illegal but also fundamentally destabilises the way that group bonds and works together. When another soldier knows who the culprit is, but fails to identify him or her, that soldier is also undermining the team and exercising another form of loss of integrity – even if he has known the offender as a friend for years. The way people at work interact, the atmosphere of co-operation and mutual respect, and the integrity required to speak up for what is plainly right and plainly wrong are no different in any organisation.

People of integrity are generally honest and genuine in their dealings with others. To act with integrity is to act in a way that accurately reflects your sense of who you are, the motives, commitments and values that you hold deeply as your own. Wholeheartedness in thought and action creates conviction and guards against temptation. This does not mean blind obedience or total acquiescence: retaining intellectual rigour is important in preventing yourself being led into taking immoral actions.

BUILD YOUR ARMOURY

Recruit People of Character

Here is a list of tools and tips giving specific advice on how to recruit the right people to your staff.

▷ The right people must be recruited who can work and bond in the manner required by the organisation, and this process must be overseen by senior management. No one is exempt from this – so it includes the CEO/Chair and their board.

▷ People change, so if they are not exhibiting the right behaviours every chance must be given to explain, coach and develop – but if the pick-up isn't there, they must go.

▷ Have a programme of personal development for every employee, not just the elite top 15 per cent. That programme needs to map out how strengths can be maximised, weaknesses corrected, potential expanded and then exploited to the full.

▷ Reward reliability and execution of strategy. Recognise and promote emotional intelligence, and make every leader face up to and deal with failures, lack of effort or dishonourable behaviour.

Team Spirit

Getting teamwork right is a must – and that means behaving towards colleagues with civility, honesty and an open-ended spirit of co-operation. Some managers in business pride themselves on their tough image – yet treating co-workers with respect and going out of one's way to be co-operative does not imply weakness: it plays to a simple human truth that people move ahead by moving together, not by standing on the backs of others. The best should be able to get ahead, they must be rewarded for doing exceptionally well and talent should not be held back. It needs to be recognised that it was a team effort that supported the star player. Only one athlete stands on the rostrum with their gold medal, but usually their mum or dad gave up early mornings to take them training and the coach was always there. This is the opposite of narcissistic, over-dramatic, bullying 'toxic' leadership seen in many organisations where senior managers have unwarranted overconfidence in their abilities, exhibiting more hubris than substance. Employers need to think very carefully about such individuals before they continue to commit the talent in the organisation into their hands.

COMMANDER'S COMFY CHAIR

Team Spirit

Take some time to review your own performance regarding 'team spirit'. You might decide that it needs further work – over days/weeks:

Are you standing on your own two feet enough?

Are you too independent, flying solo too much when a more team-oriented approach would be more effective?

Are you letting someone do their own thing at the expense of others?

High Morale – Between Success and Failure

The soul of an organisation means more than just having high morale, but there can be no doubt that high morale is indispensable. This is lost on some business leaders and economists who interpret the strength of an organisation exclusively in terms of numbers – profit, market share, share price and GNP. We are not suggesting that financial accounting is not a vital aspect, but low morale makes disaster more likely and without high morale you haven't got a chance of achieving sustained success. By morale we mean more than happiness: it is also the level of satisfaction and fulfilment and the will to overcome adversity.

> '*Morale is a state of mind. It is that intangible force which will move a whole group of men to give their last ounce to achieve something, without counting the cost to themselves; that makes them feel they are part of something greater than themselves.*'
> FIELD MARSHALL SIR WILLIAM SLIM

A survey in one of the world's largest management consultancy firms recently recorded nearly 90 per cent of the workforce did not believe in their leaders and neither were they engaged with the strategy. Yet the senior decision maker in the company did nothing to address morale. It was deemed too messy, too 'fluffy' – he thought morale would improve when sales improved. He drove the staff hard by using the carrot (upping bonuses for high performance) and the stick (liberally threatening the sack). Sales in that firm are still below target and, not surprisingly, the best talent is leaving. The focus on numbers was a short-term approach, avoiding and exacerbating underlying organisational issues of equal significance. Soul-less organisations have nothing in them with which to rise to a challenge.

INNOCENT

The brand 'innocent' is a modern-day entrepreneur's example of high morale. Three university friends became successful young men in advertising, before giving up well-paid, safe jobs to set up their own business selling fruit juices – a product they believed in. Just five years later their turnover is £35 million, on track to go pan-European and achieve a turnover of £65 million by 2006. It has 34 per cent market share and was voted Employer of the Year 2005. 'Right from Day One we decided to make sure that people were happy, as that is the way to get dedicated effort. We want the workplace to feel like home.' They all breakfast together, take holidays together, enjoy flexible working hours, interest-free loans and unpaid leave options. It is a deliberately 'playful' brand: Fruit Towers, the Head Office, has three signs at the entrance – 'Cows' to the warehouse, 'People' to the offices and 'Burglars' to the window! Their reputation attracts all the talent it needs – they don't have to incur recruitment advertising or agency costs as 300 CVs are sent to their website every week. The three founders have dared to be different, to create a firm in their own image – and it has worked. Check out their website: www.innocentdrinks.co.uk

Nothing Great Comes From Low Morale

To achieve great things you need to galvanise people's 'will' and to do that their morale needs to be high. Without this confidence and optimism there will be no step changes in performance. It is not necessary for everybody in a company to share the same fanaticism as may be found in senior leaders or founder owners, but it is necessary for a team to be composed of people who actually want to be there. A common error is to think that the limit of an employee's engagement with the firm is how quickly the clock can hit going-home time. The problem is more likely to stem from the company rather than the employee. After all, who wants to lead a life so bereft of magnificence? The person working the photocopier has a life, a history, ambitions, feelings, thoughts and desires just as much as the CEO, but how many managers take the trouble to get under the skin of all their team and really understand what fires them up? By seeing people as people, not just as cogs in the machine, they will encourage their staff to see that work is an important part of their life, not a daily eight-hour suspension of it. The first and indispensable step to achieving a state of high morale in an organisation is to build trust.

BUILD YOUR ARMOURY
Strengthening Morale

Here is a list of tools and tips giving specific advice on how to use and strengthen morale in your organisation.

▷ Check your morale and do something about it fast if there are weaknesses. Building morale requires leaders to ensure that people feel trusted and respected. Identify the leaders who do not do this and retrain them, help them to improve or move them out.

▷ Make absolutely sure that leaders are seen to lead by example, informing and inspiring their team. If not, they must be given advice and opportunity to do better and if after that they still fail – say goodbye.

To build high morale, leaders need to commit to providing conditions where their followers:

▷ Truly believe in what they are doing. Ask people to discuss if and where they believe in what they are doing and where they don't.

▷ Understand the logic of what they are doing. Ask them to relate what they do to the logic of the overall work and aim.

> ▷ Have the practical means to do what must be done. Check that people feel what they are being asked to do is practical with what they have.
>
> ▷ Work with maximum creativity and independence. Allow people to find their way of doing it without undue supervision or direction.

Trust

A recent survey showed that just 13 per cent of employees trusted the competence of their bosses. That means 87 per cent did not trust their bosses? A lack of trust means that:

- **People stop being daring**. They do not take risks, or put their heads above the parapet with novel, innovative ideas – so their companies lose the creative, competitive edge this would bring.
- **People hold back**. They leave their personalities at home. They 'do' what is needed at work to avoid getting the sack. They do not give of their whole self – so they do not engage with the customer or the mission.
- **People cover their backs**. They withhold information, do not disclose their mistakes. The result is that the organisation does not learn and there is the loss of potentially significant competitive advantage.
- **People look out for themselves**. They will not help others if it means letting go of territory gained for themselves. As a result there is regression and turf battles, rather than a spirit of pulling together to meet common goals.
- **People look around for other opportunities**. They are ever-conscious that they might be about to be 'downsized'.

They network to get out. If the market knows the business is vulnerable, competitors circle like vultures, seducing talent to leave before 'abandon ship' is sounded.

If the level of trust is low, your organisation is doomed. Trust is generated by leaders who show that they are reliable, do the right thing in times of temptation and hardship and do right by their team. Generally, contemporary soldiers respect and trust each other. This stems from good recruitment and proper investment in training, which gives them each a clear understanding of how they fit in and a fighting chance of succeeding. 'The boss' in a military context is respected because to be appointed as such he or she must have 'been there and done it', and have performed better than their peers, as judged by a remarkably fair and thorough performance appraisal system. The military 'boss' is trained to treat subordinates with respect as a matter of course – acknowledging that they rely on each other. To those outside the military, this level of mutual courtesy and respect can be a revelation. The outcome is that people feel valued and know their contribution is valued.

As part of the research for this book, we asked 100 global board directors, 'Which boss or leader in your profession do you admire?' Very few names were put forward. Comments such as 'selfish' (corrupt), 'unappealing' (grotesque), 'uninformed' (stupid) and 'inept' (incompetent) were easier to come by. Trust is not easy to inspire. Yet we all like to be honest and we all like to deliver on our promises – so what is the problem? Well, trust involves making yourself vulnerable to some degree. You have to be open to criticism, view the world from a different standpoint, realise that your opinion is just one of many, that you do not necessarily 'know' the right answers.

At TGI Friday they have what they call a 'beach ball' theory and philosophy. Imagine two people are holding a beach ball. One sees it as pink, purple and yellow. The other sees it as black, white and red. When they both move around the ball they see that they are both holding and looking at the same phenomenon – just from different perspectives. If you take too firm a stance, too uncompromising a view, you are at risk of losing the very credibility and influence you seek.

People have the most obscure reasons for not trusting someone: the fact that a person has a tattoo, an accent they can't abide, or wears button-down shirts. They might not like 'the French', or men with beards, people who look at them too directly or who avoid eye contact. There isn't a lot one can do about another person's idiosyncratic prejudices and so we tend to underestimate the effect on the company that these prejudices have over time. Most of us think we are trustworthy and therefore people will find us that way, but ask employees how many people they really trust and it may be just a handful. Superficial as it sounds, our research has shown that these factors do clearly get in the way of trust.

COMMANDER'S COMFY CHAIR
Building Trust

Take a few hours to think about 'building trust'. You might decide that it needs further work – over days/weeks.

Trust is earned by delivering on promises – what do people around you remember you having promised? (Ask!)

Trust is created by being honest – how open and honest do your team think you are with them?

Have you asked them?

Will you ask them? If not, why not? How will you ask them?

What else could you do to be classified as 'utterly trustworthy'?

How is the relationship between you and your team?

What are you doing to manage the level of honesty in your team?

Do people come to you with their problems? (If not – you have been part of a system that probably makes people who ask for help feel weak: you must make yourself more accessible.)

Who do you trust?

Who don't you trust?

What are the consequences?

What are you assuming?

Do you know them well enough to put your hand on your heart and say you are getting the best out of them?

Can you say you know categorically what worries each of your team, what delights them, their hopes, their fears?

Do you know their motivations?

Are individuals' self-esteem and self-efficacy protected and nurtured?

Are the standards of performance to be met in all values clearly articulated?

Building Trust

In part, building a company with soul means overcoming prejudices and assumptions. So, knowing this, how do you build trust? Building trust is a very tricky thing: it helps to take time to understand other people's sensitivities, their likes and dislikes, what they value and what turns them off. If you are trying to set up a trusting relationship, all parties need to agree on a basic ethical framework governing the way they will interact. The next step is to move on to behaviours. Sometimes as a leader, you have to break the stalemate of 'who is going to trust whom first'. You have to go first, state what you stand for and be a role model and encourage others to do the same. In the words of Ghandi, 'Be the change you want to see.' We look at delegation and empowerment in Secret Number Five, and the essential role of trust is at the heart of making this happen – but the leader has to start.

PEOPLESOFT

There are examples of business leaders doing the right thing, even to the extent of using their own money to compensate employees when business decisions go wrong. David Duffield, CEO of PeopleSoft, won great respect for giving $10,000 of his own money to all employees below a certain wage threshold who lost their jobs following a hostile takeover battle against Oracle. Even after his own resignation, Duffield is still active on behalf of the 3,000 people who lost their jobs. He has formed a club called The Safety Net and pledged $5 million of his own money in grants to employees in need. He has also set up The PeopleSoft Alumni Group – a website to help ex-employees find new jobs.

The shock of the Enron and WorldCom financial scandals led to a breakdown in the trust placed in many business leaders and more emphasis on corporate governance. It wasn't, of course, hard luck that brought down those companies but a moral famine – the place was awash with arrogance, greed, men with a lust for power. There were huge pay differentials in the compensation package given to senior figures compared with other colleagues and absurd deference was paid to them by other board members. Why? They were protecting their own butts.

Members of the board in firms turning over several billion pounds annually, and with over 100,000 employees, on both sides of the Atlantic can expect to earn £250,000 to £500,000 basic and double or triple that with bonuses. Their average employee might earn £30,000 with a 10 per cent bonus. In the UK, the head of the Army, a four-star general, earns around £124,000 for commanding 145,000 soldiers and directing a budget of over £5 billion. The newest qualified soldier earns about £11,000. In business, the gap between the front line worker and the head of the firm is eight times greater than that in the public sector. Maybe this contributes to making some CEOs and directors exhibit more ego than character.

Senior executives are negotiating huge payoffs when they leave, even when they have failed. This just crucifies the soul of the organisation and makes a mockery of the average, honest, hard-working employee. It is galling to 99 per cent of the firm that whoever pays them off doesn't have the courage to let them go with nothing. Business Generals need to be more candid about under-performance and look after those who are more deserving.

BUILD YOUR ARMOURY
Build Trust

Here are some ideas to strengthen the trust and the bond between team members and their leaders:

▷ Where trust is low, make sure time is scheduled in fast for leaders to get to know their team.

▷ Go off site, pick up the courage to say 'How are you? What am I doing that is helpful, inspiring, encouraging and what am I doing that hinders your performance?'

▷ Where have leaders been seen to fail to deliver on promises?

▷ When have leaders been seen not to be totally honest – what were the consequences. Find out. Act on it.

Set out ground rules of complete confidentiality and then ask some of your team to reveal:

▷ Their three greatest achievements and why. What had they overcome?

▷   Who they regard as their hero, or the quality in someone they admire?

▷ Why and how they try to behave like their hero (if they do)?

▷ Who they would like to have around for dinner, and why. What would they ask that person?

▷ Three obscure facts about themselves. (You'll be surprised! The last time we did this with a group, we found out one had run for England, one had a book of short stories published and one had learned to nurse their child through its illness – and they had worked together for between two and eight years and not known any of that about each other.)

▷ Ask everyone to answer, 'When your team gets upset with you what would they say?' And then ask the team!

▷ Find out what is important to people – ask them to list the things that are essential to their well-being and sense of purpose. Discuss 'the why'. For instance, someone might say 'Money!' Ask them what would they do with an extra £300, £3,000, £30,000, £300,000, £3 million? Then ask what that would do for them, give them, get them – and the answer will reveal what they are really seeking.

Commitment – Pull Together or Lose

A striking aspect of Armed Forces' culture is the way they have learned to establish selfless commitment to the team – at every level. The battlefield does impose extra demands on the way people must commit, yet in all organisations committed people who have a personal stake in the work that they do and see how their part is significant perform significantly better than those who take a half-hearted approach. 'Commitment' covers intentions, promises, convictions, principles to projects and relationships. Harnessing the commitment of a workforce will not happen by accident – it is a function of sound leadership and a key component of high morale. You know your organisation is strong when everyone stays around and pulls together on a bad day as well as a good day. People show that level of commitment when they have come to associate their personal success and reputation with that of the organisation. They stay because they want to, not because they have to. Have you got that where you work? As a young paratrooper General Rupert Smith acted selflessly when he saw his commanding officer was engulfed in flames. He covered the CO with his own body until the flames were extinguished.

COMMANDER'S COMFY CHAIR
Commitment

Review the following regarding the issue of 'commitment'. You might decide that it needs further work – over days/weeks.

Is every employee clear what the aims and objectives are and do they know why these are important?

How many of your people truly believe in what they are doing and engage with the mission?

How do you know?

What have you done to engage them, unsuccessfully?

What else could you be doing?

Have you asked your team, your employees, if they have the tools they need to do the job? To what extent are you all aware of what could be used to enhance effectiveness and efficiency?

What plans are there for improvement?

How much of your team's creativity and autonomy are you tapping into? Have you asked them?

What don't you know about them?

Are performance appraisals and promotions seen as fair?

BUILD YOUR ARMOURY
Commitment and Conviction

Here is a list of tools and tips giving specific advice on how to develop commitment and conviction in your organisation.

▷ Check that you have a clear, coherent vision and strategic aim across the organisation.

▷ Check that every employee is clear about the aims and objectives.

▷ Check that every employee knows why these are important.

▷ Make sure they know how they contribute to the aim and that what they do matters.

▷ Build the understanding that people know that if they fail, it will affect the team as a whole.

▷ Build an acceptance that setbacks will occur and will need to be overcome.

▷ Make sure that there is constant encouragement, support and regular reminders about the organisation's goals and objectives.

> ▷ Do random checks regularly. Is success always rewarded, and unnecessary or avoidable failure penalised? Take corrective action.

Inspiration – the Vital Spark

As well as building trust and establishing high levels of commitment, you also need to add the spark of inspiration in order to achieve the highest levels of morale. This is primarily a function of leadership. Most people will soar to new heights of achievement if they are genuinely inspired by what they are doing. This requires that leaders explain what must be done, why it really matters, and how each individual can play a significant part – whether they are the real pace-setters or those who play a more supporting role. Inspiration can come in many forms, but the most enduring and effective will galvanise the staff so that they shoot out of bed every single morning looking forward to work because they feel they are taking part in something special. In the military context, acts of great courage often come about not so much because people are inspired by the cause they are fighting for but because of the value they place in the team around them. Soldiers get up out of their nice safe holes in the ground and throw themselves at the enemy because to do otherwise would mean letting the team down.

COMMANDER'S COMFY CHAIR
Inspiration
Review the following regarding the subject of 'inspiration'.
You might decide that it needs further work – over days/weeks.

Are you inspired?

You can't hope to inspire unless you are inspired – so where are you finding, where can you find, inspiration?

What do you need to do more of to get that inspiration?

Do you know what each of your team members' principles in life are?

Do you know the things they prize above all else?

Do you know what they hold most precious?

Can you name with certainty the top three things that motivate and satisfy each of your team?

Conversely, what demotivates and demoralises them?

Is your firm doing enough about the state of morale and confidence?

What do you do when you recognise your mood is grim – how much effort and what techniques do you use to change your emotions, or do you just let them out?

When has the mood of your boss affected your work?

What is that telling you about how you might have affected others' work when you have been 'in a mood'?

Do you have 'those difficult' conversations when you think that a member of your team is moody and affecting others?

Do you pay enough attention to how those moody people inhibit others from being their best?

Are you able to shift someone's mood?

Can you move an entire group of people's moods?

Do you inspire – how do you know? What has worked well in the past?

If you are a boss, ask yourself, would your team pick you again as their leader? Why? Why not?

How many of your team would 'do anything for you'?

How many of your bosses would you 'do anything' for?

What have you done lately to earn trust?

What more could you do?

Why Soul is Important to Success

So why is soul important, and what are the risks if it is absent? Military forces across the ages have found that the most important battle-winning factor has been the soul of their people. Armies with the greatest numbers and ample equipment have been humbled by lesser-equipped opponents who were fighting with every fibre of body and spirit. The defeat of the German First Army by the British Expeditionary Force at Mons in 1914 resulted in 1,600 British casualties compared with 10,000 German losses.

Success has frequently attached itself to the side that knew what it was fighting for, was imbued with a strong sense of common purpose, and also truly believed in that cause – be it religion, country, money or land. Around the edges of the conflict are many other participants and observers who feel far less engaged than this, and so take differing views on policy and action. Will, commitment and the capacity for self-sacrifice are still proving more powerful in deciding the outcome of a campaign than technology and firepower. A great organisation, of any sort, generates power from individuals who have a joint purpose, shared ethos and vision – who join together to do something that they could not do alone to create soul in the organisation. Where you find individuals whose soul is disconnected from their actions or where the collective soul is absent, the seeds of that organisation's self-destruction will have been sown.

RITZ CARLTON

The story of Ritz Carlton is an inspiring one. A Swiss shepherd boy, Cesar Ritz, moved to Paris and stood in awe in front of the finest hotels. He dreamed of opening one that bore his name and delivered the highest standards of personal service to the most discerning guests. His philosophy was embedded in the motto: 'Ladies and gentlemen serving ladies and gentlemen.' To this day, General Managers are chosen for their attitude and inducted into the philosophy that holds, for example, that it is immoral to see the back-of-house staff as simply $11 per hour hands. They are not seen as unavoidable costs of $110 per day, or 10 hours of useful labour; they are not human 'doings' but complete human 'beings' with a family they care about and want to be with, with a unique life path and a purpose beyond their role at work. This mindset ensures that the employees, as associates of the business, do not merely give their labour, but also their heart and their soul, to the best of their ability. Every one of the 16,000 employees receives around 120 hours of rigorous training in customer service standards – equipping them to move heaven and earth for customers every day. The standards are immaculate – from dress, to cleanliness, to courtesy. At first, those standards are closely supervised and thus reinforced. Thereafter a sense of commitment and self-discipline becomes the norm.

Any level of employee can be a leader, able to influence and shape the brand and direction of the business – it isn't and shouldn't be the preserve of the few at the top. The mindset that leaders have of their team, their peers, themselves and the firm is a powerful strategic asset. The depth of soul in an organisation can mean the difference between brilliance (survival) and mediocrity (death).

Most successful entrepreneurs are utterly committed, doggedly determined, prepared to work all hours and believe that they can make a difference. Their work often permeates their private lives and there is often a sense of integrity, conviction and resilience. Leaderless firms can only look on in envy as sharp and audacious entrepreneurs such as Virgin, *Pret a Manger* and innocent enlist and retain the loyalty and extra effort of their talented workforces through the inspiration of the people at the top. If such entrepreneurs can avoid becoming so massively over-confident as to take unsupportable risks, they can build a sustainable, expanding business. These go-ahead firms often attract top talent, even if they don't offer the very best salaries or the swanky offices of their larger, better-established competitors. The same can apply to not-for-profit organisations, too, as they fire the soul and imagination of the people they engage.

The Benefits of Soul

Committed people will focus on the goal. If you get 'soul' right, you increase people's sense of belonging and that brings meaning, connection and commitment. Many people are familiar with Maslow's 'Hierachy of Needs', researched in the era of post-war austerity – when basic shelter was seen as the primary need. Over and beyond our basic needs of shelter and food, we all have three basic psychological needs: feeling connected, contributing competence and having self-confidence. Being in an organisation, engaged in a common mission, is actually one of the ways humans fulfil these basic psychological needs. We spend more time in the workplace than we do with the great loves of our lives – our partners, our children and our friends – so it is important that we meet these three needs at work. When you create commitment, people move closer to the organisational aims and you will find there is more focus and less downtime and distractions. They will find it easier to endure the ups and downs of working life, there will be less staff turnover and fewer wasted opportunities. The level of commitment in your organisation is correlated to the level of budget utilised well and profit made.

If you are leading your business, it is your responsibility to help your team connect to the purpose, the aims, the style of the organisation. This is true whether you have just two assistants or 120,000 employees. You are a leader if you influence another. So, you might be a leader of your children, your nieces and nephews, your neighbours, your community, your friends, one junior in the office, a small team or operation, or thousands of workers. As a leader you naturally help others name what it is they want to do, guide their decisions, encourage their behaviour to fit the group's or society's ethics. It is your responsibility to truly boost their self-confidence and it is your responsibility to help them uncover and develop their competence and create the environment where they can use it. By doing this and by encouraging them to think things through you are developing important components of their powerbase.

Camaraderie

Camaraderie is the kind of team spirit that a lot of businesses would die for. It is created through attention to the soul of every member of the organisation. If you want to have a team of people who have committed themselves to giving their very best, who understand how their own needs and ambitions are bound up with those of others and who are prepared to go the extra mile when required, then you must grab them by their soul. Having an organisation with soul means having people who are clear about their sense of their own self-worth and the value of those around them in delivering collective excellence. It also means that individuals are prepared to set aside some of their own wishes for the greater good of the team. This might be in a small way, such as staying an hour later to finish a project, or it could be in a major way, such as taking a post far from home to serve the collective interest. In the case of members of the Armed Forces, it can mean laying down their life:

> *'It wasn't a matter of living or dying or fighting.*
> *It was a matter of helping your friends.'*
> CORPSMAN ROBERT DEGENS, IWO JIMA 1945

Common Understanding

Get the soul right and the organisation's capacity for better, faster and more responsive decision-making will be greater. There will be a common level of understanding about what really matters and where urgency and hard work are required. There will be more certainty and confidence in the judgement of the leadership, and reduced resistance to new ideas. If you want to increase adaptability and flexibility, then you need to engage the soul. When people feel good their mental effectiveness improves – they are more flexible in their thinking, better able to understand complex information and they make better judgements. Current research shows that to make good decisions, your people need to feel good. You know this about yourself. And you know the reverse is true: bad decisions are often made when one feels bad about the job. How often do you make people feel good about themselves?

Strong Moral Climate

The partners in a major consulting firm who scored above average on behaviours conducive to building soul (the leaders who were emotionally mature, showed character, exhibited self-discipline and deployed mental and emotional resilience) delivered $1.2 million more profit from their accounts than did other partners – that was 139 per cent more than the mediocre performers. What would 139 per cent gain mean to you? Which leaders in your business need to understand themselves more, manage their emotions better, develop more self-discipline and emotional resilience?

No Soul – No Direction

There are some business leaders who really do doubt that soul matters: if the man cleaning the bathrooms doesn't give a fig, is it relevant to the business just so long as it gets clean, or to the cleaner just so long as he gets paid? And if the Accounts Clerk would rather be anywhere else, who cares so long as the numbers add up? What does it matter if the senior executives in a professional service firm hate the place – they will perform anyway for the half-a-million pound bonus on offer? To some degree, of course, perhaps it doesn't matter how content and engaged people are. Gas gets pumped, papers get shuffled and everybody goes home on time.

The issue here is a comparative one: will a company operating with the minimum level of engagement from its workforce have the same or better enduring prospects than the competitors who have people eager to work together as hard and as long as it takes to win the business? And which is the better place to spend your life in?

To see the dangers inherent in engaging people at the most basic level – they come to work, they do stuff, then they shuffle off home – you only have to look at the way big organisations can work in monopoly conditions. In the absence of competition, a single supplier of a service, such as a railway or a state bank, can become totally complacent about their customers – as they have nowhere else to go for their needs. There are still examples of firms behaving like a long-forgotten tractor plant on the Steppes of Russia producing lousy machinery really slowly, in accordance with some fixed plan determined thousands of miles away, all for a personal income entirely divorced from success, innovation and quality. What a way to lead your life.

Even in monopolies, this need not apply where the spirit, values and character are developed to instil the pride and resolution needed to achieve high standards of service. For example, the US Postal Service operates as a flagship for their nation: a beacon of good service and dedicated effort for the public good. Even without the discipline of competition there are many examples of monopolistic enterprises being highly regarded because of the attitude and dedication that infuses the workforce.

For most business leaders, monopoly conditions do not apply and success means doing well in the hurly-burly of the commercial 'battlespace', where money, labour, ideas, time and luck are all vital components. In a competitive climate, business leaders who can see beyond the immediate short term build organisations that have a better chance of surviving than the opposition. It is about who is more likely to innovate, adapt, seize market share, improve efficiency and increase profits. Which company will attract investors? Conversely, which company is more likely to be overtaken by events, adversaries and competitors and abandoned by customers?

Is the phrase 'Business-is-Business' an excuse for disingenuous and unethical behaviour? Some high-profile board wars have shown how ruthless, unreliable, underhand leadership does sometimes get its come-uppance. We have seen large companies rescued by third-generation family members of the founders, who saw the soul of the business being eroded and led a shareholder revolt.

The Blight of Fear and Blame Culture

If your culture is one of fear and blame – your organisation is on a highway to nowhere. Terror and fear can get results – it is a direct way of getting information and a medieval way of getting people to perform, at least temporarily. In the past, fear and physical punishment were used to induce soldiers and sailors to do their duty. The logic of this was pretty simple: if a soldier was more afraid of going against his own leaders than of fighting the enemy he would be more likely to make it to the battlefield. Once he closed with the enemy self-preservation alone would make him fight.

In the late 1700s Frederick II, King of Prussia, wrote: 'The common soldier must fear his officer more than the enemy.' This was a doctrine he applied with some vim: punishments included flogging, beating and making soldiers sit astride a sharp wooden horse with weights attached to their feet. Capital punishment was a feature of military life around the world – indeed, it technically still is in many armies, usually for offences such as cowardice, desertion and mutiny. The British Army shot 309 officers and men during the First World War, and this was not thought exceptional at the time. The Italian Army added the dramatic touch of executing those found guilty of cowardice by shooting them in the back. During the Second World War, the US Army shot only one of its soldiers for repeated desertion. By comparison, it is thought that the German Army executed some 15,000 of its own soldiers between 1939 and 1945.

Over the years, the military have learned that barbarous methods usually provide only short-lived and unreliable gains. People will give 'information' under torture, but any information will do – just to stop the torture – but the accuracy cannot be assumed. Soldiers fearful of brutal retribution from their own commanders may sometimes perform illegal acts, and may take revenge against their leaders in the future. Today, where inappropriate or unlawful conduct is encountered there is a duty on every serviceman and servicewoman to report it. 'Blowing the whistle' in this way may be deeply unpopular with those indicted, yet it will be applauded by the vast majority of service personnel and expected by the society they serve. The rare instances of extreme bullying, harassment and humiliation of prisoners of war in Iraq have led to criminal convictions but they remain the exception, condemned by soldiers and civilians alike.

Although the death penalty is retained as the ultimate deterrent and sanction in a few armies, including the US Army, all armies have their own prisons for military offenders. These are not the places of horror recounted in stories of yesteryear, but they do embrace a regime that is more Spartan than Spa. They are not intended to be luxurious, restful or easy-going: there is plenty of healthy exercise, firm discipline and useful retraining. Many former inmates have turned their lives around there and gone on to achieve great things.

The death sentence in business is limited to the termination of careers and social life. While no firm operates its own jails – much as some may feel like it – there are bosses who terrify their staff, sometimes abusing the power of the market position of the firm and sometimes simply because he or she is a bully who enjoys wielding the prospect of sudden unemployment. Of course, fear, including fear of unemployment, can spark creativity and initiative in the same way that a shipwrecked man might make a float from his clothing. But as modern management philosophies go, driving the workforce through the fear of losing their job is undesirable and illegal – though sadly still in practice.

A climate of fear may be a way of getting a team through a difficult patch, with the terror soon replaced by hugs and kisses all round on reaching the sunlit uplands of commercial survival, but it is not a recipe for enduring success. You can't get the best out of people if their respect and engagement in what they do is driven by the threat of punishment. As soon as that threat is lifted their attention will turn to making an exit. It is far better to create a climate where people give their very best all the time because they really want to.

Shadow of the Soul

Psychoanalytists say people have 'a shadow side' and seek to protect their self-esteem and alleviate anxiety through psychological defences. This is evident in childish behaviour (regression), denial (keep doing what they are doing despite negative consequences), rationalisation (misuse of theory or policy), bullying (repression), yelling at subordinates (displacement – they want to yell at the boss) and aggrandisement, grandeur and fantasy (when they believe their own hype).

The aspects of soul that we have described so far are important not only for sustained success, but also for the avoidance of sustained damage. Building the soul of an organisation keeps in check the darker side of human nature, especially in circumstances where power of any kind can be exercised without regard for consequences. Seminal psychological experiments have shown an alarming and counter-intuitive truth: that in certain circumstances people will ignore the 'moral compass' they would normally follow, even to the extent of committing atrocities. It seems hard to believe, but the evidence is there. Ordinary citizens can be persuaded to commit torture, and other abusive acts, on others if: they are told to do so by an authority figure; when there is group pressure on them to think and behave in a particular way; in the absence of tight rules of good conduct and enforcement of those rules; and if they think they can get away with it.

MILGRAM

In the 1960s, Stanley Milgram, a 27-year-old assistant professor of psychology, was interested to know why so many ordinary Germans subscribed to the Nazi Party, and through action or inaction contributed to the Holocaust. To find out he set up an experiment, hiring Yale undergraduate students at $4 per session to take part in an exercise about authority. The volunteer students were met by the head of the experiment, a man in a white coat, who told them that in the next room, out of sight, there were subjects who would be asked a series of general knowledge questions. If they answered incorrectly, the volunteer was to operate a switch to give them a mild electric shock, which would only sting a little. As the person answering the questions continued to answer the odd question incorrectly, the man in the white coat asked the students to increase the voltage. What is salutary and shocking is that the majority of volunteers followed instructions – even when the person answering was shouting to be released, screaming as the voltage was raised and begging for mercy. The ultimate voltage level was marked 'DANGER: SEVERE SHOCK'. Yet 67 per cent of volunteers delivered that voltage – and heard the screaming suddenly stop, whereupon the man in the white coat halted the experiment. What the volunteers didn't know was that the subjects were actors, simply providing a carefully graded response in accordance to the 'shock' that they were supposed to be given. This experiment proved that people can slip into the most horrifying acts given enough group pressure and coercive conditions – often within half an hour! Milgrave also found that when the volunteers saw their peers obey the order to hit the maximum 450 volts, the number who did the same rose to 90 per cent. When they saw a peer (an actor) refuse, the number complying fell to just over 10 per cent. When Milgram asked 40 psychiatrists how many they thought would hit the maximum, the experts said under 1 per cent. They wildly underestimated the power of social pressure to make ordinary people commit what Albert Bandura called 'moral disengagement'.

Why is this experiment important in the context of building spirit, character and values? Well, there is no more graphic example than the horrific treatment of some Iraqi prisoners by a small number of US soldiers in 2004. The world asked how could they do such a thing without attracting the attention of the leadership. Nonetheless, this is a contemporary illustration of an aspect of human life that military and business leaders need to be resolute in preventing, detecting and stamping out.

Signs of Decline

To keep an eye out for the emergence of the seamier side of human nature in the life of an organisation, leaders should look out for the conditions in which one or more people may deprive others of their dignity, suffocate their creativeness and kill their spirit:

- **A rationale is given to justify the behaviour.** In the case of the Milgram experiment, the researcher told the volunteer that the man receiving the shock had tried everything to improve his memory and this was a last resort – punishment for getting it wrong. In the case of war, the enemy is characterised as a beast, a threat to civilisation. In a recent allegation of sexual discrimination the apparently offensive behaviour of investment banker male colleagues was justified as 'just laddish behaviour – natural and a bit of a laugh' by the perpetrators.

- **Written consent.** This is given for terms of engagement that lead to abusive behaviour. It makes people feel obligated to do something even if it is at odds with their normal conduct.

- **Assigning authoritarian roles.** These create positions of power over others and can be seen in some teacher/ student relationships, prison warder roles, and in some newly promoted managers who mislead junior or impressionable staff.

- **Desensitisation**. Aggression gradually increases over time, as victim and aggressor become desensitised to the consequences of their actions. Dehumanising and de-individualising victims through joking about them, ridiculing their dress or getting them into an embarrassing predicament. The damaging effects of such actions apply whether they occur at work or in the bar afterwards.

- **Use of euphemisms and labels**. These are used to soften or conceal the true nature and consequences of behaviour. Terms such as 'softening up' or 'giving a hard time' should not be permitted to justify bullying or harassment by line managers, nor can participation 'initiation ceremonies' or 'big boy culture' camouflage assault and victimisation.

- **Lack of accountability.** Responsibility and accountability deliberately or negligently become diffuse – making the buck apparently stop somewhere else. War crime accusations in Africa, the Balkans and elsewhere show that culpability for plainly wrong actions can be apportioned between leaders and followers, between those that directed criminal activities, those who participated, and those who chose not to oppose or settled for appeasement. The same principles can be applied to the workplace: managers and all other employees must be clear about their personal responsibility for what goes on around them – and especially what is done in their name.

THE 'TRAFFIC LIGHT' ASSESSMENT

Soul Audit – Where is Your Organisation?

Maybe you already work in an enlightened organisation full of people of great character and high morale. If so, well done, you have chosen well. Many others are not so lucky. So, for a spontaneous survey of your thoughts about your firm's moral courage, cast your eye down the prompts in the table and tick the relevant traffic light.

Use the following 'traffic light' assessment to show where you are, by and large, getting it right (tick the lower traffic light), where you are some way there or where there are pockets of good work (tick the middle traffic light) and where you are not doing well (tick the top traffic light). Do that for all three of the levels of assessment – where you are now, where you are against your preferred standard and how you would perform if suddenly faced with maximum pressure, given the capability you have now.

MORAL COURAGE TRAFFIC LIGHT

Ask yourself:

A) How are we doing now?

B) How are we performing against best-practice and best-in-class?

C) How would we perform if we were put under maximum pressure with the resources we have right now?

Character

Morality – we 'do the right thing' in this firm.

Those who do the right thing get recognised in the right way and are those who do not are punished.

There is a strong team commitment.

Work-life balance – we are taking enough time out and time off to recoup.

The firm does not drive so hard that there is no time to think and refresh.

Resilience – we and the firm are good at overcoming setbacks.

Everyone shows plenty of resilience when they are tired and stressed.

Emotional Intelligence – people manage their moods so as not to affect others.

A B C
People talk directly to the moody person about changing their ways.

A B C
Charisma – people give due regard to the impression they make.

A B C
Self-discipline – there is selfless commitment to others.

A B C
Integrity – people are genuine.

A B C
Teamwork – everyone flies in formation.

High Morale

A B C
Most people want to be here.

A B C
Trust – respect is shown and felt. We look out for each other.

A B C
We go out of our way for each other.

A B C
There is a high level of commitment to the plans, principles, promises, projects and relationships.

A B C
People feel inspired.

A B C
We inspire each other.

HOW TO BUILD SOUL

Before leaders set about engaging the soul of the people in a company, it helps to begin with reliable and valid personnel assessment and selection techniques, so that the right people are chosen in the first place. Have you hired a good professional to set up such a process? It is such a first-base priority that you need to have had specialist advice. Once the team has been selected, the task is to manage the practicalities of what makes the organisation tick, and know how to build the essential spiritual strength.

Building soul is not about inviting the accounts department to shed a few thousand calories on a forced march up a soggy mountain. These techniques may, of course, help: all Special Forces, for example, have immensely high entry standards in which the benefits of dragging huge volumes of equipment over large slices of rugged terrain in bad weather play a significant part. Even Special Forces need the soul to handle all the mental and physical wounds they will accrue in a hard business. In this section we look briefly at the vital role of recruiting, how to build character through developing 'self-efficacy', and the role of a code to lay down common standards and expectations.

Recruiting and Employment

Are the right people in the right seats? Too often people are recruited by simply choosing from the best of the pile to hand, instead of casting wider and selecting against a set of standards. We look in detail at how to design effective organisations and recruit for them in Secret Number Three: Right Team, Right Stuff. Here, we will confine ourselves to the specific issue of character and the need to develop it. A thriving company needs people who not only fulfil the technical 'skill' requirements of a post but also have the personal characteristics and qualities that make them an effective, dynamic part of the team. This might mean being a good fit as part of a small group, or it might mean playing a pivotal role in the formulation of strategy for a giant corporation.

Although most large corporations generally use robust and fair selection methods, the UK is mostly comprised of small businesses. Not many small businesses have the specialist knowledge to create a good assessment process that has thought through the characteristics and values they need, let alone how to assess them reliably. This is an important part of leadership and must be done with the help of professional expertise, proper thought and diligence.

There are many other ways to engage people through their soul. One way to really know someone is to 'see them in the middle of their lives' and understand where they have come from and where they want to go, as well as the complexities in their lives at present. Getting people completely out of the role they play at work and into a completely different setting will often help people to know themselves more honestly and to show themselves to their colleagues in another light. Real, lifelong creativity and teamwork can only flow from mutual and deep understanding of each other.

So with the constituent parts of what makes up the concept of soul laid out above, we now need to move on to some advice about how to build soul into an organisation. The first point is that slogans and posters are not enough. The concept of soul must be more than cleverly and simply articulated: it must be lived – an integral part of daily life.

Ignite Self-efficacy

Self-efficacy is a sense of personal agency, a sense of 'can do', a belief that you can make things happen and really make a difference. This is an important part of building resilience. When you are down, this self-efficacy gets you up. That is why major or early achievements in life and careers are so important for developing a sense of potential capacity in senior positions later on. It is a very interesting fact that one's knowledge, skills and talent are less a predicator of success than one's self-efficacy, the self-belief in one's capability. You will notice when people have high self-efficacy, they:

- Put in greater effort.
- Get over or round obstacles.
- Persevere and are resilient after failure.
- Use coping and calming 'self-talk'.
- Manage stress.
- Are quick to take advantage of opportunities.
- Generate collective actions.
- Achieve more.

Self-efficacy refers to the judgement people make about their capability, whereas self-esteem is about the judgements people make about their sense of worth. There is no essential correlation between how you judge your capabilities and how much you like yourself. For example, people may think they cannot do a particular activity very well and yet not suffer any loss of self-esteem whatsoever as a result because they do not value that activity as important. If you have someone on your team with low self-esteem, fragile confidence and poor self-efficacy you can and have to do something about it. First of all, set aside time out to consider what they stand for, what is important to them, what are their guiding principles. Then you need to have a system or a process to check if they are living those values. People who live their values feel better about themselves and make faster, better decisions. Such processes can be forums, or the support that comes from coaching or just the challenge: Am I/Are we, living those values? How does this work relate to your sense of purpose, your view of why you are here? You can go further: think through and articulate to a chosen few your sense of mission, your aspirations, what you aspire to (the vision) and what is going to get you there (your assets). Leaders need to consider what work they have done to connect value to the tasks they delegate to others.

It is true that people gravitate towards doing something that gives them a feeling of self-worth and raises their self-esteem. This tends to lead people to do work that they are good at and feel good about. If you notice a lack of engagement in any of your team then a conversation with them should be directed at improving the value of the task to that person. The person doing the activity needs to link it with their sense of what is 'worthy' in order for them to be fully engaged. This is vital because we know that when people are fully engaged they can get into the condition of 'flow'. The concept of flow is when you are lost in deep and easy concentration, completely involved in an activity for its own sake. Conditions for flow include being stretched in a task that uses your skills.

Trust Your Intuition

As a leader, it is important to listen to your inner counsel and learn to trust it. Intuition, gut reactions, these things are now finding credence in psychological circles because of the latest brain research methodologies. As a leader, it is likely you are in front, ahead of the wave, the one with the furthest view. Others don't see what you see. Before you start to influence others, you need to be rock solid in yourself. Many people who have achieved great things say it was due to hard work and 'bloody mindedness' – a conviction, an uncompromising stance, that channelled energy so acute it cut through obstacles. The military respect intuition as something accumulated from years of knowledge and experience enabling lightning-fast understanding and decision making. If you focus too much on rational decision making you will not develop your ability to trust your intuition. Of course, we need to look at facts and listen to others' perspectives, but the people who make timely, good judgements always have faith in their *own* counsel.

The Code

Many organisations have a set of principles that lay down the framework for the way they will function. Employment law determines some of these, some are common sense and others may be specific to the role – such as the oath taken by doctors, priests and service personnel. It isn't a 'flavour of the month' activity – there are good reasons for having set principles. The value of a code is that it provides clarity and a common point of reference that explains what is expected of people. Listing values, creating a code, a common way, they all act as important guides that enable people to react appropriately, rapidly and flexibly to events around them.

Sometimes this code will come exclusively from an owner/founder; sometimes it will come from the views of the entire workforce – especially with technology now enabling greater participation. Some think it best when as many in the workforce as possible contribute. But sometimes the leadership really is best placed to create a code, explain it clearly and then expect others to follow it. Whatever way this code is constructed, every single employee must know it, remember it, think about it and live it. This sort of 'code' or 'way', whether written down or not, requires thought in construction and investment in training/coaching.

The organisation must genuinely 'live its values', making them a feature of all activity. These must be more than abstract or empty phrases to be deployed on team-building events or in annual reports. This starts at the top, applies at all levels without discrimination and requires regular investment in training and assessment. Selection, promotion, the award of bonuses and discipline should be contingent upon abiding by the spirit of the code. Leaders must regularly take stock with their staff and see where the soul of their organisation needs reinforcing or repair – then action must be taken if required to set things straight.

COMMANDER'S COMFY CHAIR

Core Values

Take a few hours to think through the following. You might decide that it needs further work – over days/weeks.

How well do you know what is expected of you?

How does that relate to what is important to you in life?

Do you know what your boss would love to see?

What does your boss need to see?

Do you know what worries or concerns the boss has about you?

As a leader, do you have conversations with your team along these lines?

In the Armed Forces it is particularly important that there is this high degree of common understanding about values because people are required to accept that there are constraints on the way they live their lives, both on and off duty, that would not apply in many civilian occupations. These restrictions must be justified by the needs of service, not relics of a bygone age that serve no contemporary purpose. The British General J.F.C. Fuller wrote more than 50 years ago about the dangers of misplaced restrictions:

> *'The old are often suspicious of the young and do not welcome criticism, yet without criticism, both destructive and constructive, there can be no progress. The easiest course to adopt is to lay down rules and regulations which must be implicitly obeyed; yet chance knows no compulsion, and such rules and regulations are apt to cramp intelligence and originality.'*

This is easier said than done in any hierarchical, monolithic organisation where change has to flow top-down and there is no scope (ordinarily at least) for 'Young Turks' to have a major influence. Cultural change may be slower in the Armed Forces than elsewhere, but this is inevitable, bearing in mind the nature of warfare and the essential differences between military and civilian norms.

So, for example, the modern Armed Forces have learned to embrace greater diversity in terms of ethnic origin and sexual orientation than was the case even 10 years ago, but they also retain appropriate constraints on the way personal relationships are formed and expressed. These are essential to preserve the fighting efficiency of men and women likely to be faced with the unique demands of war, and as such are perfectly in step with contemporary employment law. For example, a commanding officer will not retain his post (or probably his career), if he enters a relationship with his driver's wife: this would fundamentally undermine his credibility and integrity as an officer required to command with unimpeachable fairness, impartiality and judgement. He might, for example, try really hard to get the driver into the hottest combat situations in the hope that he was killed, thereby saving the boredom and cost of divorce proceedings. People will rightly be less inclined to risk their lives if they sense it is for reasons other than the real demands of the situation.

If values are given to you that you do not understand or accept, whether in the form of a code or not, and you then try to live them anyway, there is a risk of internal tension that could become a source of significant stress. This is why clearly articulating values is essential, but so is hiring people who will truly accept them. Typically, less than 10 per cent of the population can readily name their values – yet we run around all day making decisions, interacting with people, leading people, despite not being conscious of our values.

Organisations need to recognise the vital nature of having a simple, robust framework that establishes the basic rules by which all employees condition their behaviour. This is fundamental to creating a common spirit and attitude that permeates through all activity.

There is no use investing effort in building a code for an organisation if no one knows about it, understands it or abides by it. The potentially strong effect on the individual and collective soul of the firm will be forgone if all that happens is a list of desirable values is pinned up in the canteen, and it is bound to become an object of derision from those intimidated by or mistrustful of it. Handled badly, the production of a code will lead to an outburst of cynicism and parody.

In the Armed Forces, this education begins early in basic training and is repeated throughout an individual's service. Every

British soldier has a personal copy of 'Values and Standards' and every US soldier has the 'Warrior Ethos', which includes:

I will always place the Mission first.
I will never accept defeat.
I will never quit.
I will never leave a fallen comrade.

Interestingly, the US Army adds that:

> *'In a broader sense, the Warrior Ethos is a way of life*
> *that applies to our personal and professional lives as well.*
> *It makes us better people in general – better husbands,*
> *better wives, better sons and daughters;*
> *better brothers and sisters.'*
>
> US ARMY WEBSITE

BUILD YOUR ARMOURY
Build the Code

Here is a list of tools and tips giving specific advice on how to build a Code that all your people can adhere to.

▷ Have a Code that is well articulated and understood. The spirit, values and behaviour expected of people must be clearly articulated to every employee. Indeed, all new intakes should be encouraged to live these values in all aspects of their lives.

▷ Integrate the values of this Code into all activities. This requires a thorough approach to how work is done internally and externally – making sure that all communications and all internal courses are 'value checked'. That is, they comply in context, style and method to the espoused values. Talk with suppliers and check that their people and their materials are aligned to your values: if your suppliers do not match your values they will weaken your brand. If not, look for other suppliers. Make the results of the learning public to maintain focus as a 'learning organisation' and to build strong learning mindsets. Finally, senior leaders must formally review their values and the way they are being integrated into the life of the organisation, just as they review their balance sheet.

▷ Provide a common reference for all behaviour and relationships. It should be the subject of a comprehensive internal communication programme, with leaders at all levels required to brief their teams on its content.

▷ Indicate clearly to potential employees what will be required of them. The code should be a high-profile part of staff recruitment and induction, and be recognised as part of the contract between employer and employee.

▷ Introduce a process whereby people can give regular feedback on how they are living the values. This feedback should be to their boss, their colleagues, to everyone. TGI Friday has introduced a system called 'Take Five' – in which every day each employee gives three positive pieces of feedback, and two suggestions where they noticed the values could have been lived better. That process, free and instant, meant thousands of conversations were taking place about the values, by all levels, every day and it gave them the 'excuse' to introduce the subject of poor behaviour.

▷ Provide guidance for leaders to use when dealing with unsatisfactory behaviour. This should be 'audited', with senior management reviewing behaviour at least annually across the firm and publishing the results. Unsatisfactory behaviour cannot be pushed under the carpet.

▷ Provide a yardstick by which employees will judge their leaders.

▷ Personal example will be required. Where behaviour falls short of the required standard, the Code should be used as a basis for reviewing the significance of what has occurred. This makes it a set of 'living' ideas, and puts the debate in a context which everybody can follow. It may be helpful to have an 'Employment Test' to apply where something has happened that may undermine core values, for example: 'Has this behaviour adversely affected the efficiency or effectiveness of my organisation?'

▷ Build the expectation that self-discipline and integrity will be judged as a paramount quality in all activities.

▷ Let it be clearly understood that high standards of personal example must be set by managers and leaders. People mirror what is being modelled. Being in a position of authority does not mean you are in an 'integrity exclusion zone'. In fact, the opposite is true. Being in a position of authority means showing high integrity – in action. Failures of self-discipline and integrity, major and minor, must be held to account.

Integrate Your Values

There are many forms of training that can be provided to help integrate values and build soul, including (but certainly not restricted to) education in the content of a code. This can be provided by written information, formal induction and continuation courses for staff, away-day workshops and just included in straightforward and routine management briefings to staff. The greatest mistake is to skimp training in this whole area: if you accept that soul matters more than anything else to the long-term health of an organisation it implies that resources invested in getting it right are well spent.

What has worked especially well in changing a culture fast was to 'shadow' coach the entire board – staying with them all day and even going home with them at night until 'they got it'. 'Getting it' meant awareness of the difference between their intent and their behaviour and also modifying their behaviour in a way congruent with the values. For one director, this took just four days. In another case, the consultants were with the director for six weeks. But at the end of that time the board were ready to stand tall and talk about both the values and their task of imparting them to the rest of the staff in the business, all with awe-inspiring credibility. Many subordinates were moved when their leaders told their stories, revealing their values, what they meant to them on a very personal level and how easy or not it was to live them. People became genuinely inspired and within weeks 'value champions' were appointed – volunteers to create a values-based internal magazine. Within a quarter their customers and suppliers were noticing a real shift in atmosphere and behaviour. Not surprisingly, that business won an award for successful culture change.

'Living the values' that will promote success can be expected to be demanding as well as rewarding, and it must be entirely consistent with the law and the expectations of society. For the Armed Forces, it is not about reducing sentient beings to automatons dripping with bloodlust, free from the moral restraints of normal life. Unrestrained brutality may be viewed (even today) as entirely admirable in some of the more militant paramilitary groupings around the globe, but modern societies demand Armed Forces who fight legitimate wars successfully and in accordance with the international laws of armed conflict. Battles won by means outside the law, such as Saddam Hussein's treatment of the Kurdish population in Iraq or the massacres of

Albanians and Serbs in Kosovo in the 1990s, tend to lead only to more bloodshed until deep-seated injustices are dealt with.

In business, there are many examples of companies that have sought to get ahead by abandoning the law and treading on the heads of others, and there will be others in the future. The good news is that much of modern society has the good sense and the legal system to deal appropriately with those who are caught.

Education in Ethics

Every soldier and officer in the Armed Forces of today is trained in the ethics of war. This includes the philosophical and legal aspects of what constitutes a just war, as well as the internationally agreed codes that should govern how wars are conducted. For example, there are the Geneva Conventions that set out the responsibilities of an occupying power, as well as the standards for the care of prisoners of war. The education is directed at building good judgement as well as teaching matters of fact.

Only a few of the major business schools put ethics as a major part of business education. Difficult ethical issues requiring prompt and sound decisions are faced by managers all the time, yet many pass by without notice or are resolved on the basis of a limited appreciation of the ethics at stake. Ethical dilemmas generate questions about what we should do in accordance with commonly understood standards of right or wrong, and what sort of character traits (such as honesty, loyalty, compassion and fairness) should take precedence. Adherence to a high standard of business ethics benefits shareholders, increases customer loyalty, attracts top young talent and improves staff motivation.

Building self-discipline and integrity requires a top-down approach that permeates all levels and all aspects of corporate life.

In many respects the Armed Forces are better geared to inculcating these qualities. Aspirant commanders who might be idle, slothful, sullen, sloppy or selfish by nature are easily identified and fail to pass the rigours of the forces' common entrance procedures and basic training. During the initial training, the programme takes away a lot of personal liberty and fills every waking moment. A recruit is inspected, corrected and directed – those who have an irredeemably negative or lazy disposition either reject the regime and leave or are rejected.

As evidence appears about individual strength of character and the ability to bond in a team during this arduous basic training, personal liberties are restored. The common values, ethos and mutual respect thus learned are deeply rooted in all who stay the course. Military and commercial organisations both demand that where unacceptable behaviour occurs, only swift and sharp intervention flowing from the top can hope to regain credibility and confidence. Bullying in the Armed Forces happens from time to time, and when it does steps are taken to eradicate it.

Similar high standards must be applied in business, too. An investment bank sacked one of its top dealers for being so abusive to airport check-in staff that the airline wrote to the bank detailing the event. This was a highly profitable employee, yet the boss decided the person had fallen out of line with the organisation's core value of 'treating people with respect' and so must go. Many leaders would not have found the moral courage to discipline the dealer to that extent, perhaps in the interests of profitability and perhaps through being genuinely spineless, but this leader had the integrity to take the appropriate decision. It begs the question of what the 'bottom line' really is for a business: is it this year's profit or loss, or the enduring qualities of the workforce that will pay off handsomely over many years?

Reluctance to step forward when it is the right, necessary thing to do can be applied to the decisions leaders have to take at all levels. It can also be much more significant to the organisation's future, such as the manager who detects signs of serial fraud yet decides to ignore it – perhaps fearing for his own job. Moral courage is an inextricable part of leadership, and equally essential to the newest, most dispensable employee: people should expect to work in an environment free from the deceit, inadequacy and uncertainty that an absence of moral courage will entail.

General Harold K. Johnson, the US Army's Deputy Chief of Staff for Operations during the Vietnam years and later Army chief of staff, had to respond to the question: If you had your life to live over again, what would you do differently? He said, 'I remember the day I was ready to go over to the Oval Office and give my four stars to the President and tell him, "You have refused to tell the country they cannot fight a war without mobilisation; you have required me to send men into battle with little hope of their ultimate victory; and you have forced us in the military to violate almost every one of the principles of war in Vietnam. Therefore, I resign and will hold a press conference after I walk out of your door." I made the typical mistake of believing I could do more for my country and the Army if I stayed in than if I got out. I am going now to my grave with that burden of lapse of moral courage on my back.'

Time to Review

Having done well to identify the right people, to articulate clearly what is required of them, provide the right training and ensure that these values are part of everyday life, the final element is to monitor progress. The senior leadership should set aside time and other resources to conduct an audit of the soul of their organisation, based on opinion taken at all levels and their own judgements. How many management teams can claim to put this item on the agenda, even just once a year? All managers know that opinion will vary at every level and across functions, and will be alert to the tendency to blame all ills on the next level up and pass all responsibility for doing something about them to the next level down. For senior leaders, the danger of subordinates telling them only what they want to hear is as real as it is human. There is plenty of scope for managers being led, or leading themselves, to a fundamentally false view of the health of their organisation – and once the rot has settled in it can be very challenging to shift direction, without taking draconian measures, such as sacking those in charge.

Summary of Secret Number Two: Soul Matters

- This Secret goes to the very heart of the organisation and is the second of the three sides that make up the Power Pyramid.
- It shows how the spirit, values and character of an organisation and all its people are vital, even pre-eminent, to lasting success.
- If you join together the strengths of Synchronised Thinking and Soul Matters, your organisation will surely have the right ideas and the right climate to be a stunning success.
- The two main elements of 'soul' are character and high morale, and encompass many factors including moral courage, conviction, self-discipline, integrity, trust, commitment and inspiration.
- Getting the 'soul' of a company right has a financial payoff – resulting in good decision making, enhanced work–life balance, good teamwork – leading to improved performance.
- Getting the 'soul' of a company wrong leads to a culture of

blame, animosity, mistrust, lack of co-operation, low confidence and poor self-esteem – and the risk of being overtaken by competitors.

- Business Generals who focus on the soul of the company and fully engage their people in what they do can expect to out-think, outperform and outlast a competitor that limits everything it does to process and numbers.
- Achieving this advantage is within the grasp of every business, but only if it really commits itself to building the soul of the organisation on a consistent and dedicated basis. It won't happen by itself: this is an area where strong and robust leadership is necessary.

Next Secret...

Your organisation also needs the practical means to realise its potential, and so we turn to the third and final side of the Power Pyramid in Secret Number Three: Right Team, Right Stuff.

Secret Three
Right Team, Right Stuff

Get the mix of structure, technology, people and training right

'We trained very hard, but it seemed that every time we were beginning to form into teams we would be reorganised. I was to learn in this life that we tend to meet any situation by reorganising. And a wonderful method it can be for creating the illusion of progress while producing confusion, inefficiency, and demoralisation.'

(QUOTATION BELIEVED TO COME FROM THE TIME OF THE BRITISH OCCUPATION OF GERMANY AT THE END OF THE SECOND WORLD WAR, SOMETIMES ATTRIBUTED TO OTHERS – SUCH AS THE ROMAN FIGURE PETRONIUS ARBITER IN ABOUT AD 60.)

The first two Secrets have looked at the role of Synchronised Thinking and Soul Matters in creating a successful and enduring organisation. Both are essential and indispensable elements of the Power Pyramid, but by themselves they are not enough. You also need 'the right team' – the best people in the best positions – and 'the right stuff' – the correct equipment and materials for the task in hand. These are the physical and tangible element of any enterprise. So, Secret Number Three is about the third side of the Power Pyramid, the physical aspects of organisational power.

Some of this may be less gripping for leaders than wheeling grand concepts and big deals around, but without a strong understanding of an organisation's 'nuts and bolts' a Business General's success will be in serious jeopardy.

PRACTICALITIES – IGNORE AT YOUR PERIL

This is a very broad area and it is the one many leaders, managers and staff generally feel at home with. Indeed it makes up most of what business leaders have to deal with, frequently to the detriment of the other two sides of the Power Pyramid. Dealing with practical aspects such as how many employees you need, what machinery to buy, how much inventory to hold, where best to borrow money and countless other points are the stuff of everyday life for us all. This Secret does not attempt to – indeed could not hope to – offer insights into every aspect of the structures, technologies and processes that may apply to every type of organisation. In any case, there are volumes of technical and specialist advice already available. The point of Secret Number Three is to:

- Look at the importance of building the right balance in the physical and practical aspects of an organisation.
- Appreciate how each aspect contributes to the whole.
- See why and how leaders need to manage this part of a successful organisation.

It is the ability to excel at systemic and strategic thinking that sets senior commanders apart. A key leadership function is bringing together all the parts of an organisation to act in balance, unison and harmony. The greatest organisational success comes from harnessing the strengths of thinking, soul, and the practical aspects – 'right team, right stuff' – under inspirational leadership, with every part, however modest, pulling in the same direction at maximum effort. Getting Secret Number Three right turns ideas, high morale and passion into success.

Keeping the Wheels Oiled

There are many illustrations of the importance of getting the practical aspects of an organisation right – and of the complete and irredeemable disaster that may ensue from getting it wrong. These potential benefits and risks exist in every form of organisation, but for the Armed Forces the consequences can be pretty stark. History can relate many campaigns that were a disaster for one side. Often this is not through any failure of will or courage – it is the result of the practical aspects going awry.

FRANCE 1870–71

When France declared war on Prussia on 15 July 1871, it was a triumph of pique and emotion over reason. Prussia had worked hard to provoke France into such a declaration and was better prepared for battle. Prussia had an exceptional system for the massed mobilisation of its men of fighting age, coupled with brilliant use of the new railway system to concentrate forces in accordance with a well-conceived plan of operation. French arrangements for conscription were far less efficient, resulting in new armies being formed as they were being sent to the front. This led to chaos. When the battle began, there were 250,000 Frenchmen opposing 300,000 Germans – and the latter continuing to build up more quickly.

French artillery was the old-fashioned type and had to be loaded from the front, whereas the Prussians fielded the new, quicker-firing, breech-loading weapons. The French used cavalry against well-positioned infantry – leading to many premature deaths amongst the mounted soldiers. Above all, the Prussians showed decisive skills in planning, moving and concentrating their forces under pressure. They had thought hard and long about tactics, built a 'General Staff' who were among the best in the world at planning and conducting campaigns, and trained their soldiers – regular and reserve – to a higher common standard. This was 'right team, right stuff' in action. As the Prussian military leader of the day, Field Marshal Graf Helmuth Von Moltke, wrote: *'In the long run luck is given only to the efficient.'*

In business and the public sector there are many organisations that have gone down because they got the practical aspects of their operation hopelessly wrong. There are just as many examples of the 'well-oiled machine' delivering exceptional results, whether that is defined in terms of profits, growth or benefits delivered.

TESCO

Tesco, the British supermarket chain, is a particularly well-oiled commercial machine. In a recent poll, Sir Terry Leahy was selected as the 'people's choice' for most-admired CEO, winning with twice the number of votes of his closest competitor. In 2003 he was voted Fortune's European Businessman of the Year. Yet 10 years earlier, Tesco was widely derided for its 'pile it high and sell it cheap' branding – dating back to the strategy of founder Jack Cohen in 1919. Sir Terry joined in 1997, just after Lord MacLaurin left as Chair.

Lord MacLaurin had always advocated close personal contact with his managers – he led the way and insisted his senior manager left the ivory towers of head office to go to one of the 800 stores to chat to, enthuse and thank his managers. This meant that all 1,600 employees knew the vision of the business clearly and could contribute to a cohesive plan to make it happen. Sir Terry conceived and led a return to a strong and expanding retailing presence, both in the UK and internationally, selling more than just food.

This new strategy was executed with impressive vision, judgement and a military-like zeal. In just two years, Tesco stole the march on Sainsbury's and had a full 20 per cent lead in sales on their nearest competitors. Much of this gain came from greater square footage with the new Metro and Express store openings, but they also won the race in terms of sales per square foot. The marketing of the no-frills, 'every little helps' pitch attracted those who were cost conscious and the loyalty 'Clubcard' proved to be a killer for the competition. Tesco launched a better service initiative, promising that a new check-out would open if there was more than 'one in front' in the queue. It all encouraged people who had defected to Sainsbury's or Waitrose to try Tesco again and to spend more.

Sir Terry looked to the workforce for new thinking, listening to a wide range of views that culminated in 'The Tesco Way': a core ideology, a code, and a leadership ethos (in our terms, he got to the soul of the company). Then he turned to logistics and spent £250 million on supply systems, upgrading facilities and using existing resources more efficiently so that, for example, two deliveries a day would mean reducing the incidence of 'out of stocks'. He wanted to empower and build authority in his store managers, so he introduced a programme where managers spent a week in a store filling different low-level functions. This developed greater empathy across the workforce and clarity about what could best be decided upon locally.

Under Sir Terry Leahy's leadership, Tesco management were united behind a shared vision and common values, able to operate with greater autonomy in local decision making. He had paid attention to logistics, IT, people, culture, training, customers, sites, suppliers, lorries/kit – improving them one by one in a united, no-compromise effort. It paid off handsomely in record sales and profits.

Of course, in business nothing stands still. Like any winner, Tesco will need renewed effort on all three parts of their Power Pyramid (Synchronised Thinking, Soul and the Right Stuff) to stay ascendant in a tough market.

BALANCING CORE ELEMENTS

All organisations, large and small, have to find and maintain a balance between the many functions that contribute to 'right team, right stuff'. Specialists in finance, human resources, information technology, operations, production, pensions, research, and marketing all play an important part, but the leadership must understand something about all of them and so orchestrate the mix that works best. Having an organisation held hostage by, say, the fixed views of the finance department, just because the financial director has the ear of the CEO, is a sign of weakness and an indicator of incipient organisational failure.

It is about leadership and relationships: people – especially experts – need to be convinced not only about what they need to do, but about what they are not to do. It is the combination of character, communication and brain power of a Business General that creates the relationship with the director/employee/customer/client/patient – not just specialist knowledge. The requirement is to build a great team where it is the power of the whole effort that counts:

> *'An army is a team. It lives, eats, sleeps, fights as a team.*
> *This individuality stuff is a bunch of bullshit.'*
> GENERAL GEORGE S. PATTON

The core elements of 'Right Team, Right Stuff' are:

- Organisation
- Technology
- Infrastructure and logistics
- People
- Training
- Leadership

We will look at each of these in turn.

Organisation

The shape and the culture of the organisation must match its purpose. Any endeavour that brings two or more people together requires some form of organisation. Organisations can be large or small, hierarchical and heavily regulated or flat and anarchic – and all points in between. They can be carefully and deliberately designed, or left to grow like a spider plant. They will all change over time, but the issue is will that change be managed in detail or abandoned to the ebb and flow of whim and fortune. Throughout the life of an organisation there will be good times and bad times. Some of these will be within the gift of the leadership to control and some not. Companies can manage what goes on in their offices, not the hurricane that devastates their customers.

For Business Generals at all levels and in all walks of life, the shape an organisation takes, the way it works, its culture, the way it is kept aligned to its purpose are all matter for conscious thought, direction and management. This mix – and the spade-work it requires – is the way to great results.

> *'If you have knowledge, let others light their candles with it.'*
> WINSTON CHURCHILL

What Should Go into the Mix?

Military organisations have developed over a very long time, which brings both advantages and weaknesses. In most armies, there is broadly universal acceptance that a platoon of around 30 troops under an officer is a basic building block. These are formed into companies of around 100, and then battalions of 650. A battalion commander will come to know all the names and key contributions of all 650 – even those (especially those) who are a walking potential disaster.

Even today, the ideal composition of a simple platoon is the subject of considerable and detailed scrutiny and debate: how many of each type of weapon or store to carry, the best distribution of radios and vehicles, the right mix of ranks and trade skills, and how best to train it to peak effectiveness. Whatever is provided, the soldiers will be quick to complain if they feel anything is missing, shoddy, or too heavy. No detail is too small: combat underwear now has silver in the fabric in the interests of hygiene after days in the field without a wash.

ORGANISATIONAL DESIGN

The debate about Organisational Design (OD), even at the lowest level, needs to be influenced by:

- **History**. What happened in the last battle will inevitably shape the preparations for the next battle. This means looking at what didn't work so well, and learning from the mistakes, as well as what did.

- **Technology**. What new piece of technology will make the team more effective? How could and how should technology influence organisation and method? How do you avoid being seduced into buying a technically magnificent but impractical device? How do you avoid the mistake of developing technology and machinery that is massively over-specified for what you need? What will be the cost in time and training to learn to use the technology properly and safely?

- **Thought and Information**. What are the theories the staff are actually using day to day, and what are the theories they are meant to be using? In the Armed Forces there is a constant search to refine or replace organisation, tactics and procedures with better ways. There is no absolutely right answer, but there are some absolutely wrong ones and spotting the difference can be hard. This is where the effort put into Synchronised Thinking pays off.

- **Social norms, dynamics, and culture**. How are people relating to each other at a 'social' level? Do the relationships between them enable a full and vibrant flow of information, or are they locked in a deadly silence caused by mutual antipathy? Do people bond and bind together in a common pursuit of wealth and happiness, or are they circling like vultures waiting for the next corporate casualty? Are people just cannon fodder for the next bout of inter-departmental warfare? Does the 'way things are done around here' act as the oil that lubricates or the treacle that makes things turgid?

- **Resources**. Affordability and competing agendas for the potential use of resources (especially money) are key points to decide on. As the Armed Forces are paid for by taxpayers, the requirement to prune and justify human resource costs is a considerable pressure on the leadership. Shareholders exert much the same discipline. There needs to be a transparent, robust analysis and dialogue about what resources are needed to be successful at least cost. These should be well informed by accountants, but not necessarily decided by them.

COMMANDER'S COMFY CHAIR

Examine Your Organisation

Take a few hours to think about the following questions in relation to your organisation. You might decide that it needs further work – over days/weeks:

Look at the aim or purpose of the organisation – in outline, what needs to be done to get there?

What are the tasks to be performed?

What are the skills needed to carry them out?

Look at the history of your organisation – what is smooth, well oiled and slick and what is messy and turgid?

Look at what needs to be done – how can that be clustered into roles? (Brainstorm to get some creative new ideas; do not automatically switch back to how it was done before.)

How many people will you need?

What knowledge, skills and attitudes/values should they have?

What is the best plan for suppliers, outsourcing and procurement?

What is the information that needs to flow?

What resources will those roles need to be effective? (Challenge your thinking.)

How will you train, embed and discipline the Synchronised Thinking?

How might technology facilitate decision-making and help to turn input into output ?

How will you recognise and reward potential in your business and encourage it to grow your people?

What about the culture and climate that might hinder achievement ('red light' conditions)?

What will you see and hear if things are not working or require further investigation ('yellow light' conditions)?

What will you see, hear and feel when conditions are such that people can get excited, release their potential, keep learning and want to stay ('green light' conditions)?

How can you keep your ear to the ground?

How are you going to get unadulterated, quality information so that you know when to adapt and change?

The greatest strength in the way the Armed Forces plan is the intellectually robust approach taken to making the case for each role. Once the analysis is complete and senior-level approval received, detailed documents show exactly what entitlement a unit has – and this is what the taxpayer agrees to pay for. A unit has a document that lists the personnel, technology, information and kit it is entitled to. This is the basis on which recruits and more senior staff are allocated to posts and equipment is procured.

Choosing Resource Priorities

All branches of the Armed Forces have a mechanism for properly debating where resource priorities should go and where shortfalls in recruiting and training are acceptable. For example, in recent times the Air Force has looked to see how to transfer aircraft maintenance tasks to private contractors or other parts of the public sector, thus reducing the number of more expensive service personnel. Has such a robust approach been taken in your organisation?

As a result every post in the Armed Forces has been subject to scrutiny and conforms to a broad vision about where people should be applied and how the organisation as a whole should operate. This includes everything from the four-man team operating one tank to the complete armoured division of 20,000 people and 5,000 vehicles. The detail is really important: if the members of a British tank crew found that they had no means of making hot water there would be considerable and understandable unhappiness. If loading the gun on the tank required someone to be no more than one metre tall but with the upper body of a champion wrestler, recruiting gunners would be a challenge.

The weaknesses in military organisation planning stem from the challenges of a hierarchical system. Despite the Armed Forces' pride in being thorough and forward-thinking, ideas from the young and junior can get knocked back – albeit rarely – by the attitude of 'we didn't need that in my day' or 'that's how it's always run and it works'. Failing to challenge assumptions is the biggest risk to getting Secret Number Three: Right Team, Right Stuff right. Default settings and habits need to be questioned overtly, explicitly and systematically. Alongside the reluctance to confront an uncertain future is the tendency to make comprehensive plans based on the certainties of the last battle. A huge amount of effort and training goes into shaping the thinking, judgement and intuition of officers and soldiers, and once an idea has taken root it can be difficult to modify or remove.

Planning for Peace and War

For industry and the public sector alike, one of the things that gets in the way of thinking about the future and managing change is the constant pressure of daily activity. Even when war breaks out, peacetime requirements for detailed accounting of the use of resources can be hard to drop – to the immense consternation of people at the front faced with shot and shell.

> 'My Lord, if I attempted to answer the mass of futile
> correspondence which surrounds me, I should be debarred
> from the serious business of campaigning. So long as I
> retain an independent position, I shall see no officer under
> my command is debarred by attending to the futile
> drivelling of mere quill-driving from attending to his
> first duty, which is and always has been to train the
> private men under his command that they may without
> question beat any force opposed to them in the field.'
>
> THE DUKE OF WELLINGTON TO THE SECRETARY OF STATE FOR WAR
> DURING THE PENINSULAR CAMPAIGN.

For the Armed Forces there are lulls during and between conflicts, natural moments to think things through. But in business, in hospitals, and in many other services, there is not that luxury. Most businesses are on the commercial battlefield every day. The daily pressures of operating a factory, store or department are only too evident. The challenge of Organisational Design is the reverse of that faced by the Armed Forces: there is no time for leaders to break out of the rigour of day-to-day activity to take stock and plan ahead.

This leads to one of three possibilities: incremental growth in lieu of root and branch review and reform, a huge shock to the business when some major new factor that could have been foreseen and managed is allowed to spring up as a nasty surprise, or the abrogation of organisational matters to in-house or external experts. Delegation is better than abrogation, but it is important that leaders do not discard their responsibilities for this area.

So, while the Armed Forces have the luxury of time and resources to consider the design of their organisation in detail, there are also reasons why achieving the most balanced and effective organisation is not necessarily straightforward. Businesses not only have different pressures, but many have no Organisational Design, or model, at all. The structure is simply the result of how it has turned out – possibly influenced by who happened to be around at the time, by trades unions or by what constitutes normal or best practice in the industry.

The short-term imperative to worry about this does vary. Businesses enjoying a period of growth and profit may be less inclined to cut staff than one trying to stave off financial disaster. In the long term, poor Organisationalal Design can be a major contributor to failure if it makes a business too expensive or lacking in flexibility and creativeness.

Watch the Horizon

So time needs to be built into the programme for keeping an eye on the horizon. The usual way is either to squash it in, in a hurried, cursory, or curtailed fashion, or get a long-term study done by a few people who are either not good at, or too far removed from, the daily work. The result is either a statement of the blindingly obvious or plans that appear to come from another planet. This is not good; Business Generals need to recognise that they must be engaged in Organisational Design over the long term and lead a full debate. This is about building the foundations for enduring success, not an unfortunate distraction.

In the USA over 95 per cent of small businesses fail within five years. In the UK the picture is nearly as bad. The overriding problem is not thinking through all the integrated aspects of the business, which can be ascribed to a lack of experience or thought. For example, most crashes involving business-to-consumer (B2C) dotcom firms in the 1990s were the result of having poorly conceived business models. In what has been called 'The Fatal Attraction', these firms were good at luring people to their sites, but failed to turn them into customers or failed to deliver. Entrepreneurs are generally a hard-working lot, full of passion about their product. Some, usually those that fail, just want to make a quick buck and/or do not manage their risks.

Boo.com

Boo.com was one of the first companies to attempt to sell fashion and sports clothes over the Internet. Apparently the company spent $135 million before it even went online, constructing the most aesthetic site, and building up hopes of limitless possibilities for Internet sales. Boo spent a lot on the marketing and look of the site, but customers seemed not to value that – they were looking for value and fast service. The software was thwarted with problems – so customers could not navigate through the site easily to make a decision to buy. And many sports manufacturers chose not to sell their merchandise on the site. Tales abound of how the company tried to expand into 18 plush offices in 18 countries before they had even tested the market. Their financial director left after just two months, having seen the writing on the wall. The two Swedish entrepreneurs (a poetry critic and a model) eventually closed the business with what they called 'overwhelming sadness'.

Having a mechanism for designing an organisation, and then overseeing it in action is a core function of leadership. British Army expenditure and the issues that surround it are not only heavily scrutinised by the Treasury and Parliament, they are also regarded by commanders as an essential aspect of combat capability that warrants their close interest. 'Capability' here is the key word: it is not numbers and size that will completely define the power of any part of the Armed Forces; it is overall effectiveness that matters.

> *It's not the size of the dog in the fight,*
> *it's the size of the fight in the dog.*
> MARK TWAIN

THE 'TRAFFIC LIGHT' ASSESSMENT

What Is the State of your Organisational Design?

Use the following 'traffic light' assessment to show where you are, by and large, getting it right (tick the lower traffic light), where you are some way there or where there are pockets of good work (tick the middle traffic light) and where you are not doing well (tick the top traffic light). Do that for all three of the levels of assessment – where you are now, where you are against your preferred standard and how you would perform if suddenly faced with maximum pressure, given the capability you have now.

ORGANISATION DESIGN TRAFFIC LIGHT

Ask yourself:

A) How are we doing now?

B) How are we performing against best-practice and best-in-class?

C) How would we perform if we were put under maximum pressure with the resources we have right now?

Technology

A B C
○○○
○○○ We are using the technology we have to its capacity.
○○○

A B C
○○○
○○○ We have done enough training to exploit its potential.
○○○

A B C
○○○
○○○ The technology is serving us well.
○○○

A B C
○○○
○○○ The technology will still be serving us well in the long
○○○ term.

Information

A B C
○○○
○○○ Our leaders are getting honest information.
○○○

A B C
○○○
○○○ Our leaders are getting timely information.
○○○

A B C
○○○
○○○ Our leaders are getting the right amount of information
○○○ and are not overloaded.

A B C
○○○
○○○ The information is managed well.
○○○

A B C
○○○
○○○ There is adequate access to knowledge.
○○○

People

A B C
○○○
○○○ All our staff are the right people in the right jobs.
○○○

A B C
○○○
○○○ The staff skills match the organisation's aim.
○○○

○○○
○○○ Training and development are seen as a priority.
○○○

○○○
○○○ There is 'collective training' – that is, the different
○○○ levels and departments meet to develop the same
      understanding of core subjects such as infrastructure,
      culture, information processing, and delegated powers.

Logistics

○○○
○○○ All leaders have an understanding of the logistics from
○○○ beginning to end.

○○○
○○○ All leaders have an appreciation of the different
○○○ logistical functions in the organisation.

○○○
○○○ We have the right equipment.
○○○

○○○
○○○ We have enough reserves for a rainy day.
○○○

Organisational Design and Diversity

International co-operation and diversity bring opportunities,
but they also bring frictions, which can slow things down.
Contemporary business, like most of the activities of the modern
Armed Forces, is conducted in a multinational environment. This
is particularly the case in Europe, where many nations with different languages and laws may join together in an alliance, whether
that is to build cars or conduct military operations. Multinational
corporations have to manage the linguistic, cultural and social
implications of having staff originating from many different
lands, even if there is a strong core from one country. The same

occurs in large-scale military ventures, with the added pressure of generally short notice to get organised and leave to fulfil the mission.

The commander of a multinational force must take account of the differing contribution each nation will make to the force, by giving them roles they are willing to accept and capable of fulfilling. The commander must use the mix of forces that nations elect to provide, which may or may not fit the requirement as specified, and allow these forces to operate as they have been trained to do. The same challenges apply to mixing investors and assets from several national contributors into a multinational venture. Building the European Airbus involves technically advanced contributions from the major aircraft producers of several countries. Having one firm make, say, the wings in one country and another construct the fuselage in another country, both working together in English – mother tongue of neither – can lead to problems. For military staff deploying to a new operation, blending together officers and soldiers from many nations into an effective headquarters organisation is a test of character – especially when they have never met before. There are big challenges, like using English as the working language, the wildly different military cultures, different sets of standard operating procedures and even different standard measurements.

ISAF

The International Security Assistance Force (ISAF) set up in Kabul, Afghanistan in a rush over Christmas 2002 comprised 3,500 soldiers from 19 nations. The smallest contribution was fewer than 10 people, the largest more than 1,500. The British general in command was able to take his own chief of staff, but

supported by a Turkish senior intelligence officer, a French
operations officer and an Italian personnel chief, and had a
German-led brigade under his command. All dialogue
with the Afghan authorities was conducted via interpreters (of
varying degrees of hopelessness) and orders were issued in
written English.

Multi-cultural appreciation and interpersonal sensitivity have
ended disputes and allowed more people to feel valued, giving
them a voice and the chance to offer their contribution. Multi-
cultural sensitivity is also needed in order to understand
customers. The EU now includes some 25 countries but it is still
not a single market. Borderless exchange and common currency
help facilitate the mechanics, but it is still a polyglot place, where
one size does not fit all.

IBM AND DIVERSITY

IBM has shown that multi-cultural appreciation and diversity is
not only a moral and social imperative, but also a strategic one –
that there is a link between diversity and competitiveness. IBM
has paid men and women the same for doing the same job and
worked to offer equal opportunities since the thirties. It has
been an ongoing commitment to equality in step with society's
evolving ideas on what it means to be 'equal'. For instance, it was
one of the first companies in the UK to offer pension rights to
same-sex couples, and they run Mindset workshops for men that
lead to a better understanding of what it feels like to be in the
minority, the general preferences and tendencies of women and
how a diverse workforce is better. All this has enabled the

company to attract and better retain very talented employees from a broad range of backgrounds and the other advantage for them is that their workforce relates to and enjoys broad customer appeal.

Your Culture Is Key

No look at Organisational Design is complete without recognising the fundamentally important role that the prevailing culture of the business itself plays in enabling or inhibiting success. All firms need a culture that has a shared core ideology, shared beliefs, assumptions/goals, and common ways of doing things, or else people will find it hard to know what they stand for, or be able to connect to them, and to commit to them. MORI polls have shown that if you want low turnover of talented employees, high customer loyalty, high productivity and increased profit – you'd better pay attention to the cohesion in your organisation.

The top-performing organisations have engaged, cohesive cultures that are well aligned with the organisation's vision. They enjoy half the rate of staff turnover of talent, enjoy twice as much customer loyalty and achieve a third again more productivity and profit than those with fragmented or disengaged cultures. Quite simply, where the culture inhibits people giving their best – it costs dearly. Every leader should be concerned about this, and know exactly what culture is needed, which parts of the organisation are living the desired culture and which parts are merely giving it a passing nod – and do something about it.

It is easy to slip 'culture' into the corporate lexicon without actually knowing what it is or doing anything to build a good one – just as some espouse the ethos that 'people are our greatest asset' as they crush them into the carpet. Culture is not just 'the way people do things around here' – that is too superficial an explanation. You have to look deeper, at what makes that 'the way people do things around here'. People have all manner of assumptions about why we do certain things in a certain way. The difference between a person's intent and their actual effect is often a whopping chasm.

To understand culture, you need to break down assumptions and barriers to reveal the inner layer of individuals: their fears, their habitual defences, confidence, rationale, philosophy, faith and beliefs. All those components go into the complexity of why a person, a group, a company 'does things' in a certain way. And all those complexities contribute to resistance to change the way 'things are done around here'.

SONY

Akio Morita-san, the founder of Sony, set out to create a firm and a supporting culture that was to make Japan known for quality. This was at a time when 'Made In Japan' meant poor copies, obsolescence and lack of style. The goal was admirable, it transcended even Sony itself and, alongside the technological wizardry of his co-founder Masaru Ibuku, Morita-san set about creating the first quality Japanese brand. He even moved his family to the US so that he could get into the mindset of the US customer market. His legendary energy and zeal to build a brand that transcended boundaries brought Sony to the place it is today – one of the enduring business legends.

Changing Culture Systemically

People and cultures can change – and fast – but it is not a job to be underestimated. The degree and depth to which people change are determined by various factors: national identity and character are quite robust, as is the grip that their fears, their defences and their beliefs have on them. Cultures are changed when the right questions are asked and time is set aside to listen to the answers; when appreciation and forgiveness have healed old wounds; when people have been helped to let go of ideas/beliefs that are no longer appropriate to hold on to; and when people have been able to share their values and their dreams. Such approaches have changed cultures that embrace tens of thousands of employees within months – one of our clients won the UK's Chartered Institute of Personnel Directors Award for doing just that.

The timing has to be right, and people need to be made aware of the cost of not changing. It is possible, with inspirational leaders, to question assumptions and beliefs in a way that lures them to the desired place, to generate a spirit of 'can-do' in every individual, to build a collective will to do things differently and to capitalise on both collective intelligence and individual strengths to adapt and survive.

Culture change needs to be systemic and reinforced at every turn. There are no shortcuts and it cannot be done half-heartedly. There need to be reminders, full alignment in all processes, all courses, all communications, and strong and repeated reinforcement – 'catching people doing it right' and 'catching people doing it wrong'. The leadership must set an exemplary model for their staff to follow.

Spirit of Community

While it is important to capitalise on people's individuality and their strengths in creating a community and building a collective spirit and drive, we do believe that there have to be some core values and ways of doing things that must be signed up to by everyone. Stubborn cynics who refuse to at least try to do things differently will act like poison in the system and will need to be moved on. Making someone redundant is not easy, yet it becomes non-negotiable if you want to sustain forward momentum in culture change. Creating a culture is never easy and if you compromise by letting some individuals off, your efforts will be doomed.

It is possible to manage organisational culture if it is seen as a dynamic, complex system: it cannot have rigid or static rules. Sensitive management of culture takes into account all the competing forces and is fully inclusive in its analysis of what is happening in the system – so that a balance is achieved that is truly aligned to the organisation's vision of itself and what it wants to achieve. Leaders have to stand back now and then to see the whole picture.

It takes cognitive, emotional and practical intelligence for a leader to get the culture right. You need to have your ears and eyes open, have the courage to deal with dissenters and yet maintain a wise perspective on driving through change. A crisis usually occurs when there has been a chain of mistakes and leaders have been too full of their own ego, too myopic to see the trouble. Where the culture is mis-aligned there will be conflict, wasted effort, and unintended and undesired consequences. To deal with that wastes more time and effort.

AMAZON

Jeff Bezos, who is both CEO and Chair of Amazon, has seen the company from its conception, through the times when it was eating up money to the point when it became a $6 billion business, making profit. Bezos is said to have done it through focusing on the customer and innovating constantly.

A pioneering culture was created with groups of people permanently assigned to dreaming up new schemes. Many ideas led to blind alleys but some opened up new avenues. The zest for entrepreneurial culture was too unstable for some and they left, but Bezos kept to his philosophy. Because of this, the business is renowned for its speed of evolution and the engagement of the workforce who did stay. They are still innovative: the 'Look inside the book' initiative, where customers can browse through the contents of thousands of books, and the work they are doing to customise their offering to the Chinese market. Now it is time, however, to keep an eye on the competition as shopping.com and eBay have an eye on this market.

Sub-cultures Can Co-exist

The Army, Navy and Airforce have different cultures – for good reasons: they employ different kinds of people to operate in different tactical conditions. Similarly, as companies expand into new countries and markets, decentralise, enlist in joint ventures and merge, they have to accept multiple cultures within one firm. But there is still room for sub-cultures to co-exist, and indeed they add value.

An organisation needs to be 'one face', like a photo mosaic where from afar the composite looks like one image, but when viewed more closely can be seen to be made up of individual photos. Managers create their own cultures all the time in their teams of six or seven, so it could be said that there are as many cultures in your enterprise as there are managers. This is only desirable if they contribute to the collective picture in a way that doesn't disrupt the common thread.

DELL

Michael Dell started Dell Computers in 1984 while still a teenager and brought it to seventeenth place among the US top 50 firms by the year 2000. Now he is said to be worth $17 billion and his business created $50 billion in sales in 2005. His early philosophy was to make a computer for every purse and every purpose and sell it directly to the consumer. Yet he held firm to his vision and created a culture of improvement where he is said to have told his staff, 'You can celebrate for a nanosecond – and then analyse for hours how we can do it better.' As a consequence, Dell has blazed a trail in the cut-throat personal computer market. Michael Dell has a naturally uncharismatic style – and makes a virtue out of it. The story goes that he said to a senior player, 'See this? It is square and so am I.' He had the moral courage and character to be who he was, to grow into more of who he was and create a culture in which everyone was expected to sacrifice their own ego for the good of the business. There was the famous 'two in a box' tactic, where managers paired up to share both the success and the blame together. This was insurance against creating a blame culture. The leadership ethos and morale component was strong.

Choose Technology Carefully

An essential part of getting the 'right stuff' is making the best choices about technology. Good decisions on technology may lead to great success, and bad decisions inexorably to failure – no matter how motivated and clever the workforce. The Armed Forces across the ages have always sought the battle-winning weapon that will sweep their enemies before them, ideally without the need to break sweat or shed blood. Various weapons have held sway for a time: the English longbow that destroyed the French army at Agincourt in 1415; the development of gun- powder and artillery, from the first serious use of the cannon in the fifteenth century to its decisive hold on trench warfare in the First World War (1914–18); the evolution of seapower – first on the water and then under it in the vital submarine campaigns of both world wars; the advent of airpower from wobbly stringbags in 1910 to the precision weapons of today; and, of course, there are the horrors of nuclear, chemical and biological weapons of mass destruction. It is generally the case that as each new weapon 'system' appears, its early years become a battle between those who can see its potential and those who cannot.

> *'Aviation is fine as a sport. I even wish officers*
> *would practise the sport, as it accustoms them to risk.*
> *But, as an instrument of war, it is worthless.'*
> GENERAL FOCH, ALLIED SUPREME COMMANDER IN THE FIRST WORLD WAR.

There then follows a period as the new weapon enters service when the technology is so fragile and immature that its effectiveness is limited, and it requires more investment, courage, some luck and great vision to deliver the full capability.

BIRTH OF AVIATION

In the First World War, the British Army was slow to recognise the potential of fighter aircraft or understand the importance of air superiority. Allied pilots had to concentrate on army support roles – reconnaissance, bombing and strafing – to the exclusion of all else. By contrast, the German High Command realised how dedicated fighter squadrons, filled with 'Top Gun' pilots, might sweep the Royal Flying Corps from the skies. The propaganda value did not go unnoticed either. Many German 'aces', notably charismatic Baron Manfred von Richtofen, became celebrities on both sides of the lines. It was only as British losses mounted to unsustainable levels – culminating in 'Bloody April' 1917, when an allied pilot's life-expectancy was counted in days – that the British began to adopt the German strategy, just in time to turn the tide.

The challenge is to see how technology can offer new, better ways of getting the job done. For example, fighting terrorism around the globe needs a different mix of technology from that required during the Cold War in Europe. To no one's great surprise, the result is often a compromise: some legacy is retained and the new equipment is perhaps not extended to its full potential. Money will, of course, play a part. In a democracy that is accountable to taxpayers, no branch of the Armed Forces can afford to buy everything it wants in the quantities it would like.

The greatest technology that the current generation of Armed Forces are wrestling with is 'Network Enabled Capability' – harnessing the full potential of digital information technology to allow forces to know more about their situation, to make better decisions and to act faster and more effectively. In theory, this means building resilient information networks that run from Government buildings to the front line trench, and bring together 'sensors' (radar and satellites), decision makers (at all levels), and 'shooters' (weapon platforms on land, sea and air). It should allow a general in Washington and London to look at the same real-time battle picture, and pass instant instructions based on it to their commanders in the field. It already allows a Predator unmanned air vehicle flying over Afghanistan to be remotely controlled from Florida, even to the extent of firing precision missiles at a target. At this rate battles will be fought from the poolside.

Blending new technology onto old platforms has its challenges: the new digital system put onto a British Challenger tank initially meant the tank commander was able to speak to everybody except the driver, thereby rendering the vehicle immobile. These teething troubles are to be expected and will be overcome, given time – and cash. The financial traumas associated with developing new platforms such as ships, submarines and aircraft are well documented every year by the governments of every developed nation that looks to maintain 'first division' forces.

Technology Pitfalls

Look at technology in your organisation. There are some basic choices to be made: for example, there is no point acquiring equipment that confers an unnecessarily large advantage at huge cost when a more modest one will do. The potential range of technologies to be exploited far exceeds the capacity and enthusiasm of the financial director or bank to satisfy. As many projects require a huge investment over many years to bring to fruition, decisions over what to buy and what to forgo will leave a legacy that might last 30 years. This is true of many capital-intensive businesses, such as oil companies and aircraft manufacturers. Decisions on where to invest taken today may dictate revenue streams for decades hence. Leaders may have to take these decisions based on imperfect or conflicting information, having found themselves being pulled between the fanatical desire for innovation by scientists and engineers on one side and the cultural resistance to change by the 'old guard' on the other.

Keeping Ahead

Just as it is not possible to invest in everything at once, so it may not be possible to keep up even in all 'vital' areas. This is especially true now that many areas of technology are propelled by commercial pressures alone. For example, the surge in development by INTEL and Microsoft is neither funded by, nor geared to, military requirements. Worse, because of the need to freeze the design of equipment in order to get them approved by Government at an agreed specification and price – and then actually built to a common standard – many items may be out of date in comparative terms before they enter service. This is especially true where information-based technology is concerned: it is often a case of buying yesterday's radio today and bringing it into service tomorrow. This means leaders have to decide whether to wait or to buy equipment now that may not be state-of-the-art, but is good enough for the task it is required to do. Compatibility is a huge consideration. You might upgrade one piece and then find it will not talk to your other pieces or to other sites/people you need to contact.

Risk Management

With uncertainty and technical challenge comes risk. The Armed Forces can sometimes spend huge amounts on a project only to find that it is a huge white elephant – a multimillion-pound device that turns out to be of no use at all. Missile programmes often end like this. There is also the risk that just as a new system reaches service, a cheap and readily available counter-measure will appear to neuter it overnight.

Managed Obsolescence

Any organisation has a set of basic equipment and stock that it may well have to phase out over time, mixing the old with the new as it enters service. The British Army, for example, has some armoured vehicles in service that are now older than their driver's father – but which carry state-of-the-art radios, weapons and equipment. It is just not possible to have everything new at once – the pain of equipping an army is not that much different to the pain of equipping a teenager. The trick is to strike the optimum balance.

Balancing Current Activity and Investment

The Armed Forces cannot borrow money the way a business can: they rely on a flow of cash from the taxpayer – either directly, or indirectly via Government borrowing. This may make the management of peaks and troughs in investment harder than in the private sector. The challenge for senior defence leaders is to establish how much money can be allocated to investment in future capability and how much is needed to sustain current activity. You can buy more aeroplanes for tomorrow if you spend less on pilot training today, but then you may find you have no pilots left capable of flying the new machines effectively. It is important to factor the full costs of operating equipment into the case for acquiring it in the first place, or it may transpire that the shiny new submarine has to stay tied up in port because it is too costly to run. Business faces the same dilemma, but generally has greater flexibility in how it reaches an outcome. For example, you can shift production to cheaper countries, or sell poorly perform-ing enterprises, or borrow more money.

COMMANDER'S COMFY CHAIR
Managing Technology

Take some time now to review how well you are 'managing technology'. You might decide that it needs further work – over days/weeks.

What are your priorities at the moment as regards technology?

Where is the edge of technology in your field?

Are you keeping up with technology?

Have you directed research into the most promising future options?

Where is the balance to be struck in your organisation between upgrading equipment and carrying on with what you have?

Have you looked into the full range of possibilities, taking into account the views of all relevant parties?

How can you balance running costs with the need to invest for the future?

For how long will your planned investment pay off?

What are the risks of making the wrong decision?

BUILD YOUR ARMOURY
Making Technology Work

Some tips for managing technology in the context of 'right team, right stuff':

▷ Make sure you are clear what technologies exist in your arena (now and on the horizon) that might confer decisive advantage. The best options can be explored if they look promising enough, within resources. If the competition can do this much better, the future may look rather bleak – so do something about it.

▷ You need to retain a healthy scepticism about how well new technologies will work initially and the claims made about their ability to sweep all else before them. Because a scientist says something is possible does not mean it can actually be made to work at reasonable cost. Generally, the more mature the technology the less risk is associated with using it. However, against this is the risk that if you leave it too late to change, you may lose an important competitive advantage.

▷ Manage the balance between investment for the future and running current activities carefully, to deliver the best available mix. Investment in the other two sides of the Power Pyramid – 'Synchronised Thinking' and 'Soul Matters' – is just as important as investment in new equipment.

▷ Expect there to be some resistance to change in your organisation where a new technology promises a completely new way of doing things, or renders obsolete a long-established organisation or process. It requires intellectual rigour, patience, creativity and determination to manage technological change, and a degree of ruthlessness to kill off outmoded practices – in the best interests of both taxpayers and shareholders.

TRANSFORMING YOUR ORGANISATION'S PHYSICAL POWER

The key factors in transforming your organisation are people, technology, innovation and training. Here are some techniques you might try:

People
Keep thinking about what level of skills and experience you will need in the future and which of your staff assessment techniques

have the highest proven reliability and validity. Do this regularly
– not once every 10 years!

- Check what is getting in the way of promoting the best talent.
- Test a few performance reviews – look back at a sample, question the honesty and the outcome.
- Make induction tougher. Get rid of those who do not fit; get rid of those who perform earlier rather than later.
- Don't worry so much about what people can't do – exploit what they can do.
- Conduct peer reviews every three months.

Technology

Think carefully before purchasing new technology. It can be seductive but could stay there, barely used.

- Ask people their views about the equipment they need!

Innovation

Allow a culture that is occasionally chaotic, messy and makes mistakes – or there will be no capacity for innovation.

- Assess the climate for change. If your workforce is cynical or prefers the status quo, bring in outside experts to give a fresh perspective on the need for new products or processes.

Logistics

Check the alignment of logistical support with the rest of the organisation's aims and processes.

Training

Make sure training is the last thing to be cut. Do evaluate training needs, evaluate the trainers, what is learned, what is remembered a few weeks later, what behaviours have changed as a result one month later, what business impact training has yielded after six months.

- Think about what you want every single person to know, do, be, think, have an attitude about – and train every single person in that.
- Train everyone to the same level as soon as possible. You need to ensure the majority get into the habit of doing things the new way or they may slip back into the old way.

Infrastructure and Logistics

These two topics are too important to leave to others. Logistics, in particular, is often seen as that unsexy, uncool and slightly grubby thing that backroom people do. This is a big mistake. Business Generals should take a very close interest in it, whatever their field. There is no point investing in the finest production machinery money can buy, only to stick it into a crumbling shed that renders it impossible to operate efficiently or safely. Nor is there any point operating this world-beating facility without the means to keep it supplied with raw materials and transport the goods it produces to market. These things have to be managed as a system, and that includes factoring in the people dimension both from a soul perspective (Secret Number Two) and a practical skills viewpoint.

In a big firm it's usually no good asking the man who works out the most efficient regime for a machine to do the tax returns and produce the advertising as well. The fact is that dry though many of these subjects may be, they are decisive in navigating that fine line between success and failure. An organisation is likely to need advice on these subjects from outside experts from time to time, but they require leading and integrating into a coherent organisation. Leaders need to know enough about what they do to guide them sensibly and listen intelligently to their opinions –

before squeezing them some more. Military commanders forget this at their peril:

> '...logisticians are a sad race of men, very much in
> demand in war, who sink back into obscurity in peace.
> They deal only with facts but must work for men who
> merchant in theories. They emerge during war because
> war is very much fact. They disappear in peace,
> because in peace, war is mostly theory.'
>
> [UNKNOWN]

The Armed Forces are major users of land, capital and logistics. Land is used for living and working facilities, the storage of stocks and equipment, headquarters, training, research and much else. In western countries much of these non-combat functions are being privatised or run by other parts of the public sector. It is usually only in countries where universal conscription is still the norm that it is cheaper to fill every post with service personnel. As noted previously, if cash is spent on large capital projects, such as luxurious offices, it cannot be made available to fund new equipment, training or better pay. The pressures to keep infra-structure and logistic costs down are no less in the Armed Forces than they are in a commercial company, and the methods employed to do so have much in common.

In battle, you can never have enough stuff. Ideally it needs to be in such abundance that losses from enemy action or a rapid change of plan can be sustained without jeopardising success, and it is usually logistical factors that circumscribe the art of the possi-ble for a commander. The idea of 'just in time' logistics is deeply unappealing in battle: it smacks of brinkmanship, verging on a gamble. Governments, like shareholders, take a slightly different view: although generals might like a warehouse bulging with spare ammunition, unless the case for this is truly compelling, stocks are likely to be kept to a minimum. This eases the burden on the taxpayer, but at the risk that the Armed Forces will be under-resourced in the event of a crisis.

In peacetime, the Armed Forces must estimate what they need to prepare for future conflict. The results are clearly a mixture of intelligence, analysis, judgement and wishful thinking. There will always be a tendency to try to over-insure, which the Government of the day – whether money or policy led – then usually overturns. The resultant risk is that not quite enough stuff is held to deal with the next crisis, especially if industry cannot crank up production quickly enough. This applies to boring things such as diesel fuel, food ration packs and uniforms, as well as high-tech equipment such as missiles and tanks.

Another major constraint on contemporary military logistics is the venue for the campaign. Gone are the days when an army on foreign soil was expected to forage for all its food and supplies from the hapless population, although this could feature in some respects again if battles were fought in rich cities (and it is how terrorism sustains itself).

NATO's Approach to Logistics

With this degree of challenge in mind, military logisticians have formulated some basic principles. These are also a useful check-list for commanders to use when testing plans for flaws and flexibility. There are many possible variants that could be cited, but we offer the NATO mix below, which speak for themselves:

- Foresight
- Economy
- Flexibility
- Simplicity
- Co-operation

The cross-over between logistics in the Armed Forces and in civilian organisations is getting greater as measures are taken to streamline the way an item gets from 'factory to foxhole'. The aspiration is that information technology will enable commanders to make smarter decisions about where stocks are held and how they are moved to the point of greatest need, instead of relying on leaving stockpiles all over the battlefield. Done well, this should translate into lower and cheaper stock levels, a smaller requirement for expensive movement assets, and less likelihood of troops/aircraft/ships running out of supplies in the middle of battle. Done badly, it will mean too little stock, in the wrong place, at the wrong time.

Business Generals at every level should make a point of learning enough about the logistics of their organisation to know how it liberates or constrains what can be done. They need a grasp of how questions of supply, production and distribution affect a business, so that they make realistic decisions that are neither too cautious nor too optimistic. The trick is to strike a balance between knowing what the real limits of capability are, and not letting single-issue experts limit the horizon through a certain natural conservatism. In other words, it is quite all right to ask your logistical staff to do something that is impossible in their eyes but within reason in yours.

Infrastructure

The military need lots of buildings on home soil. The challenge is that the fighting element, with some important exceptions such as the airfields that defend the homeland, only need these places when not committed to operations. Buildings are needed to house soldiers, their families, vehicles, stores, for training facilities and so forth – but none of them contributes to fighting capability in conflict, and so tend to be seen as something of an unfortunate overhead. Worse, when faced with hard choices about expenditure it is often the case that property maintenance is sacrificed to pay for new equipment, better training, or even pay. This can result in some distinctly unglamorous accommodation, and much-needed improvements postponed until some time in the future. Business, too, must strike the right balance. Sales staff may be on the road most of the time, but may need an office from time to time. A civil engineering company must accommodate staff when not on the building site. At other times they are paying for empty offices.

Leaders in business or the military must think hard about what they want from their infrastructure, and see it in the context of the organisation as a whole. In some cases, buildings and fittings only need to be safe and functional – such as temporary accommodation on a road-building project. In other cases, the building is an essential part of motivating staff and customers; it needs to inspire confidence and creativity and make the business stand out above others. This could be reason enough for a unique steel and glass palace in the heart of a capital city. The staff of any organisation will be inclined to desire the latter, the taxpayers and shareholders perhaps the former.

Leaders must also see how their infrastructure contributes to the efficiency and effectiveness of their organisation, and how it fits in with their people, culture and process. The choice between open-plan, hot-desking, or cubicles really matters to the way people work. Shifting cubicle-dwellers into a hot-desk regime will necessitate cultural and practical challenges, and if the aim was to save costs the risks to effectiveness and morale will also warrant consideration. Of course, there is a bottom line: the law lays down minimum standards on health and safety that are non-negotiable.

People ARE the Business

> *'The credit belongs to those who … spend themselves in a*
> *worthy cause; who, at the best, know the triumph of high*
> *achievement and who, at the worst, if they fail, fail while*
> *daring greatly so that their place shall never be with those*
> *cold and timid souls who know neither victory nor defeat.'*
> PRESIDENT THEODORE ROOSEVELT

Earlier in this book we looked at what goes on inside people's heads: the way they think and the way they feel. Under the banner of right team, right stuff we need to consider how well people cope with the practical tasks of the organisation. This means recruiting the right skills and characteristics for each role, and providing the right training for individuals and teams. The military do not skimp on this; it is crucial to their success. How well have you trained your people to do their job? If your answer is 'not well', then there may lie the key to your organisation's future.

Recruiting the staff an organisation needs in a competitive market requires careful planning. The Armed Forces know that they must attract enough young people of the necessary quality to fill a range of jobs, and do this in direct competition with every other employer. As the demographics change, so does the scale of the challenge. The Armed Forces track the demography of their population to see well in advance what the market for school leavers will be like and how the forces might need to change to attract and retain them. Today's recruits may well have very different expectations from those their generals had when they joined up.

The circumstances are much easier in quantitative terms where selective or universal conscription is in force, such as in the USA during the Vietnam War of the 1960s and 1970s. In the

UK, conscription following the Second World War became National Service. The terms and manner of recruitment affect much more than the motivation of the new staff. Conscripts are subject to a code of discipline that includes a degree of compulsion. In the business world, trainees and apprentices are required by the terms of their contracts to do what is required, however much they would rather not. This can lapse into casual indifference about how conscripts and trainees are treated. There are mixed views among those who underwent conscription or National Service. Some recognise that their short military career gave them skills and attributes, perhaps rather painfully, that have helped them in later life. Others feel it was an utter and degrading waste of time and propelled them into a lifelong hatred of all things martial.

Business leaders need to be wary of building a climate in their organisation that would be more applicable to conscripts than volunteers. If staff have an alternative to working in an organisation that treats them as if they had no choice, they will eventually exercise it. If they feel they have no real alternative (because other employment is scarce), they may put up with more – but are unlikely to give their best or feel loyalty to the organisation as a whole. Even the cutting-edge financial services, where success is all about how much money is made in competition with others, are taking a risk if the relationship with employees is based exclusively on cash and bonuses. Teams may decamp to the highest bidder without notice; key players may make their exit when it suits them, regardless of where this leaves everyone else. Office life becomes an ordeal by fire, where personnel work themselves into the ground before cracking up in their mid-thirties from ulcers and exhaustion. Human life spans of 80 plus years are not uncommon, so why go to work in your twenties like a kamikaze pilot?

Recruiting volunteers for the Armed Forces is different from conscription. People choose to join up of their own free will and commit to all the exigencies of service – the rain, the wet, the fatigue, and the risk of injury and death. They accept these conditions in return for the perceived benefits and attractions. These include: a sense of joining a highly credible organisation, a change from previously humdrum lives, adventure, variety, regular pay, a trade, money to pay for college later, and much more. Everybody has to accept that by joining the Armed Forces they will be subject to limits that do not apply in most civilian occupations. Foremost among these is giving up the right to elect not to serve on the spot as soon as shot and shell start falling. When it is raining you still have to honour the commitment you made when the sun was shining.

Having recruited volunteers, the Armed Forces have to find ways to retain them. Highly demanding and technically advanced jobs such as fighter pilot, nuclear submarine captain, and tank regiment commander require many years' investment. So it is no good being brilliant at recruiting youngsters only to find that two years later they have all left bored, battered and bitter. It not only takes time to train people, but also leadership roles demand a mixture of training and experience. A soldier aged 19 engaged in his first conflict needs the example of a corporal aged 23 to know what to do and to stand the stresses of battle. The people element of right team, right stuff involves getting the right people in and then developing and using them so that they want to stay. This won't be everyone, many will serve for three to four years before heading back to the comforts of civilian life, but enough must be retained to maintain the structure. Getting the people aspect right includes:

- Recruiting to fill a well-designed structure.
- Retaining people with a balanced set of incentives.
- Training people to do the job to the best of their ability.

Not investing in training is short-sighted. Other than at baseline salary level, people put more value in being developed than a little bit more pay. Firms who develop their people have better-trained, flexible and loyal staff.

Recruitment

How do most organisations recruit? Some do it by informal and unstructured chats over lunch, others by over-formalised interviews, others still by family tradition, and the best by a well thought-out, validated and reliable structure. Some take the first person with broadly the right qualities and qualifications, and some simply hire the cheapest labour on offer. Others will only recruit those who fit well-researched criteria, using assessment-centre techniques that use the most reliable and valid procedures with complete transparency.

In most western countries the law takes a hand in this, prescribing limits on discrimination and opening up equal access. The degree of government influence varies from country to country, but policies that encourage employment for ethnic minorities, women, young people, old people and the disabled are now commonplace. The trend is towards asking interview questions that only and directly equate to the role, sometimes at the expense of depth and of full and effective analysis of the individual. Some of our own research findings show that early life influences are among the most important drivers and inhibitors of performance behaviours, yet it is deemed incorrect by the Chartered Institute of Personnel Directors (CIPD) to ask about early family life.

Business leaders need to identify whether their chosen recruitment method is effective enough to really uncover a candidate's strengths. A recruitment policy that works purely on the basis of 'bums on seats' will get exactly that: enough people at the price, but with no guarantee of quality and commitment. Choosing the best of a mediocre lot will only saddle you with mediocrity for a long time – you have to be disciplined and wait for the right candidate. Most people start off a new job full of good will, but it is how the job is designed that releases or depresses their strength and personality.

Everybody has their favourite call centre horror story, where the person representing the bank/insurance firm/telecommunications company has become so automated that they have begun to sound like an alien on a mission to test the human capacity for irritation. And firms wonder why this provokes aggressive behaviour in their customers! Do the customers *want* to pick up telephone calls from Indian or Chinese call centres? It might look like cost management at the start but when customers walk away it will look like folly. Leaders who have thought about job design and organisational structure will be better placed to hire the right person for the right job. Typically, this includes an organisational chart, a description of the purpose of the role and how it is related to other jobs in the firm, the job content – what they have to do, responsibilities, accountabilities and performance criteria as well as the personal specification – the competencies (skills, values, attitudes, beliefs, knowledge, traits) that a successful applicant will need. The Armed Forces, like many other organisations, use specific job descriptions in recruitment campaigns in order to compare the merits of competing candidates. The result is that the requirements of a military cook are as well articulated as those for a vehicle engineer or bomb disposal expert.

Any business, however small, can benefit from such a procedure to form the basis of recruitment and then, once recruited, their performance analysis. There is also room for expert judgement – that rapid, intuitive appraisal made by people experienced in the business, who know intimately what needs to be done and have the vision to know how the work may change over time. This should not replace the robust assessment procedure completely, but it certainly has a place.

Recruitment, of course, is a two-way process: the volunteer candidate is interviewing the organisation just as much as the other way round. Honesty and openness on the part of the interviewer are essential, so that prospective employees know what they may be submitting to and candidates can select-out if they feel the job isn't right for them. For the Armed Forces especially, it can be difficult to portray accurately and vividly the realities of operational duty, but this is not an excuse to gloss over or glamorise what the work might involve.

Leaders in all organisations need to consider what overall package they wish to offer to potential employees. There are real competitive advantages in doing more to engage people than simply handing over a pay packet. It really matters who they work alongside and how they work together, and high (and expensive) staff turnover and absenteeism usually indicate that this could be handled better.

Retain the Best or Watch Them Leave

The Armed Forces would far rather retain more and recruit less. It is cheaper, capitalises on training and experience, and reduces uncertainty about who will be filling the ranks when the next conflict breaks out. This is especially important where the investment in training is lengthy and rarefied: replacing a bomb disposal expert means training from scratch; there is no competitor to poach from. The trick for the Armed Forces is to come up with a mix of incentives to encourage people to stay. Part of this mix is the salary: few volunteers will stay if they think they are being taken advantage of compared to broadly similar occupations in civilian life. But nobody serving in today's Armed Forces expects to get rich. This was not always the case. Recruitment incentives over the ages have included a promise of booty. Loot was parcelled out on a sliding scale from commander down to most junior soldier, leaving the former well-heeled for life and the latter incapacitated by drink for several weeks. This no longer applies, but the nearest commercial comparisons appear to be the stripping of a former state company's assets in some privatisation deals, and the rich rewards heaped on the legal profession by epic-length public inquiries.

The mix of incentives for servicemen and women has to be a blend of meeting reasonable material expectations – pay, housing, health care – and satisfying their professional and personal ambitions. This will include graduated training from novice to expert level, job variety, and increasing responsibility for those selected for promotion. It will also include sufficient time with families and for sport and recreation. The biggest inhibitor to retention in the Armed Forces is overcooking: soldiers, sailors and airmen sent away too frequently to sustain a normal life, with insufficient time to recuperate and train between operational tours. In the British Armed Forces, six-month tours away from home should come around every 24 months. In the US Army in Iraq it is not uncommon for soldiers to be away for over a year, and then come back for another tour in less than 12 months. That is hard labour: nobody enjoys being cash poor *and* time poor for long. Many civilians work away from family and friends during the week, or on projects abroad, but usually the pay increase makes it worthwhile.

In other organisations, the package of incentives should be easier to design. Money will obviously feature but, increasingly, so will other factors such as holiday allowance, medical insurance, working hours and office facilities. Many firms are finding that flexible, personalised benefits are especially popular. These include being able to defer holidays, or take extra days off unpaid, having subsidised health care, an interest-free loan scheme, or a concierge to carry out personal tasks. There is still a lot of debate on performance-related pay – some are in favour, while others regard it as a disincentive unless the culture is one of perceived fairness.

All of these incentives are frills around the edges because TRUST or rather, distrust, is the fabric that meshes people to do the things together that they could not do alone. A study in 2005 by one of the world's largest actuaries, Watson Wyatt, showed that a mere one-third of British workers trust and have confidence in their senior leaders – that means a full two-thirds don't trust or have confidence in their leaders. We shouldn't be offering dry-cleaning when the basics of what makes people commit and give the best of themselves is so absent. These statistics for the UK are about the worst in the world, significantly worse than in the US.

Training – Invest or Watch the World Go By

Employers cannot take for granted that the people they hire will come cheerfully to work armed with a full suite of skills. Many need considerable training to be effective employees in even the most straightforward appointments. British businesses live with a false sense of security. During 2005, the UK had the fourth- biggest economy in the world, the lowest unemployment for a generation; inflation (which was running at 20 per cent in the eighties) was as low as 1.6 per cent; and the interest rate was stable at around 2.4 per cent. The UK also enjoyed growth (forecast at 2–3 per cent) rates on a par with the US, and a record 18 million of the 55 million-plus population own their own home. It is a picture of success, yet in 2005 Britain exported only 8 per cent of its Gross Domestic Product. Much of this manufacturing decline can be blamed on the low skills levels of much of the workforce, just as highly efficient competition has stormed in from the fast-developing Asian economies. With China and the world's developing countries set to export half the world's manufacturing output, it is essential that western, developed economies fight back with knowledge and technology – and that means investment in learning.

We need to acknowledge the existence of a skills-shortage ticking time bomb. We need more professional and technical staff, and more entrepreneurs. Nearly a quarter of all employers admit that the skills levels of their workforce are inadequate. The result is that projects are often delayed simply because they cannot get the staff needed to start them. Training ought to be the answer, but a staggering two-fifths of employers still offer no training to their employees. The problem applies to senior staff too. In 2004, over one-quarter of managers of public limited companies had no training at all. Of those that did, only 5 per cent had more than 20 days' training (some had just four days). Senior UK managers typically are less well educated than their German counterparts, many of whom completed a commercial apprenticeship and took a PhD before going into business. British managers are often technically weaker, which means they are not as good at understanding and managing complex processes, which in turn makes them less adaptable and less marketable.

In-depth, immersed, long-duration training has become overlooked, almost passé, in the battle to build competitiveness. This is absurd, and flying in the face of the methods used in the best countries elsewhere in the globe that are getting ahead. Many business managers think that they can ill afford to spare five days to go on a course. Yet the military put their leaders through a year's course to start with, followed by further training sessions lasting up to a year. Therein lies the difference – a couple of days versus a year. The outcome is that business leaders are often not fully competent, can't be followed with absolute trust and can't be relied upon to show robust value-led core decision-making and behaviour.

What little training there is in business is often poorly conducted and evaluated. It is startling how most firms do not use a systematic process of training evaluation. The data for determining the success of training is weak and does not feed back into improvements in training design. Training is often remote from the day-to-day job, and delegates, however enthused when they leave the session, do not see through the behavioural changes they commit to. What is needed are compelling reasons for improving transferability from the class to the meeting room – through systemic, repeated training, just-in-time feedback, proper support and challenge from peers/boss/coach.

There is also a trend towards decentralisation – allowing business units to ask for the training they need. That can be like waiting for people to ask for life insurance. They need a nudge – indeed, coercing. Allowing training to dribble through a population over a long time will not create the momentum, the critical mass needed to bring about a significant culture change, and a palpable shift in behaviour. Sheep dipping, as it has been called, means sending huge drafts of people for training. It may smack of indoctrination but it does create critical mass and we have seen businesses transform when everybody has been through a similar shared experience, emerging with shared goals, shared perspectives and a willingness to share challenge and support each other.

Make Your Induction Count

Induction in the Armed Forces is tough. In business it is a breeze – a nice get to know you, get your feet under the table; so light it barely registers as induction. Some get nothing – leaving the newcomer feeling unrecognised and vulnerable. In the Armed Forces you are not forgotten – but neither can you hide. Is anyone hiding or forgotten in your firm? Induction is the time to socialise people into the way of the organisation, putting meaning into *why* they are there and *what* they are contributing to. It is a potentially invaluable time, sadly lost to the wind in many organisations. It is also the time to test whether the new arrivals are indeed up to the job.

INDUCTION

The National College for School Leadership has initiated a Head Teachers' Induction Programme that is state-of-the-art. Each new Head Teacher can design their own programme based on their needs analysis. They attend workshops and are given a coach (a peer) and a mentor (an experienced leader) who will offer support on orientation and socialisation into the role, facilitate reflection/feedback and make introductions. The initiative includes 6-10 full days of thinking and articulating vision and purpose; generating new understandings on leadership learning and developing leadership learning skills and habits (Synchronised Thinking) and forums where they can engage in professional dialogues and exchange perspectives and ideas in a safe environment (Right Team, Right Stuff). They are also encouraged to regularly lead collaborative reviews, look at the moral territory of the dilemmas they might face and understand the emotional climate of the school (Soul Matters).

Business Generals will recognise that systemic under-performance costs more than training. Entrepreneurs are ambitious, have vision and confidence and often have little actual experience in what they are doing, but their curiosity and passion help them to learn how to do things quickly. They break the mould and drive through step changes in innovation and performance. What are the immediate and long-term costs to your organisation of not investing in sufficient learning?

The training requirement outside the Armed Forces will obviously vary with the role of the organisation. Big, complicated, high-risk organisations such as oil refineries have a high bill for individual training and collective skills, both to carry out normal business and to be prepared for emergencies. For the average commercial organisation, the need for training may be more modest. But it is important not to neglect it, nevertheless.

BUILD YOUR ARMOURY

Investing In Training

Here is a list of tools and tips giving specific advice on how best to invest in training:

▷ Make sure your induction training makes a big impact. Induction training orientates new employees to the company structure and values, their role in it, the expectations placed on them in terms of conduct and efficiency, and what to do if something goes wrong. Some of this is covered by legislation; some of it should be designed by leaders to ensure the best fit between the staff and the firm.

▷ Provide individual training and test recruits to ensure they are ready for the tasks they will face. This might mean a long apprenticeship, or a few hours' tutelage if the equipment is relatively simple. For instance, train then test a secretary on PowerPoint presentations, diary management, note taking. Don't assume they have these skills already or ignore it if their skill level is not up to standard. Where appropriate, there should be a planned progression that introduces more advanced training in line with the experience of the employee. (You can't bake bread until you know how to make dough.)

▷ Consider collective training. That means everyone from top to bottom goes through the same socialisation or functional training together, so that the team is well balanced, with everyone clear about how they fit into the whole and how to work with others to best effect. This not only applies to posts that require close team work, such as paramedics, but also to every office in an organisation. How many firms try to get along with their staff working like semi-autonomous automatons, duplicating and complicating the progress of the others, rather than acting as cogs in a well-oiled machine? Collective training need not be elaborate and can include short periods of training, led by the leadership at every level, that focuses on explaining the intent behind current business activity and improving understanding of the processes that support it.

▷ Demonstrate new or misunderstood equipment, so that it is used as intended. How many computer networks are brought to their knees by the ministrations of an unskilled yet enthusiastic (senior) member of staff poking about in its set-up?

▷ Hold longer periods of training, away from the office or shop floor, to improve group understanding and team-working skills. These can focus on practical skills and/or the group dynamics of leadership.

▷ Have a deliberate policy of succession that trains deputies for the next level up. This allows vacant roles to be filled quickly. The Armed Forces assume that leaders will become casualties and so prepare their subordinates to step up at a moment's notice. What happens in your firm if a key manager falls sick tomorrow? Are there people trained, cultivated, ready to step in?

Leadership: Making Right Team, Right Stuff Work

We noted at the start of this Secret that leadership was a key component of right team, right stuff. It needs serious deliberation and direction from the leaders of an organisation to establish the optimum blend of organisation, technology, infrastructure and logistics, people and training. Once set up, any organisation will be engaged in a continuous process of change, sometimes evolutionary and sometimes more stepped and dramatic. Keeping a well-oiled machine requires constant analysis and effort, especially when faced with fierce, agile competition.

As the leaders of their organisation at any level, Business Generals will need to think about what they need to be and what they need to do if they are to succeed. Part Two of this book provides some thinking and techniques that will help in many aspects of leadership. We look at the question of leadership specifically in Secret Number Seven. For now, we need to look at leadership from the perspective of understanding some of the roles this entails, how to avoid doing it badly, and the importance of accountability. We also need to examine the vital importance of good information flow to a healthy and successful organisation.

COMMAND AND CONTROL – MYTH AND THE REALITY

In the Armed Forces, Command and Control is not a euphemism for an unlimited and unquestioned autocracy. It is about maintaining clarity of roles, powerful leadership, decision precision, clear boundaries, optimum information flow, empowerment and accountability – all in the most difficult conditions. Whatever the shape and size of an organisation, it needs inspiration, information and decisions to flow freely around it. The utter brilliance of the CEO has to be communicated to the marketing staff, the production engineers, the finance experts and the logistics team. They need to be able to tell the boss how well they will deliver the plan, or that it won't work. In the Armed Forces, there are well-founded means established for delivering the closely related, but different, requirements for command and control.

Command

Command is the function of the leader, at every level. The commander in the Army, Navy, or Air Force, or commanding a mix of all three, is responsible for delivering the objectives set by the Government. General Tommy Franks commanded all US forces in the Iraq Theatre of Operations in 2003. It was he whom the President and the Secretary of State for Defence rang when they wanted to pass on political direction or hear about progress. The commander is the person who takes responsibility for deciding on the plan, for making things happen, and is then held accountable for the results.

This role is replicated at every level of command down through the Armed Forces: there are divisions commanded by generals, and battalions commanded by lieutenant colonels. At the lowest level in the Army, a second lieutenant in command of a platoon has the same responsibilities in principle as the general at the top. To command effectively, an officer will require some indispensable leadership qualities and essential skills, including the ability to see the situation clearly and provide clear direction to the organisation about what needs to be done and why, and then lead the people to success no matter how great the stress and uncertainty. The same requirement for command exists in all organisations. Somebody must be in charge, responsible for working out what needs to be done, setting this out clearly and then making sure it happens:

Do We Really Need to Have a Commander?

Leaderless groups were experimented with in business in the 70s and 80s, resulting in an abrupt loss of efficiency; much 'real work' simply wasn't done. In psychological terms, it seems people have an unconscious, irrational need for someone to take on the parental role and when that is denied to us, the rejection generates a feeling of incomprehensible loss that can result in infantile behaviour.

Groups do naturally let a leader emerge, but this is often based upon poor judgement heuristics, i.e. who talks the most and/or sounds the most confident is deemed leader! Studies show that the shy are often seen to be less intelligent by their peers, the unassuming are perceived as weak and stereotypes are quickly assigned. The leaders that emerge from leaderless groups are often the result of ruthless competition between the aggressive few and may not be the leaders that would be the rational best choice if the group openly and honestly talked about the candidates' strengths and weaknesses in order to lead to the best all-round choice.

A transparent system for selection and promotion to command positions ensures a better person/role fit. A leader is needed to show the way, which direction to head in and why: the naturally bossy and aggressive may do well with the first part – the direction – but unless they have learned to have great communication skills, they will fail at the 'why' part.

Control

Control is the whole suite of supporting functions that enables commanders to turn their plan into results, and monitor progress along the way. This includes a whole range of functional staff roles that are complicated and challenging, occupied by people who are indispensable – but not actually in command. Accountants, lawyers, information technology experts, logisticians, bankers and many others fall into this bracket in the commercial sense, as do intelligence experts, engineers, supply specialists, aviators, communicators, medics and many others in the Armed Forces.

The CEO of a company has to fulfil many of the responsibilities of a chief of staff. Many of the best CEOs, for example, are taking a more strategic and less functional role, and are certainly not mere bean counters. They are becoming involved in strategy, operations and performance, creating business models and driving value generation. Who fulfils the function of a chief of staff in most businesses? There needs to be someone who pulls the work of the firm together, who is not also responsible for all the functions of command. Chairs or CEOs, for example, who get bogged down in the detail of working out how cash should be allocated to various projects, or how many new computers to buy this year, are almost certainly not making best use of their time or talent. Worse, they may expend so much energy on the detail that they fail to master the big picture – or simply burn themselves out – with disastrous consequences.

Somebody should replicate the role of the chief of staff in most large commercial organisations, but this is clearly not the Chair or, usually, neither is it the CEO. A general manager may exist, particularly in the public sector, and an executive assistant may play this role in the private sector, but neither is the equivalent of a fully fledged military chief of staff. The issue of command and control is slightly different in the corporate world from the Armed Forces. The Chair and CEO in a business are usually seen as two discrete roles and responsibilities to be filled by two different people. The Chair is there to ensure corporate governance and compliance. The Chair should set the board's agenda, making sure accurate and timely information is provided and that the concerns of all directors are heard. The board covers the work that it alone should do and not lose itself in managerial detail. The Chair should identify the development needs of directors, be the front for the financial media, and ensure that the directors understand the views of the major shareholders.

In principle, this is something a good CEO could do too, but experience suggests that the scope for corruption, expediency, the drive for personal reward, or susceptibility to undesirable pressure from fellow directors means that there are conflicts of interest inherent in one person having both roles. There are personality, skill-set and stage-of-life differences too in the essential characteristics of a Chair and CEO. Generally, a Chair leads a board for an average tenure of three years; he or she does not recruit that board and must be seen to be fair to each of them. Unimpeachable fairness, maturity of judgement, diplomacy, the wisdom gained from wide experience – these are the qualities of a successful Chair. (They don't have to be over 60: some young people who have lived through tumultuous experiences in the industry can be great Chairs.) Many Chairs are non-executive, making only short and superficial incursions into the daily life of the business.

A CEO, on the other hand, is responsible for the conception and execution of strategy and is much closer to the detail of the business. However, he or she does not usually oversee the detail of execution as well – that is left to individual directors, who remain individually accountable to the board. The Chair is more like a Secretary of State for Defence, who oversees and holds the Armed Forces (the business) accountable and who is in turn accountable to the legislature (the shareholders). The CEO is like the Chairman of the Joint Chiefs of Staff in the US: the professional head of the Armed Forces and the senior serving serviceman, responsible for making the Armed Forces perform well and develop successfully.

Whatever the precise definition of their roles in a company, the Chair and the CEO are two mission-critical roles, generally requiring different qualities. The incumbents will look to achieve different things in different ways. They need to complement each other and the quality of the relationship, especially trust and co-operation, between the two is vital.

Bad Leadership – Is This You?

There are some common failings in command in all walks of life, applicable to Chairs and CEOs, as well as Generals. They can be broadly categorised as follows:

- **The Figurehead** maintains a weak grip on the situation around him, too remote from his key staff, and incapable of providing effective leadership. Instead, huge effort goes into enjoying the trappings of appointment (cars, offices, golf club memberships) and making off with a wholly unjustified pension pot.

- **The Showman** is great at conceiving and selling ideas, but weak at designing them into a workable strategy or plan and then making the organisation deliver. He provides about 10 per cent of the command requirement, leaving others to fill in the rather obviously large gaps. He may well capture the attention of the media, and also probably move on between firms quickly before he can be accused of failing to deliver on the razzmatazz.

- **The Technocrat** is the reverse of the Showman. He has been appointed as a result of his proven success in managing detail or being a master of his specialism but is unable to master the other vital aspects of his role: the need to see the big picture, how to take advantage of it and inspire the people to seize the future. Instead of command, the organisation gets micro-control of process without vision or inspiration.

- **The Invisible Man** is truly a brilliant man, fully the master of his situation and brimming with initiative, but wholly incapable of persuading his organisation to follow him for want of any skill at all as a communicator. Just as a leader will generally fail if he is all presentation and no substance, so he will probably fail too if he has substance but also a personality bypass. Successful leadership requires the ability to inspire more than prodigious capacity to inform by memo.

There are other possible versions of weak command: the point is that the commander, whether in the Armed Forces or in business, needs to deliver the full set of command responsibilities if he or she is to succeed. How many business leaders see themselves in this role?

Armed Forces and Accountability

In the Armed Forces, commanders take full responsibility for the work of their headquarters staff and how their subordinate units carry out their plan. There is no room for blame or for failures in command to tumble downwards or sideways. How does that equate to your industry? Individual success or failure at any level is acknowledged by a thorough system of personnel appraisal reporting: awards for success and removal from appointment for significant failure. Of note, however, is that removal from appointment is usually from a particular job, not from the service as a whole – unless a crime or serious misconduct justifies that. The civilian parallel is not to sack people for just failing, but to redeploy them to a more suitable role.

The actions of the Armed Forces are also held to account by defence ministers, who will in turn be required to report to their Parliament, and by bodies such as NATO and UN councils, where a multinational operation is concerned. Accountability extends to reviewing what has happened and why, and to ensuring that public money has been well spent and accurately accounted for. Naturally, there will be scrutiny by the media, too.

Business Generals have similar responsibilities, although rather than Parliament the primary focus will be the scrutiny of investors, shareholders, potential customers and markets. The relationship between the Chair of a global company and his or her major institutional shareholders, and the relationship between, say, the US Chairman of the Joint Chiefs of Staff and the President and his Executive, have much in common.

Where are the bounds of accountability for the leaders of

commercial companies? In Secret Number Two the case was made for the importance of moral courage and integrity, among other qualities. Business leaders should identify themselves as being responsible for more than the current bottom line. They must balance long-term investment against short-term return, and be prepared to be the public face of their organisation in good times and bad. For this, in the commercial world, they may expect to be rewarded handsomely if they succeed – although why they should expect to leave with more than a train ticket home if they fail remains something of a mystery.

BATTLE RHYTHM

A key element of the command-and-control process in a military organisation is battle rhythm, the routine through which information and decisions are passed. This ensures that commanders have a means by which they tell their subordinates what is wanted and subordinates tell the commander how they are doing. It also ensures that supporting detail (of which there is a lot) is also passed and presented efficiently.

What is the beat of your battle rhythm? Part of the answer is regularity. The tempo of information flow in the military on operations is faster and more consistent than it is in business.

In a high-tempo operation, it will be usual for a Commander to be briefed by key staff and subordinate commanders first thing in the morning and again in the evening. How well are you and your leaders kept abreast of movements or events?

In a large force the staff will there in person and the subordinates, perhaps many thousands of kilometres away, may attend by video conference. In addition, there will be regular face-to-face gatherings of the Commander with his subordinate commanders to discuss policy, resources and other fundamental aspects of the mission. This includes pithy criticism where appropriate. How does this compare to the way your firm operates? Is your leader there, face to face, discussing policy, resources, morale? Do they act on the information they receive?

In a military campaign there are briefings, written and verbal, to all members of staff so that they know in general terms at least what is going on. This process is essential to building common purpose, spreading inspiration and preventing rumours from taking hold. In each case the aim of a meeting is to convey or build a common understanding of the situation and how to act to remain in the ascendant. This is not micro-managing but *essential* communications to calibrate focus and energy.

A vital supplement to military battle rhythm are the visits senior commanders make to their subordinate units. This face-to-face interaction provides a chance for the senior leaders to check progress for themselves, to sense the state of morale and to verify the written reports they receive. It also, and equally vitally, allows the workforce to see the person in charge – this should boost motivation and confidence. In combat operations, senior military commanders may spend the greater part of many days doing just this. Some have gone down in history for their ability to inspire as much as inform.

COMMANDER'S COMFY CHAIR
Leadership Quality

Think back to the last operation/important activity in your firm and ask yourself:

When did you last visit your main players?

Did you discuss policy, maintenance of the aim, commitments, resources?

Did you check to verify what you were told?

Did you go out of your way to speak to people not 'presented' to you?

What did you do to manage the confidence of the team?

What did you do to *inspire* them?

Think forward to the next operation/important activity in your firm and ask yourself:

When and how can you visit your main players?

How are you going to discuss policy, maintenance of the aim, commitments, resources?

How are you going to verify what you are told?

How are you going to speak to people not 'presented' to you?

What are you going to do to manage the confidence of the team?

What are you going to do to inspire them?

Don't Just Counting Pebbles – Keep an Eye on the Sea and Sky

It is essential that clear and effective command is not bogged down in the process and minutiae of control. The welter of supporting operational detail, about, say, stock levels, equipment condition, personnel returns and intelligence detail, can be passed along functional lines. Good team members will take the initiative to raise points of detail only in exceptional cases, otherwise keeping them out of the commander's head. Cluttering up the Business General's head with questions and details that team members ought to be able to deal with is poor followership. It serves not to impress but to annoy and detract. In turn, the Business General needs to show the team that he or she trusts them enough to make reasonable decisions.

Technology can be abused here: it is very easy to squirt limitless quantities of information or ask inane questions of a Commander using email, perhaps in an attempt to impress him with the volume of work or their attention to detail. This serves only to clog up the Commander's mind with mental fluff and impede the clarity of thought and expression that is their purpose.

Some Armed Forces have unfortunately developed a battle rhythm where the Commander is confronted with information overload, and any sense that he is unable to manage this is seen as a sign of weakness. Much better to have an Admiral, General or Air Marshal with the time to read the newspapers, be intuitively brilliant and ring his kids, than one who knows how many man-hours of patrolling took place yesterday and that there is a shortage of canned fruit – yet hasn't spotted that the enemy is on the march at his rear.

There are clear parallels here with other organisations, commercial and public. It seems that many have not consciously worked out what battle rhythm they need to get the right information flowing throughout the staff, or how to structure the content of meetings to keep them useful. Instead, too many ad hoc meetings are held to discuss everything that happens to be on the minds of people attending.

> *'We need to learn to set our course by the stars,*
> *not by the lights of every passing ship.'*
> GENERAL OMAR NELSON BRADLEY, 1893–1981, US ARMY, SECOND WORLD WAR

E-mail is vital for the provision of timely, accurate and relevant data, but it cannot make up for or replace broken management relationships. Striving for the broadest possible consensus is fine for politicians, but not a necessary condition for turning a profit. Copying e-mails to voluminous address lists can sow confusion, attract superfluous comment and breach the requirement for confidentiality when forming new or novel plans.

Commanders in all organisations need to be clear about at what level they operate: although modern information technology allows the battalion commander to issue instructions to individual soldiers he is a fool if he does so. There are company commanders and platoon commanders who will do this so much better, leaving the battalion CO free to get on with the really important decisions. If subordinates receive unstoppable flows of detailed instructions from the top of the shop, they will quickly establish that ignoring them is an entirely successful approach, safely assuming that the imperative will pass and be rapidly succeeded by another great idea from up on high. They will then run the risk of missing the truly important instructions that will make the firm great.

It is up to the subordinate to question the flow and not just ignore or delete or they run the risk of being ill-informed and will not serve their leader well. Are you receiving too many e-mails? What are you doing about it? Are you copying in lots of people? Are you asking what they are doing with them?

BUILD YOUR ARMOURY
Command and Control

Here is a list of tools and tips giving specific advice on how to apply the principles of command and control.

▷ Analyse how command and control responsibilities are allocated in your own organisation. Is there a commander?

Do you need a chief of staff to pull things together? Are these roles clear to everybody? Then stick to them.

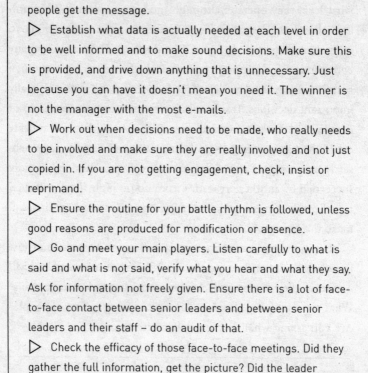 Analyse what you need to send out and when.

▷ Check that this information is being used properly.

▷ Work out the level of information you can cope with, and when you want it – and tell people. Manage that ruthlessly until people get the message.

▷ Establish what data is actually needed at each level in order to be well informed and to make sound decisions. Make sure this is provided, and drive down anything that is unnecessary. Just because you can have it doesn't mean you need it. The winner is not the manager with the most e-mails.

▷ Work out when decisions need to be made, who really needs to be involved and make sure they are really involved and not just copied in. If you are not getting engagement, check, insist or reprimand.

▷ Ensure the routine for your battle rhythm is followed, unless good reasons are produced for modification or absence.

▷ Go and meet your main players. Listen carefully to what is said and what is not said, verify what you hear and what they say. Ask for information not freely given. Ensure there is a lot of face-to-face contact between senior leaders and between senior leaders and their staff – do an audit of that.

▷ Check the efficacy of those face-to-face meetings. Did they gather the full information, get the picture? Did the leader manage the confidence of the team, did they reiterate purpose and aim, did they inspire? This applies to all managers – middle managers to Chairs and CEOs must get out and about.

Summary of Secret Number Three: Right Team, Right Stuff

- This Secret covers the practical aspects of an organisation – its people and equipment – and makes up the third of the three sides of the Power Pyramid, alongside Synchronised Thinking and Soul Matters.

- This Secret shows how to improve the basic elements that underpin all organisations – the structure, technology, people and training – that must be joined into a cohesive and seamless whole.

- A basic understanding of infrastructure and logistics is vital if all the elements are to mesh and not clash. A Business General who neglects these fields is storing up trouble for the future.

- People – and their knowledge, experience, skills and ideas – represent a valuable resource that is often underused in many organisations. A well-planned training system can bring out their best.

- At the heart of Right Team, Right Stuff is the idea of Organisational Design – creating a knowledge base that takes in past experience, current technology, specialist information and resources to make decisions for the future.

- This helps ensure that an organisation's equipment and skills base are regularly updated to meet future challenges, without being weighted down by unproven systems and technologies.

- The well-organised Business General may need to draw on experts for the know-how needed to make the constituent parts of Right Team, Right Stuff work well.

Next Secret...

Part Two looks at the Business General's leadership skills in the round, examining – among other things – how the experience of the Armed Forces can be applied to seize the initiative, and improve planning and decision-making, leading to true and effective delegation and empowerment. Part Two opens with Secret Number Four: Dynamic Manoeuvre.

Part Two

Secret Four
Dynamic Manoeuvre
The fastest way to achieve decisive advantage at least cost

'If your enemy is secure at all points, be prepared for him.
If he is in superior strength, evade him. If your opponent is
temperamental, seek to irritate him. Pretend to be weak,
that he may grow arrogant. If he is taking his ease, give
him no rest. If his forces are united, separate them.
If sovereign and subject are in accord, put division
between them. Attack him where he is unprepared,
appear where you are not expected.'
SUN TZU, THE ART OF WAR

This Secret is a synthesis of tried and tested military learning, a
methodology that has led to success many times in finding 'the
fastest way to achieve decisive advantage at least cost'. All it takes
is a little dynamic manoeuvre. You just need to apply it intelligently to suit your own particular situation. It is about a method
– almost a philosophy – of looking at any challenge with an eye
for finding the most creative, unexpected and effective way to
bring about success. The thinking we offer you in this chapter
will enable you to be:

- Wise to what others are up to.
- Completely clear about what constitutes success over your competitors.
- Able to identify the best route to success, seizing opportunities at the best time and place.
- Able to manage and deal with risk.

THE LEADERSHIP DILEMMA

We start with a short survey of some of the main dilemmas that leaders face when taking an organisation into the future.

Taking the Stage – Without Being Upstaged

Dynamic Manoeuvre has a lot to do with knowing your enemies and outwitting them. You may not see your competitors as 'enemies' (and we are not recommending animosity or physical aggression). You may even think you have no competitors. A lot of companies are moving away from the notion of beating the competition and instead looking at ways to work alongside, in an alliance, with previous competitors. There are valuable tips arising from how military forces assisted peaceful collaboration between former foes arising from, for example, the post-IRA ceasefire in Northern Ireland and successful NATO-led peacekeeping in the Balkans.

The key point is that unless you are aware of others' strengths and intentions in your potential market, you could find yourself being ushered away into failure and obscurity just as you think you are about to take centre stage. Before taking the stage to front up your offering to the audience, you need to be absolutely sure your own house is in order and know what your rivals are capable of. Does everyone involved understand the play, the plot and their part in it? Are you fully resourced and does the team have the necessary energy and agility? Can it manage hard days with reserves of strength and understudies for key players? Are you sure that you know what gives life to your organisation? Are your leaders taking charge in a conscious way – reflecting on the action, helping others to make sense of what is happening?

COMMANDER'S COMFY CHAIR

Know Yourself

Before you know your enemy you must know yourself. Review the following. You might decide that it needs further work – over days/weeks.

How comfortable are you with the fact that you are a leader and that you will be watched, modelled, mimicked, gossiped about?

How comfortable are you that your actions are copied?

How sure are you that what people are copying from you is helpful?

Think about your behaviour this week, last week – would you be entirely happy if the people around you copied your behaviour?

Do you know how others see you and what impact you make?

Can you name your 'intent' – what you stand for, what you value, what your priorities are in life and what you want to contribute – or do you need to take some time to think these things through and record them?

Have you worked to close the gap between your intent and the effect you have actually made so that you can be authentic as well as successful? If these questions raise issues for you, Part Two of this book will help you to identify the answers.

Shifting Terrain, Territory, Enemies

Advances in technology and transport have turned many businesses upside down, around and even out of their original homelands and markets. The shift to establishing, for example, new manufacturing plants and call centres in China and India is all part of contemporary globalisation. And whether or not this works as a long-term strategy, what is certain is that it is never really a case of 'business as usual'. The play is being rewritten even as you stand on the stage in front of a critical audience – so you have to improvise. In order to improvise you have to read the signs around you, take what you have got to work with and transform it.

Both the Armed Forces and the business world must deal with living, breathing and proactive opposition. They are both required to find winning solutions set against the realities of the world as it actually is, not how they would like it to be. The business realities of today are often a surprising shift away from how things were yesterday and we have to manage that, not try to pretend it isn't so.

The Armed Forces have to work with what they have got once engaged in battle and they must win against determined opponents who are out to heap disaster upon them. They need to do this whatever the geographic challenges, in a world constantly being reshaped by changing politics, shifting demographics and economic swings. Businesses have to defeat fierce competition to win customers who are, in turn, being shaped constantly by the ebb and flow of the circumstances in which they live and work. Success is about being the best in relative terms, and sustaining hard-won advantage against competitors who work just as hard to get ahead. Even Microsoft has to keep an eye on what clever new software some bright sparks are knocking up in bedrooms around the world.

INTUIT

This software company really did start on the kitchen table. It was a start-up that grew to challenge the giant Microsoft and won the attention and loyalty of 25 million customers. It now has 6,000 employees and is worth $1.4 billion. Intuit destabilised Microsoft's hold on personal finance software with its product 'Quicken'. It was a good product, but it was the stealth and intelligence with which Intuit managed to meet customer needs that turned this great idea into a profitable, sustainable business. Success was so strong that it led to comprehensive market dominance – a modern-day David triumphing over a high-tech Goliath. The story of Intuit's rise is a real drama. There were moments of disaster (the product launch), of high risk (make or break investments) and long days of unrelenting hard work. The lesson is that inspiration and perspiration are not enough. Intuit had a strategy that was smart and cool, it kept its customers in full focus, understood their needs and applied that knowledge. Intuit chose its people well, and recognised and rewarded them appropriately (large bonuses for those who out-performed others). Its operational rigour and attention to process improvement was also exceptionally good.

Differences in Pace and Tempo

The Armed Forces are not engaged in battle all of the time (although they must be in a state of constant readiness) whereas many businesses must meet heavy demands on them day in and day out. Some academics suggest that the structures and cultures of the part of a firm that is looking after the traditional business, to sustain and exploit it, should be different from that part of the business that is constantly looking at ways to re-invent itself. But this seems like needless complexity. There should be enough flexibility in the system to enable the company to build on the past as well as face the future. This means dealing with the critical 'high energy' periods of intense activity as well as finding the time for contemplation, analysis and testing.

Predicting the Future – Based on the Past

Technology is evolving all the time and the Armed Forces have to keep pace with what is on offer. As major conflicts tend to occur at intervals in history, new technology can only be tested now and again in situations of high drama – experimentation and simulation can only ever provide limited assurance. It is hard to draw confident conclusions about what will work for sure in the next conflict based entirely on what worked or didn't work in the last, no matter how much theoretical testing and agonising is done. There will be a natural reluctance to part with equipment and method that worked well previously on the unproven promises of some new and unproven alternatives – especially if lives are at stake.

However, there are ways to start to tackle this dilemma. For example, BAE Systems has created a Battlespace Management Experimentation Centre for its customers – it uses people-in-the-loop real-time simulations and involves customers in identifying the problem and working on a solution together. Many businesses fail to engage their customers in defining the future, despite the fact that where the interests of businesses and customers diverge there is a significant risk of investing in the wrong equipment.

As business is 'in battle' every day, facing continual challenge, business leaders should find it easier than the military to keep abreast of changes in ideas and technology and be able to define and read the situation well at any given time. They don't have to wait for a major conflict to arise in order to test their thinking in action. In fact, too many CEOs are so busy with their heads buried in the details of the moment that they do not manage to look towards the horizon. Many businesses are rather slack at gathering intelligence on their competitors and working out exactly how they can achieve enduring success on a relative basis.

COMMANDER'S COMFY CHAIR
Think About the Competition

Take a few hours to think about the subject of 'competition'.
You might decide that it needs further work – over days/weeks.

Can you name your competitors – and say exactly why they are the competition?

What they are doing better than you?

What value do they have in the eyes of the customer?

What are you assuming?

Do you know where you sit in relation to your competitors?

What are their strengths?

How can you avoid/circumvent their strengths?

How can you minimise or neutralise the effect they have?

Have you clearly identified the competitors' points of weakness?

How might you get into a position to take advantage of their weaknesses?

What could you do to make some rapid gains against their weaknesses?

If you were really wise, what would a smart move be that would

break the competition's will to compete and ability to sustain
an organised or cohesive organisation? How could you 'win
the battle by breaking the will of their commander and
causing mayhem in their HQ?' What would surprise the
competition?

What illusions do they have about your weaknesses?

How could you add to that deception?

What else could you do to be original?

Are you clear about where you want to be?

Where do you want to be in the eyes of your customers?

What are the external factors that could impede your success?

Do you know what strategy your competitors are following?

Do you know for sure what your clients and potential clients
think of your competitors?

What are the internal factors that could interfere with your
success?

> '*Neither a wise man nor a brave man lies down
> on the tracks of history to wait for the train
> of the future to run over him.*'
> US GENERAL AND PRESIDENT DWIGHT D. EISENHOWER

The Armed Forces have the advantage of many hundreds of years
of serious research, evolving thought and practical experience of
combat to draw on. It can be hard to turn theory into action in
any environment, but having a well-formed and tested theory is
at least a start. We saw the value of consistent and joined-up
thinking in Secret Number One: Synchronised Thinking in creating a powerful organisation. Secret Number Four adds to this by
revealing one of the core and enduring approaches to warfare
that has a record of consistent and significant success, and

explaining how it can achieve the same in business or any other form of competitive enterprise.

What Do You Want from a Winning Theory?

Whatever your organisation, there are certain basic outcomes that you need from a theory or an approach if it is to be worth adopting. This applies to the General charged with invading another country or keeping an invader out; and it applies to the CEO required to maximise profits; the investment banker looking for increased return on capital; or the manager employed to build a better health service. You want one that:

- **Yields decisive success**. The method must deliver the results you need with the greatest possible certainty. You don't want to try ideas that lack strength, logic or coherence. You are certainly keen on imagination, novelty and surprise – but only in so far as they contribute to an assured result.

- **Delivers quick results**. You want to achieve your goals as quickly as possible in the circumstances. A major fear is that delays may put the outcome in doubt, costs will be higher and the competition will have more opportunity to strike first or retaliate.

- **Is affordable**. You naturally want to achieve the required result at least cost. For the Armed Forces, this cost will be measured in casualties and the expenditure of equipment and ammunition. For business, it will be measured in terms of cash, disruption to services or manufacturing, morale, land and capital equipment. Governments think in terms of money too, of course, but must also consider reputation and votes. In all cases, there will be the question of: what else could be done more usefully with the resources expended?

- **Out-performs the opposition**. The theory must be a better one than the competition's or, if the competition is following the same theory, you must be able to do it better. The key element is to out-think the opposition. To be better at understanding what is really going on, to display more ingenuity and insight, to be faster at deciding what to do, to issue instructions more clearly and concisely, and – vitally – to be able to implement them faster and more effectively.

  If you are an Admiral fighting an enemy fleet, you want to see them first, get in the best position to attack without being spotted, sink them all with surprise and unstoppable force, and then break away with no casualties and without being traced. At no time should the opposing Admiral know what's going on or be able to put together a reaction, until he finds himself bobbing about the sea in a lifeboat. Having done this, you will expect a knighthood and a happy, prosperous retirement as a military expert for Sky TV.

  If you are a CEO of an electrical retailer, you want to take a range of fantastic products to the customers that no one else can offer, at unmatchable prices yielding huge and sustained profits, leaving the competition in ribbons while you enjoy dominant market share. As a result of this you will expect bonuses that leave the otherwise contented shareholders a little pale, and a retirement filled with golf in the sun and a string of highly paid, low-stress, non-executive directorships.

- **Manages risk**. Even a great and successful theory cannot eliminate risk entirely. Taking risk is a necessary part of achieving in all walks of life. Theory must nonetheless identify how to measure and manage risk, so you know the odds and can plan in advance how best to respond to them. This is a vital part of dealing with any worthy opponent or competitor. Also you cannot ignore the potential role of Lady Luck or her sister, Countess Cock-up. A military commander has to cope when small things go wrong, such as a tank breaking down and temporarily blocking the main route to an objective, as well as bigger problems such as the enemy successfully mounting a surprise air attack. The business leader has to anticipate problems such as machinery breaking down, and the competition planning an advertising campaign timed to draw attention away from your brilliant new product launch.

MANOEUVRE WARFARE

The list of a theory's desirable attributes sounds very attractive – and may seem rather obvious – so is there a theory that encompasses all these features and can be used in practice? The modern Armed Forces have fleshed out a theory of 'Manoeuvre Warfare' that is designed to do just this. Understanding the theory is straightforward: putting it into action on the battle-field with all its uncertainty, complexity, friction and fear is naturally harder – but when it is done well, history records that it has stunning results. Transferring this to commercial practice is easily done: the theory of Manoeuvre Warfare applies as much to making goods or providing services as it does to crushing the state's enemies. Its implementation in business should be a good deal more straightforward than launching an invasion.

The basic idea of Manoeuvre Warfare has been around for centuries: find the way to crush your enemy with the least amount of fighting or, better still, none at all. It is much better to position your forces in such a way that your opponent realises the game is up and surrenders, than to have to batter into him and slug it out until the victor is the last man standing. If a bloodless victory is not attainable, the fighting should be directed so as to lead to the most rapid and decisive victory at the least cost. This will generally mean not charging straight at the enemy's strongest point.

When General Schwarzkopf, commanding Coalition ground forces in the Gulf War in 1991, sent his leading divisions around the flank of the Iraqi forces he was using a manoeuvrist approach. When Napoleon sent his cavalry to charge straight at British infantry and artillery at the Battle of Waterloo in 1815 he was going for the slug-it-out option. Intuitively, as well as historically, the idea of taking an unexpected or indirect approach must make sense. Instead of hurling all available combat power at the opposition in the hope or expectation that a muscular and direct use of force will bring success, how much better it must be to find the enemy's point of greatest weakness, to manoeuvre forces towards it so intelligently and so swiftly that the enemy cannot keep up, and then to strike him so effectively that the battle is quickly and decisively won at least cost.

The alternative is both unattractive and historically painful. A battle of attrition, where two sides engage head-on and fight it out until one side runs out of the will to continue or the means to do so, would normally be expected to be less predictable in outcome and result in higher costs to both sides.

BATTLE OF THE SOMME, 1916

The British attack on the Somme began on 1 July 1916. Over 142 days the British Army lost some 415,000 men, killed, wounded and taken prisoner, and their German opponents lost around 650,000. On the first day, the British assaulted after an artillery barrage lasting a week that used around 1.7 million shells, crossing ground slowly on foot that was heavily waterlogged whilst heavily laden with equipment, walking into impassable stretches of barbed wire (despite the heavy shelling), and straight into the teeth of German machine-gun and artillery fire from men who had endured and yet survived the bombardment. No wonder almost 60,000 British soldiers were killed, wounded or taken prisoner on the first day alone. This was clearly fought as a deliberate battle of attrition, and perhaps in the circumstances of the time there was no real alternative.

Blending Manoeuvre and Attrition

It would be a mistake to think that simple 'manoeuvre', just the movement of resources, can deliver success alone. Although a broad distinction can be drawn between a Manoeuvre Warfare approach and a battle of attrition, in practice they usually have to be blended by a skilful commander and so are not mutually exclusive. The art is to manoeuvre until you are in a position to have a decisive effect at the most telling point. The manoeuvring has created the right conditions for the battle to take place. But it may be necessary to conduct operations based on attrition at some stages of a conflict. So although organisations aspire to the advantages of the manoeuvrist approach, they have to acknowledge that through choice or necessity a battle of attrition may have to be fought.

BATTLE OF BRITAIN

During the Battle of Britain it was essential that the Royal Air Force shot down the Luftwaffe faster than British aircraft and airfields could be put out of action. By defeating the German air attack through successful attrition in 1940, Britain was able to maintain the territorial integrity of the British Isles, which could then become the launch platform for the manoeuvrist D Day landings in Normandy in 1944 (most Germans thought Calais more likely). The attrition was a hard, but necessary precursor to manoeuvrist success. As the British Prime Minister of the day said:

> 'I have nothing to offer but blood, toil, tears, and sweat.'
> WINSTON CHURCHILL

So the point is that although organisations may aspire to the advantages of the manoeuvrist approach, they have to acknowledge that sometimes through choice or necessity an attritional battle may have to be fought. The trick is to do so at a time, place and cost of one's own choosing and to avoid being drawn by an opponent through design or accident into a slugging match.

The philosophical approach of Manoeuvre Warfare is carried forward into the way operations of war are actually conducted by the practitioners on the ground, in the air and at sea. It means that a commander will look at the enemy with a view to finding the best way of defeating him, not just settle for the most obvious or familiar way. For example, when required to attack, a battle group commander in charge of around 30 tanks and 30 infantry fighting vehicles, and with artillery, engineers, aircraft and logisticians in support, will search for ways of getting behind the enemy's positions.

> 'The more efficient a force is, the more silent and the more subtle it is. Love is the subtlest force in the world.'
> MAHATMA GANDHI

Dynamic Manoeuvre in Business

The basic idea of Manoeuvre Warfare is easy to grasp when applied in a commercial context, when we call it 'Dynamic Manoeuvre' (DM). Rather than tackle the competition head-on in a battle to see who can win on a like-for-like basis, you would probably prefer to find a clever way of winning more customers, bigger market share, better profits and higher growth. Most business leaders would naturally go for the latter. From the perspective of an entrepreneur looking to make a fortune, or a large company looking to grow quickly, the idea of Dynamic Manoeuvre in business has great appeal.

GLAXOSMITHKLINE

The £30 billion merger between Wellcome Glaxo and Smith Kline Beecham, one of the largest in commercial history, resulted in the creation of GlaxoSmithKline (GSK) with a staff of 100,000 employees and a turnover of £17 billion. Such a bold move needed to show decisive payback early on. Apart from cutting costs by shedding duplicate jobs in sales and back-office functions, CEO Jean-Pierre Garner's first move was to boost the research and development departments by turning them into six autonomous centres of excellence, with rewards for the most successful. This approach encourages precisely the dynamic thinking that Manoeuvre Warfare demands from the Armed Forces. The competitive environment for GSK is intense. The heat is always on to maximise profits from new drugs before competitors can begin marketing generic products as soon as patents expire (currently after 17 years in the USA). The firm must be ever mindful of potential side-effects as regulatory bodies have the power to halt production of any drug where safety is in question. Half of all sales are in the USA, so a weak dollar can depress profits. Some of the risk is managed by ensuring that no individual drug represents more than 12 per cent of total sales. GSK was also the first business to discount products to the poor in the USA and Africa, a move that is socially responsible and also builds empathy with customers, laying the foundations for future markets.

DYNAMIC MANOEUVRE

The principal components of Dynamic Manoeuvre are that:

- The leadership shows creativity, originality and surprise in setting the goals and objectives of the organisation. Just settling for doing the same thing slightly better is never considered good enough. Dynamic Manoeuvre must be understood and practised at all levels of leadership.
- The leadership is constantly open to finding an unconventional or unexpected route to financial success, by maximising surprise and innovation, such as moving into an entirely new business field or market.
- The organisation is able to operate its decision-making processes faster than any of the competition – and fast enough to keep ahead of the market and other key variables. Once a decision is made, it is implemented swiftly and fully by a fully briefed and engaged workforce.
- All levels of the organisation are encouraged to contribute to finding new, innovative and intelligent ways of boosting the organisation and its activities. From the CEO to the most junior employee, each person looks at what they have been

asked to do and tries to find a better way of achieving the desired effect.

- All possible lessons are learnt from past successes and failures and faithfully employed in future activities.

The principles of Dynamic Manoeuvre can be used in both mature markets and developing ones. For example, the market for new cars in Western Europe and the USA is now at saturation point, where the differences between products and price are marginal. Here, Dynamic Manoeuvre can be seen in the approach by some manufacturers to make money by lending customers the cash to buy a new model and selling expensive after-sales support, with margins on the car itself kept tiny (even negative). In developing countries where widespread private car ownership is relatively new (most notably China with 30 million cars now and perhaps 130 million in five years' time) there is more scope for striking deals that will dramatically outpace the competition in the way cars are made, marketed and sold on a rising scale.

In principle at least, we might expect business to be good at identifying winning methods and putting them into practice quickly. Experience suggests that this is not necessarily the case. As we highlighted in Secret Number One, look at how many businesses crash and burn after only a few years of trading, how even large, long-established enterprises can go into terminal decline, and how new enterprises often repeat the elementary mistakes of their predecessors. There are others that have made a real success of reaching for the stars, and are well placed to take up the challenge of Dynamic Manoeuvre.

3M

The principles of Dynamic Manoeuvre can be clearly seen in action at 3M, one of the world's most consistently innovative firms. 3M use 'story telling' as a means of keeping the innovation culture alive and recently this approach has even been transferred to business plans. Leaders tell stories explaining where they want to go, rather than just giving a list of objectives. By doing so they have found that their listeners find it much easier to identify with the mission. The firm believes in creating the space and freedom for entrepreneurship to flourish. Staff are encouraged to have a go at anything that takes their fancy, perhaps even moonlighting outside their normal role for up to 15 per cent of their time. The authors of the better ideas win a board sponsor and the opportunity to convince a multi-discipline team of accountants/designers/engineers that the idea has commercial application. They may even receive $50,000 for people and equipment in order to develop the idea. Few companies have such a systematic way of generating innovation. 3M's objective is that a quarter of its revenue will come from products conceived within the previous five years. This ensures that it is constantly reinventing itself.

RISK MANAGEMENT

Dynamic Manoeuvre means taking risks. It is rarely possible to be strong everywhere and in order to reap the advantages of Dynamic Manoeuvre a Business General must accept some potential weaknesses. Where this comes from internal factors, such as the way resources are mustered or the effects of low morale in the workforce, steps can be taken to minimise the impact. Where the risks come from outside the organisation they can be harder to manage but just as threatening.

Employing Dynamic Manoeuvre in business or any form of organised activity is first and foremost an attitude of mind. Of course, technical aspects are important too, such as efficient communications, good logistics and well-run financial systems. When working well, these practical aspects make an organisation agile and efficient – able to change direction quickly and smoothly without losing efficiency – and have good co-ordination. But at its heart, Dynamic Manoeuvre means leaders thinking clearly about where they want to go and the best way of getting there. This is about leaders taking the time to think things through and to think smart, mustering all the creative energy, willpower and flexibility they can.

Dynamic Manoeuvre means you as a Business General developing your ability to be shrewd, and to be ingenious. It is about being loose enough on your feet to engage in the dance, the theatre, the jazz of it all.

Build Your Armoury
Improvisation

▷ When the competition is unpredictable or when you are in new territory, there is no script, to follow – so each person must improvise. This involves using the resources you have to create agreement on what it is you have to work with and agreement from others to go along with you while you build a coherent, spontaneous story. Stories engage people, give meaning.

▷ Part of the skill of improvisation lies in what is called 'bricolage' – where you build a solution with what you've got, not waiting for the ideal, but using what is in front of you. Entrepreneurs are good at bricolage – they do not wait for a full and detailed analysis if they are confident enough about their intuition, moving swiftly and making things happen while the time is right. Of course, there is risk in this – and sometimes failure will follow – but equally seizing the moment can reap huge dividends. Many professional advisers hesitate while they wait for the right information or the ideal situation to appear – by which time it is too late. It is much better to go when the time is right with 80 per cent of data than to wait for that elusive 20 per cent more.

▷ Improvisation is applicable both as a metaphor for successful business leadership and as a way of seeing and equipping yourself as an individual to deal with changing situations. To be good at improvisation, you need to let information flow freely and not block it, to listen well, be lateral, be authentic, and go with the chaos from which great creativity often emerges. It relies partly on letting experience, good and bad, build successful intuition.

▷ Improvisation is a highly collaborative act between those who engage and those who sit watching, agreeing to go along with the interpretations. Improvisation deals with the unpredictable and with 'the now' as it hasn't been written. You can't wait for the intuition, you have to create it. It draws on spontaneity in creating the 'what next'. It is about 'saying yes' to whatever comes up and making it your own, adding the 'and...'. It is more to do with intuition and experience than planning. It is better with experience, but experience comes with having a go. Improvisation is an intense, dynamic attitude and skill that suits people looking for an opportunity to deliver a crushing win.

COMMANDER'S COMFY CHAIR

Dynamic Manoeuvre Tool Box

Dynamic Manoeuvre is in part a philosophy and in part a guide to best practice in planning and in operations. Take some time to consider your organisation in terms of DM. You might decide that it needs further work – over days/weeks.

What is the purpose of your organisation?

Is your current activity meeting this?

Is it the best or only way?

Are there better, alternative ways to satisfy the purpose?

Are you fighting a battle of attrition?

If so, at what cost?

Can you afford the costs?

What would be a more manoeuvrist approach?

Would it be more decisive, quicker, or cheaper?

Who in your team has the capacity to find the new, unorthodox and decisive way to success?

Is there dead wood holding your team back?

What are you going to do about it?

Are you clear about the risks and how to manage them?

Whom do you consider to be a great leader of the past?

What would they see/say/do in your circumstances to be creative, original?

Who do you rate as wise, informed, insightful?

What would they see/say/do in your circumstances?

How agile is your organisation?

What contributes to its agility and what holds it back?

What would surprise the market?

Is the tempo of activity and the energy level at your work enough to be able to 'move and fight' in a way that no competitor can keep up with?

Who/what hinders that energy and pace?

What/who helps it?

Where could the organisation work at a higher tempo?

How resilient is your team?

What can you do to help them sustain operations? (There is no point manoeuvring with skill to strike the vital point only to then have to stop from exhaustion or lack of resources.)

Protection and Risk Management

In applying the DM approach, the business leader must be clear what risks he is taking, and how he will handle problems that might arise. A risk for which there is no remedy available should it materialise is just a gamble. Risks can take many forms but, for example:

- Cash flow dries up.
- Suppliers fail to keep up deliveries essential to production.
- Competition produces something new out of the blue.
- Currency fluctuations occur.
- There is dramatic technology change.
- Natural disasters or war happen.

You will need to assess the risk to activities honestly and fully, and then monitor what actually happens carefully. The vital role for you as leader in this respect is to be able to readily accept when things are going astray and to take decisions to do something about it – even if unwelcome. In many ways, the cruellest test of a leader is to have to face up to incipient failure and take urgent steps to do something about it. It is often easier to pretend it isn't happening, or that it is someone else's problem. There are many examples of businesses and other organisations failing as a result of becoming over-exposed in one way or another. An illustration from the Korean War makes the point:

KOREA

In 1950, during the Korean War, the US forces under General Douglas MacArthur successfully landed from the sea at Inchon, in a stunning manoeuvrist example of how to surprise and dislocate an enemy. In conjunction with British and other forces driving up from the South, they quickly drove the North Korean People's Army up to the Thirty-Eighth Parallel. However, US-led forces then pressed on Northwards, despite warnings that further movement over the Thirty-Eighth Parallel would bring China into the war. In great secrecy, General MacArthur's forces were attacked by 30 Chinese Divisions, and compelled to fall back 150 miles – losing Seoul, the capital of the Republic of Korea, in the process. The risk of Chinese involvement had not been fully understood or thought through, and when it materialised led to disastrous consequences.

BUILD YOUR ARMOURY
Dynamic Manoeuvre

Some tips for managing technology in the context of 'dynamic manoeuvre':

▷ Build on the Power Pyramid. You cannot manoeuvre intelligently and with agility if your organisation is subjected to weak, incoherent or circular thinking, or is poorly motivated or

staffed by insufficiently trained people. The Power Pyramid
(see Secrets One, Two and Three) provides a model for making
your organisation strong enough to execute Dynamic Manoeuvre.
Make sure all the ideas are well understood throughout the
firm (Synchronised Thinking), are put into action by a committed
team pulsating with high morale (Soul Matters), through
excellent processes, equipment, training and logistics (Right
Team, Right Stuff).

▷ Use improvisation. Teach your organisation to work
spontaneously, collaboratively and creatively – to feel okay with
unpredictable results.

▷ Create true entrepreneurship, where the qualities of seeing
opportunity, taking courage, managing risk, having confidence
are exhibited in an extraordinary way at all levels of the
organisation by the 'ordinary' employee. Creativity and
inspiration are not the preserve of particular job titles.

▷ Audit your strategy. Check that your corporate strategy or
business plan identifies and exploits strengths and minimises
weaknesses in the way it sets out how to achieve success.

▷ Find your competition. Success in a competitive market is
about being better than the others in a relative sense. This means
that leaders must know who the competition is and what they are
doing. It is essential that leaders have their heads above their
desks and are well versed in what is going on in new technology,
industry best practice and looking for new ideas – both at home
and abroad. Well-focused networking is time well spent, whether
it is with other leaders, academics or even politicians. The aim is
to be as sure as possible that you have the initiative and the
capacity to surprise the competition – not the other way around. It
is a constant effort, in the same way that a military commander
will monitor the intelligence picture as a matter of constant
importance. Are you confident that you are on top of this?

▷ Deplete the will of the competition. Attack the mind as much as the wallet of your competitors. They must be made to feel they are distinctly second rate as a result of the high-tempo way your products and services are launched. Competitors who feel – rightly or wrongly – that they cannot compete or keep up are likely to fail. The will of the competition to stay in the market, their stamina, effectiveness and the cohesion they need to operate on a par, should be eroded by the power of your own confidence and performance.

▷ Focus on the customer, not just the process. Check you know what your customers want in all aspects – what they will consider as value added to a product that will tempt them away from other offers, and how much extra they will pay. Once you have identified what they need, or think they need, work out how to give it to them. The DM approach includes finding a new, better way of giving customers what they already have and/or finding a completely new way of grabbing their attention. Do you want to be the organisation that made cassette tapes better and cheaper than anybody else, or do you want to be the organisation that thought of the iPod? Are you sure that you are not guilty of just cleverly refining a process that delivers something people are really not interested in?

▷ Let your customers know you. Do not hide your light. There is no point having a brilliant idea or product if it is a secret from the people who need it. Build your image so that you are prominent in the minds of potential customers, and condition the market to desire what you offer above any alternatives. List what you do now to get your message across and identify how you could do it better.

▷ Know your customers' points of resistance and their soft spots. When you examine your customers, find out where you can pitch your products and find a better reception with less resistance. The DM approach means not labouring to break through your customers' thick skin if you can find a more subtle way of getting under it.

▷ Know what will constitute your decisive success. You must be clear about what defines success for your organisation before you can work out how to achieve it. You must also be clear that the ideas that lead to success today will not necessarily last forever. Leaders must be as interested in what comes next as doing well today.

▷ What you do successfully today will not necessarily bring success tomorrow. Check that you are not pinning the future on doing the same thing as today, just in a different colour. What are you assuming? Where could the next surprise come from?

▷ Think flexibly about alternative routes to success. If organic growth is proving difficult, how about growing by acquisition? If the market for the existing product is saturated, why not convert the assets and workforce into something else entirely? DM means finding the most effective and least expensive route to success, not slavishly following the present road.

▷ Don't battle it out in a war of resources. Do not settle for competing on a like-for-like basis, where margins are squeezed to the point where the activity becomes virtually profit-free, unless this is done as a temporary tactic from a position of relative strength – such as a big retailer using a price war to gain territory, or to squash a smaller or weaker competitor. Attrition has its place, but is not the tactic most likely to succeed in the long term.

▷ Concentrate on a synchronised effect on the customer and the competition. Combine offering a new product or service with: repositioning yourself in the market-place through a well-timed campaign to create awareness and demand, supported by availability, delivery and after-sales support. Bringing all these disciplines together is the task of the Business General, just as a military general must co-ordinate firepower, manoeuvre and logistics. Have the successor product already in the pipeline, to be ready tomorrow when today's idea has run its course.

Summary of Secret Number Four: Dynamic Manoeuvre

- This Secret is the first to look specifically at the vital leadership skills that a modern Business General needs today.
- It explains how an approach known as Dynamic Manoeuvre can help you to prepare for all eventualities in an ever-changing business world, including the ability to take well-managed risks.
- Dynamic Manoeuvre means building an attitude of mind to seek out the most effective – but not always most obvious – way of achieving success.
- It is about finding ways to captivate the customer and catch competitors off guard, rather than slogging along the conventional path and battling it out with rivals toe-to-toe until exhaustion decides the winner.
- Dynamic Manoeuvre, and the methods that flow from this philosophy (described in Secrets Five, Six and Seven), give an organisation a better chance to win comprehensively, and to do so more decisively, more quickly and at lower cost than before.

Next Secret...

For Business Generals operating in a large and complex organisation, a key component of leadership is the art of delegation and empowerment, and this is the subject of Secret Number Five: Mission Management.

Secret Five
Mission Management
The art of delegation and empowerment

'The best executive is the one who has sense enough to pick good men to do what he wants done, and self-restraint enough to keep from meddling with them while they do it.'

PRESIDENT THEODORE ROOSEVELT

That delegation and empowerment unleashes the full force of the talent that an organisation possesses has underpinned fashionable management theories for a decade or more. So there is nothing new about the idea. Of course, people work better if given the freedom, encouragement and responsibility to really 'go for it'. But attempts to implement this approach have often been poorly articulated, piecemeal and ad hoc – ending in misunderstanding and failure. Secret Number Five: Mission Management shows how the Armed Forces make delegation and empowerment work, and how you can do the same in your own organisation.

The Myth and Misconceptions of 'Command and Control'

We have already dispelled some myths that persist around the idea of the military and 'command and control' in Secret Number 3. This expression is still sometimes deployed in a rather derogatory way by people convinced that Armed Forces are led by authoritarian monsters – who direct every single action of an unthinking and servile band of automatons. Such a view reflects the slimmest grasp of military history – and invariably indicates the speaker has had no direct contact with contemporary Armed Forces.

For example, it may once have been the case – say in the seventeenth century – that the British Army maintained order and discipline in the ranks through the lash, access to drink and the promise of booty. But that was how much else of life was ordered then too. The idea that the British or US or French military are still run along the lines of some form of antiquated authoritarianism, where commitment from subordinates is obtained by fear of retribution, is just not tenable. As we have seen in Secrets Number 2 and Number 3, this would not lead to effectiveness in battle, and who would volunteer to join up anyway? The ridiculous but popular view that one man rigidly commands and controls the work of others is insulting – soldiers, sailors and airmen are neither docile nor stupid; they wouldn't stand for being treated as such.

'Command' actually means the exercise of leadership and 'control' refers to the more functional aspects of leadership and management – like coordination, regulation and administration. But the key point is that to win in battle (on land, the sea or in the air) requires people to be completely, freely and consciously committed to the task and to their team. Anything less leads to weakness and vulnerability under pressure. So, of course, there is discipline and, of course, orders are issued and obeyed, but it is done so intelligently and voluntarily: people do difficult things because they know why it matters, not because they are frightened of their own side.

So when we talk about military command and control it is important to drop the connection to any illusions of slavish automata and draw on the real advantages of how the modern military get things done. In this Secret we will give you the opportunity to pick up on how Armed Forces do empowerment and delegation, and in so doing gain the motivation, commitment and levels of empowerment that come from real passion – the kind many large and small businesses are dying for.

Some companies still follow low-trust, macho, command-and-control management styles that kill innovation and commitment. Juniors do not trust the leadership and the leadership use fear and threats as the prime 'motivators' because they do not trust the workforce. Just as abused kids often go on to abuse others, so juniors model the behaviour of senior management. Lack of trust simply encourages staff to move to the highest bidder, so high staff turnover becomes the norm. There is little that can change this without proper attention being given to modelling correct behaviour. Conscious leadership is called for to challenge the status quo. High trust and respectful environments have a greater impact on the financial 'bottom line' than great designs, new technology, clever strategy or quality control.

The Quaker values of the firm Cadbury (now Cadbury Schweppes), 'working together to create the brands people love', are lived by the entire workforce and have contributed to their sustained success over 200 years. No surprise then that taking an ethical approach is their main corporate ethos. Their super-friendly website is a marvel: by displaying the names and pictures of their management team it gives the impression of a transparent, open, accessible style.

Getting People and Culture Right

Firms without strong professional Human Resources (HR), like many City firms – especially those in investment advisory and management, investment banks, private equity – have cultures that have been described as mercenary and callous. They often lack real diversity and are blatantly sexist and racist. As equal opportunity becomes a given demand, these firms are going to have some sharp wake-up calls as more top talent sues them and even more leave them. Looking after people and the culture is not left to HR in the military – everyone does it; but in business it is HR who need to lead the way because they have the knowledge and methodology.

Empowerment Today – Trust, Respect and Reciprocity

The two fundamental components of empowerment are trust and respect. We discussed in Secret Number Two how levels of trust in many firms are often appalling, yet most studies into competitiveness show that trust significantly affects organisational effectiveness and performance. Trust is an intangible resource. Without it the potential for passionate engagement in staff cannot be released.

Studies in social psychology have also shown how reciprocity is a robust and natural human condition – we give back, sometimes in a roundabout way, what we think we are getting. Today, with the concept of 'employment for life' a distant memory, longer hours squeezing our work-life balance, and the insecurities that result from mergers, acquisitions, downsizing, redundancies and outsourcing, a great deal of *negative* reciprocity is generated in organisations. On top of this, the 'fat cat' culture of senior leaders creaming off million-pound bonuses, even though they have crumpled shareholder value and sacrificed their employees, does nothing but add yet more to a climate of 'negative reciprocity'. You cannot have empowerment unless your moral climate is good.

As a general rule, people attracted to volunteer for military life tend to want to serve and are clearly not motivated by the prospect of big money. Military leaders are committed to the ideals of a 'Serve to Lead' (the Sandhurst motto) culture. The men and women serving in uniform expect and require their commanders to know them well and to treat them with dignity and respect, and on this basis they undertake to follow them to their best of their ability – even into danger. Not many people say that about their bosses in industry. Yet in business, people have been convinced of the merits of empowerment since the 1980s. It certainly suits the enterprise age, where entrepreneurial, flexible and innovative patterns of behaviour are needed. The question is how to achieve it to the mutual satisfaction of employer and staff?

A 'Social Contract'

This idea of a 'social contract' in the military underpins everything else. There is a well-understood basis of mutual trust and respect that binds leaders and followers together and prepares both for the rigours and perils of combat. Where this trust is broken, as it has been occasionally by acts of bullying and discrimination, only radical steps to identify and put the problem right will do – otherwise operational effectiveness is fatally undermined. The military have found this recently when bullying and torture of a few has seriously undermined the image and reputation of the entire force.

Many businesses struggle to get empowerment right because they fail to establish the basic relationships between leader and follower as a priority. There is little point building an elegant model of corporate empowerment if staff are too busy watching their own backs. In some respects it is slightly easier for the military as they offer longer-term security of employment, so long as individual performance is up to the mark. If business continues with the culture of long hours, lack of job security and often no real care and investment in employees' careers, then it must face up to the fact that creating trust will be complicated, and perhaps well nigh impossible. A system of empowerment produces trust and the trust generates the conditions for more empowerment – a virtuous circle, but it needs to start somewhere.

Making a Start

Changing a firm from a culture of 'dog eat dog' to 'empowerment' is not easy. People are bound to be sceptical about where the boundaries really lie and uncertain where they stand if they take risks or make mistakes. Trust and risk are linked. Where firms want their people to be more creative, innovative and take more personal risks – then they need to work on creating strong levels of trust. People hold on to information to protect their job and their power, and part of your mission as Business General is to encourage people to share knowledge. If your firm needs people to be trusted more or to take more risks in order to seize advantage, as a Business General you need to:

- Invest in people's development and train them to be competent.
- Embed the organisation's values and reward people for really living them (financially and with personal recognition).
- Eliminate as much 'office politicking' as possible.
- Develop open communications, so that ambiguity and uncertainty are reduced and people feel they belong.
- Encourage, reward and insist upon fairness, consistency and

transparency in performance management and grievance procedures.

COMMANDER'S COMFY CHAIR

Taking Stock

Take a few hours to ask yourself the following questions. You might decide that further work is required – over days/weeks.

Do you feel genuinely empowered?

Have you consciously empowered your subordinates? Have you told them?

Have you refrained from interfering in matters that you have delegated?

Do you trust your peers?

Which of your bosses do you respect and why?

Who don't you respect and why not?

What work has been done to identify the values and ethics of your organisation and ensure they are understood and lived?

Do you personally set an example of 'living the values'?

How well do you know your team as people?

Are mistakes seen as an opportunity for learning for everyone?

Empowerment as it is used today in businesses is about task and operational delegation, but unless it is backed up with proper training and appropriate reward systems, leaders should not expect employees to jump for joy when they have been 'empowered'. Many times it feels more like abandonment. Staff often say they feel they are being challenged, dumped on, given more responsibility without being given the necessary support, and without any apparent prospect of benefit to them.

Empowerment cannot be installed in a culture that lacks trust, doesn't invest in training, where information and decision making is not clearly defined and well-managed – without trust people won't buy into it and rightly won't believe the rhetoric. You have to get your house in order first.

If the average tenure of a CEO is less than four years – often in firms where many of the employees have been there most of their working lives – where is the mutual obligation, the history of trust that is vital to create the conditions of empowerment? Where trust has been actively promoted within an organisation it has usually grown organically over time and results in something special that cannot be readily imitated by competitors. It becomes a vital asset in creating enduring value. Most firms list trust in their statements of values. In a survey, some 75 out of the top 100 UK and US firms had it. But how many firms really make it happen?

The military community at unit level lives together, dines together, knows each other's husbands/wives and children like a well-knit, yet mobile village. They have concern and respect for each other as individuals within a large organisation. This makes it easier to use the transformational model of leadership, rather than merely obtain compliance through contractual and transactional models.

DELEGATION AND EMPOWERMENT

*'A general is just as good or just as bad
as the troops under his command make him.'*
GENERAL DOUGLAS MACARTHUR

When an individual does something entirely alone there is no doubt about who is in charge. Whether he or she is hopelessly indecisive, torn by inner turmoil about what to do next and why, or completely confident and on top of their job, a person working alone is entirely responsible for making decisions about what they will do and how they will do it. That is how it should be, but we often see people of low emotional intelligence making all sorts of excuses for the drivers of their behaviour, and those with poor character pinning the blame on others or things outside their control.

Individuals

People at work (and at home) should expect to 'own' their own behaviour and teach others to do the same. By owning behaviour we mean acknowledging it, controlling it and taking responsibility for it and its outcomes.

Small Teams

Much the same sense of control applies to small groups where the leaders can see every other member of their team. They can issue instructions about what to do, explain in detail how it will be done and then monitor progress with 100 per cent clarity. This was broadly the position of a military commander for hundreds of years: he could see the whole battlefield from a vantage point and so direct the battle in detail. He could not, of course, supervise or assist every part of the fighting directly – but by confidently relying on his units to execute commonly understood and well-practised drills in response to his instructions, the commander could anticipate how his instructions would be carried out in some detail. If he said 'Charge', they charged. If he said 'Fire', they fired. Only if the enemy proved too strong might this confidence be misplaced.

The Challenge of Scale

The problem is more difficult when it is no longer possible for one leader to oversee the detail of every task, either because it is spread over too large an area for one person to keep an eye on, or because there are so many moving parts in the organisation that a single brain simply cannot manage every aspect in detail. This does not stop people trying: we can probably all think of an organisation that is so dominated by the person at the top that staff lower down worry that they are doing things the wrong way, and that every decision has to be referred upwards. As a result, morale is poor, people feel cramped, vulnerable and undervalued, and productivity is low. The person at the top then thinks the staff are incapable of showing initiative and that the answer is yet more prescriptive direction and closer personal control. Meanwhile, the organisation slides towards mediocrity, and is buffeted by the slipstream of more agile and cohesive competition forging past to seize the glittering prizes.

The Case for Delegation and Empowerment

The theoretical case for delegation and empowerment is powerful. If every single person in the organisation is allowed to exercise their powers of critical thinking and given decision-making autonomy within broad boundaries of task and values, then they can become awesomely more productive, creative and effective. This is a huge advantage over employees waiting to be told in detail what to do at each step and exactly how it is to be done.

Empowerment and delegation of responsibility requires trust, respect and long-term thinking, but all too often the opposite is the case. If leaders at the top don't let go of the ball often enough, however much they may toss empowerment theory around, their subordinates will not have the freedom they need to be successful. If subordinates fail to live up to the expectations placed upon them, or are unable to do so through lack of training or support, then either nothing at all will be achieved or the wrong things will happen. In companies where employees are squeezed to deliver short-term results at any cost to the long-term picture, mistakes are not tolerated, and radical or creative steps are made to look like disruption and delay, then none of the positive effects of empowerment will accrue.

It is well proven that success becomes more likely when individuals have the freedom to think and act as part of a well-practised team. In military terms, even at the lowest tactical level, for example where a team of four soldiers is sent to seize a small objective, if the individuals in the team can select their targets and decide where and when to move, there is a greater chance of success – provided they are bound together by a common spirit and purpose, are well trained and know each other well enough to work together instinctively.

Nowadays, military campaigns may be spread over huge parts of the globe with many nations contributing sea, land and air forces to a coalition. So it is impossible to make anything happen without empowerment. It is important that the commander at the top sets out very clearly his 'road map' to victory and what he wants each major part of his forces to achieve. It is just as important that this commander does not think that he can personally direct every aircraft, ship, team on a blow-by-blow basis. And once the battle has been joined, commanders at all levels must expect the enemy to do his best to interfere with the plan and for the situation to change – and they must be prepared to seize the initiative and act decisively rather than wait for detailed fresh instructions from the top. On the battlefield, like crossing a busy road in the rush hour, hesitation can be fatal.

The same parameters apply in business. As more large companies compete in a global market place and run their operations across several continents (finance in London, advertising in New York and manufacturing in China), so the leadership must find a way of directing and controlling diverse functions and responsibilities. The board must set the direction and then empower operating divisions to deliver results, dealing with the competition and other challenges as they see best in their particular circumstances. When we are looking for business solutions it isn't only management theory that helps, but also looking outside in a comparative sense for a fresh perspective. Businesses do not often put considerable effort into forming theories that will lead to guaranteed victory in the way the Armed Forces have, but they can now learn from their results. While some have their own MBA or send large proportions of their senior managers to business schools – they study finance or marketing and not their *own* firm.

The Armed Forces' Experience

The Armed Forces have not found the *one* theory that always works – just some generally good principles. This is really no surprise: wars are not subject to immutable laws like gravity; each conflict has a different mix of circumstances and factors, and rarely does a commander have a perfect view of what is going on (and if he did, historically speaking there is a good chance of him leaping to the wrong conclusions anyway). There has been profound disappointment that no magic recipe exists, and the search for a wonder weapon to bring guaranteed victory has been just as fruitless. (We can discount even nuclear weapons here: they may have the power to be wonderfully decisive in a conflict, but a weapon that leaves all the participants and their territories toasted has significant limitations.)

Part of the challenge for Armed Forces in their search for methods that will bring success is that they are not all made up the same way. An army that is made up of hastily conscripted civilians given only rudimentary training and little equipment is self-evidently a different organisation from an Army filled by fabulously well-trained and equipped volunteers of many years' practical experience. The former will need to be given limited tasks and significant guidance in the field; the latter will be capable of complex manoeuvres and have no doubt about how to go about it – to the point of resenting interference in its affairs.

The same differences apply in business: if you are digging the Panama canal by hand then a vast manual labour force can be handed a shovel and carefully orchestrated by a small team of experts; if you are building the ships to sail through it then the workforce will be a far wider mix of intellectual and manual skills, all of which need careful integration. The way an organisation operates is bound to be affected by the nature of its composition. The more complicated it is, the more can go wrong.

> *'The military machine – the army and everything related to it – is basically very simple and therefore seems easy to manage. But we should bear in mind that none of its components is of one piece: each piece is composed of individuals, every one of whom retains his potential of friction … A battalion is made up of individuals, the least important of whom may chance to delay things or somehow make them go wrong.'*
> CARL VON CLAUSEWITZ

For the Armed Forces of the more developed countries, which obviously have much in common with the similarly well-established and experienced commercial enterprises of their societies, there is no doubt that there is considerable scope for delegation and empowerment. This is because most are all-volunteer organisations where people serve for a number of years – and many for their whole working life. Even those that still take a conscripted element will have all-volunteer officer and non-commissioned officer cadres. Well-organised and trained organisations make delegation and empowerment more effective at all levels of command, right down to the crews of single vehicles and right up to the leaders of multinational forces in conflict drawn from the armies, navies and air forces of several countries.

The Requirement for Balance

How do you strike the balance between holding direction and decision making at the top of an organisation, with the risk of stagnation and paralysis, and delegating to lower levels, at the risk of lack of consistency and even chaos. This dilemma prompts the same essential questions in any organisation.

COMMANDER'S COMFY CHAIR
Balancing Direction and Delegation

Review the following regarding the need to 'balance direction and delegation'. You might decide that it needs further work – over days/weeks.

How much decision-making can be delegated in your
organisation, leaving others to decide what to do within clear
boundaries?
How much freedom should subordinates have in deciding *how* to
carry out their assigned tasks?
How can leader and follower know that they are all pulling in the
same direction?

MISSION COMMAND

There is a system that works now in well-practised use with the military and tested in the most extreme conditions. It is the theory of 'Mission Command'. Like the few really great theories, the basic idea of Mission Command has been around for some time – at least 800 years – during which time it has evolved with experience. The theory of Mission Command has already crossed cultural and national borders, and been tested in a variety of military situations over time. It can cross the border into business rather more effortlessly.

Mission Command is the system of delegation and empowerment used in the Armed Forces today and has come about through necessity. If forces were to cover large distances and fight in different places simultaneously, a system was needed that delegated responsibility from the top yet led to distributed action focused on a common aim. In the absence of modern communications, this meant choosing between limiting the campaign to specific, detailed instructions that generals had to follow explicitly and report back on, or giving the generals a task to achieve and sending them off to get on with it.

The Genghis Khan Approach

The latter was the pattern adopted by Genghis Khan in the twelfth and thirteenth centuries in central Asia and on the fringes of Europe. He launched his generals off in different directions with the requirement to meet up at a place and time in the future, having conquered all enemies in their path. Success was not only the result of effective delegation from Genghis Khan to his subordinates, but also due to the emphatically powerful way they thought and fought in exercising that freedom on his behalf.

Nelson

Vice Admiral Horatio Nelson fought naval battles between 1797 and 1805 that were characterised by aspects of what is now known as Mission Command. He issued short, simple instructions and trusted his subordinate captains to act in conformity with the general idea he had given them. Nelson is still admired as a leader because he won the hearts of his officers and crew, he remembered their names, visited them in hospital, wrote to their mothers, and he trusted them. He explained his goals clearly and then let them get on with it. If they took initiative, he supported them. If things went wrong, he defended them. By articulating his strategic purpose and believing in the team to make a contribution, he was playing to the highest common factor – not micro-managing to cover for the lowest common denominator.

'Auftragstaktik'

Modern development of the idea of 'Mission Command' fell to the German Army in the early twentieth century as 'Auftragstaktik'. It conveys the method whereby a commander makes clear his intent and broadly how he wants this met, then leaves it to his subordinate commanders to find a successful way of achieving it. This is the central idea of Mission Command as adopted by the British and US Armed Forces today.

AUFTRAGSTAKTIK

For the German Army during the Second World War, the theory of 'Auftragstaktik' was not just an abstract concept – it infused the way they fought, both in the successes against Poland, France, the Low Countries and Britain in 1940–41 and in defending against the Allied attacks after D Day in 1944–45.

The doctrine emphasised the importance of low-level initiative, encouraging commanders at any level to take decisive action when faced with a difficult situation rather than wait for orders and help from above. When forced off a position, the German Army would almost without exception mount an immediate counter-attack with whatever men and equipment were available – knowing that early and determined reaction would catch their enemy off-balance. They did this rather than wait to put together a bigger, slower and more organised counter-attack, by which time the enemy would have had time to dig in. In the last year of the War, the German ability to put together 'Kampfgruppen' (Battlegroups) of men from any source: soldiers, sailors, airmen, support troops and even youth groups – equipped with just a few tanks and large calibre weapons – and to mount stiff local resistance, was hugely significant in slowing the Allied Advance. Just a small, well-led group could delay the movement of a US or UK formation over five times as large and far better equipped.

Mission Command in Practice

Mission Command, as practised today, means that Armed Forces apply a system of command and control at all levels that follows the same core principles. At its core it is simple, although here we start to tease out some of the finer, subtle aspects that help it work so well.

The Intent

The superior commander decides what he wants to achieve and why. The Aim to be achieved may be given to the superior commander by the Government or left to him to work out alone. He explains this to his subordinates, so that they know the mission and can grasp the purpose behind it. Together the mission and purpose constitute the Intent that will drive all planning and action. Defining this is generally the most important and creative contribution of the superior commander to the process of designing and implementing a winning plan. In expressing his Intent the commander must convey succinctly *what* the force must do to succeed, so that everybody knows what they have to focus on, and *why* it matters, so that everybody knows the purpose behind all action. This is generally for superior commanders to do personally – preferably face to face – rather than leave it to his staff. The superior commander does not, as a matter of principle, also now tell his subordinates in detail *how* to do their job.

> *'I suppose dozens of operation orders have gone out in my name, but I never, throughout the war, actually wrote one myself. I always had someone who could do that better than I could. One part of the order I did, however, draft myself – the intention. It is usually the shortest of all paragraphs, but it is always the most important, because it states – or it should – just what the commander intends to achieve. It is the one overriding expression of will by which every thing in the order and every action by every commander and soldier in the army must be dominated. It should, therefore, be worded by the commander, himself.'*
>
> FIELD MARSHAL SIR WILLIAM SLIM

The Concept

Having settled clearly on his Intent, the commander now sketches out his plan as a Concept. He will make clear what separate tasks need to be achieved, and how they fit together. Some of this will depend on what resources are available. This is akin to the concept of 'strategic fit' in business. Usually, not everything can be accomplished at once within the means at his disposal, so some tasks are deliberately planned to be done concurrently and some will equally need to be done sequentially. In outlining how his plan works the commander carries out the following:

Thinking 'Two Levels Down'

When spelling out the Concept and deciding on the missions for his subordinates, the commander will consider the essentials of the plan two levels down. A division commander will decide what his three brigades should be able to accomplish with the three or four battlegroups they have within each brigade. This constitutes a broad feasibility check, to ensure that subordinates are not being given an impossible task for the resources they have been allocated. This doesn't mean that the task will necessarily be easy: it may even be highly dangerous and unpleasant, but it will be *possible*.

Isolating the Main Effort

In describing his Intent, the commander will also designate a Main Effort – the most important task for achieving success, around which everything else will pivot. It is this that will attract a proportionately greater share of resources such as additional firepower or engineer support, and which subordinates know they must support if in any doubt about what to do. The Main Effort can change as a battle progresses, but it needs always to be clearly understood.

Giving the Missions

Missions are invariably a statement of *what* is required to be done (the task) and *why* (the purpose) and are based on the Intent and the Concept. The Missions do not tell the subordinate *how* they are to be achieved; that is left to them to work out within the resources allocated. These Missions are the basis on which the subordinates now go on to make their own plans, framing in turn their own Intent, Concept and Missions to their subordinates.

Thinking 'Two Levels Up'

Each level of subordinate commander will be aware of the Intent two levels above. A battalion commander will know what his brigade and then divisional commander above him require. By knowing the overall context in which his role is cast, he can make sensible decisions in the heat of the moment when it is not possible to refer upwards for guidance or direction. He will use his judgement and initiative to modify the plan as the situation requires in accordance with his understanding of the Intent, communicating what he is doing as soon as he can. By knowing the *purpose* behind the task, a subordinate can act intelligently and decisively in the heat of battle when the situation changes. Because he knows why he is required to do something he is well placed to work out how to evolve the plan as it unfolds in response to enemy interference.

Dialogue and Back-briefing

Mission Command is not just a question of a commander issuing an Intent, a Concept, and some well-crafted Missions to subordinates, before adjourning to the nearest hotel and awaiting news of victory. Where this has occurred, Mission Command has become cynically referred to as 'decide, delegate and disappear'. There will be an expectation that once a commander has issued his instructions he will begin a process of discussion and back-briefing with his subordinates. This is a two-way process: subordinates can ask questions, bid for more or different resources and clarify points of co-ordination w.. neighbouring units.

By being briefed on how the subordinate has elected to fulfil his mission the commander can be confident that his intent has been understood and his plan will be supported by well-thought through actions. If he is not satisfied, he can suggest a better plan – or if necessary remove a subordinate who is not up to the job. Of course, at the end of the debate, a subordinate must be left in no doubt about the conclusion – even if he doesn't like it. By using this part of the process in a disciplined way, you can be sure that a mission, a project, a plan is seen the same way by everyone on the team and that every member understands their role in it.

Mission Command and Delegation and Empowerment in Business

Many businesses have a system of delegation and empowerment: some well thought through and some that are little more than slogans. The system applied by the Armed Forces can be applied to virtually any setting and offers the following advantages:

- It applies at all levels in an organisation, so leaders at every point understand their contribution and that of others. It creates an 'auditable' chain of integrated direction and decisions.
- As leaders recognise what they are being told to do from above and think 'two down' below them, all missions and tasks complement each other and are matched by resources.
- At each stage, leaders should make clear to their subordinates how much freedom they have within the general principles of Mission Command. This can be tempered by things like expe-rience and the need to synchronise effort across different parts

of the organisation. The key point is that subordinates must be given the maximum degree of freedom possible to deliver the desired outcomes, and they must be clear about any 'red lines' that may need to limit this. Clarity and confidence will result.

Mission Command and Modern Communications

We said at the start of this Secret that it was the challenge of commanding battles beyond the vision and capacity of one leader to control that promoted the ideas that grew into today's Mission Command. Do modern communications mean that the requirement for such distributed control has lessened?

The Long Screwdriver

Nowadays, it is possible for a General sitting in his capital city to observe a battlefield thousands of miles away through satellite and other aerial imagery, and to talk to any commander on the ground, in the air, or at sea at the touch of a button. The capacity of modern data communications to acquire, store and move vast amounts of information makes it possible for the most senior US Air Force General to know up-to-the-minute details of all aircraft serviceability and activities around the world. Does this mean we can do away with subordinate commanders, leaving the Generals to run warfare directly from their offices to the man in the trench, in the cockpit, or on the bridge?

In our view, the answer is not straightforward – but there are great risks in using effective modern communications as a reason for undermining the empowerment offered by Mission Command. There may well be scope for 'de-layering' command structures where a tier of commanders and their staff officers does not add much value to the process of conducting and supporting effective operations.

In our view, the power of modern communications can substantially reinforce the strengths of Mission Command, making the system more effective through better transmission of information to the point of greatest need. Communications can certainly end up being used to undermine Mission Command in action, but it seems highly unlikely that this can be construed as a step forward.

BUILD YOUR ARMOURY
Mission Command

Some tips for Business Generals on implementing the Mission Command approach:

▷ Leaders have vision, they know what they want to achieve and why: their Intent. As a Business General, work on the way you communicate what you want to achieve and why – write it down, or tape record it and ask people to play it back to see what they took in; play the tape back to yourself.

▷ Leaders must articulate their Intent in a way that ensures others can understand it. As a Business General, go out and test how your previous messages of intent have been heard and remembered. Use that as feedback to frame your next message. Make sure it isn't dull – you need to excite them.

▷ Frame the outline Concept of how you will achieve your Intent clearly and concisely. How well do teams in your organisation know the concept and the Intent behind it, two levels up and two levels down? Install this as a process and watch how effective it is.

▷ Allocate well-defined Missions to your subordinates. Each should comprise a task and its purpose, and should be matched by an allocation of adequate resources and a

clear understanding of the boundaries where they have freedom
to act.

▷ Gain the confidence, experience and judgement to know
what/when to delegate. Where can you find that guidance –
perhaps through a mentor? Use key performance goals and
monitor closely – stay close to the detail and make sure they are
back-briefing you with updates.

▷ Listen carefully to your subordinates' views – and challenge
them on what they are *not* saying. You will need to show the
self-confidence and humility to trust and respect their views.
Be prepared to modify plans where this is required.

▷ Watch carefully for how people follow your instructions.
Good followers trust the judgement of good leaders, respect
them and expect to follow their instructions fully and
honestly.

▷ Ensure that there are no negative repercussions for anyone
having the courage to take calculated risks and 'doing it in their
way'. Think of Nelson. Help people to keep focused and
committed through the bad times. Encourage initiative when
faced with the unexpected.

▷ Ask, check and organise the right training and assessment
to give them a chance of being competent. Ask them what
equipment they need to do what they are being asked to do.

▷ Take a hard look at your team. Are they motivated, reliable,
resilient and committed? How can you, as their leader, get
them there? What are you doing to manage the confidence of
the team?

▷ Encourage staff to take responsibility and work out for
themselves how their tasks will be accomplished. Make sure
they look for lessons to be learned in the actions they take and
how they turn out.

▷ Build a process where all parties find, circulate, access and use all the relevant information available for their task. Check this happens as a matter of course and doesn't stop the minute you take your eye off the process.

▷ Analyse where risk is managed. This works best in Mission Command if risk is shared by leaders at every level, rather than allowed to drift downwards through an organisation.

▷ Even in the midst of action – celebrate successes. Don't rush it. The Japanese know how to wrap and present a gift. Do not underestimate the value of a ritual gathering to praise, of a gentle gesture of appreciation, of medals, certificates, awards.

▷ When building and developing your team, identify those people who can thrive on the scope for independent, well-coordinated action needed to make delegation and empowerment work. The first step is to be sure your people know what is expected of them in this regard, and then train them in the techniques. You will soon see who has the potential to exploit the system to achieve brilliant results, and who cannot advance beyond being told what to do in detail (see the section on training that follows).

Training for Mission Command

For Mission Command to work it requires that every level of command is trained in it. There must be a common and intuitive understanding of how the theory works and how to do it in practice.

In the Armed Forces this is achieved by training individuals first and then by training collectively as formed units. This 'collective training' rarely happens in business, as different levels of hierarchy prefer to train with their own. To follow the military example would mean that individuals on the board would learn first, then from each level *and then, each business division, unit, and department would go again – as a collective group.*

For example, an officer recruit at the UK's Royal Military Academy Sandhurst will be schooled in the basic tenets of Mission Command, and Brigadiers some 20 years ahead of them will receive more advanced training relevant to their enhanced command responsibilities. An armoured brigade will train all its commanders to employ Mission Command in its training programme, beginning at the lowest level and culminating in the Brigade Headquarters itself being put through its paces.

Part of this training is about accepting that there will be failures as a result of inexperience and misjudgement. It is vital that commanders do not instil a 'no-failure' approach amongst their subordinates, otherwise they will become risk-averse even in peacetime.

Some disasters may be necessary in training in order to improve the judgement, confidence and resilience of commanders in war. Even when committed to operations, it is wise to 'blood' new commanders and their forces with easy tasks first, where possible. This bridges the gap between what is possible in training and the full horrors of the battlefield, without shattering confidence or breaking inexperienced units.

How Confident Are You in the Team?

For a leader to delegate a task to a subordinate implies a reasonable degree of trust between them. That leader must have confidence in a subordinate's ability to understand what is required, to make a sound plan in accordance with this, to deliver it in execution and to provide honest feedback. This includes the vital ability to make the right decisions under pressure, to seize the initiative without reference when a fleeting opportunity presents itself and – just as important – to accept it when the current task is not the most important or glamorous. The commander must be confident that a subordinate will not use the independence offered to duck difficult responsibilities. How confident are you of your team's ability to understand, plan, execute the plan and give honest feedback? What are you doing to manage the confidence of the team? What more could you be doing?

What are People not Telling You?

For a commander and subordinates to make good decisions they need the best information they can get. This requires a systematic and thorough approach to creating good 'situational awareness', which includes: a picture of the enemy's intentions, strength and capabilities; knowledge about the environment in which the conflict will be fought (terrain, climate, routes); and information about own capabilities (equipment repair states, ammunition holdings and so forth). It is important that this information flows freely between levels of command, otherwise commanders will operate from different assumptions about the challenges that they face. It is just as important that nobody expects to receive perfect information at any stage. Waiting for complete knowledge before acting is usually handing the opponent the initiative: the trick for commanders is to know when they have enough information with sufficient confidence to make a decision and act – and to do so faster and more flexibly than their opponent.

Managing Risk

Risk in the military is managed by considering the following criteria:

- **Initiative**. What offers are you blocking, what initiatives are you not seizing? Think of your biggest challenge at the moment: what would be a creative response? Commanders are expected to use all their powers of initiative when planning their battle and in commanding forces once fighting has started. Mission Command empowers subordinates to find the most innovative, creative and devastating solution to achieving the effect required of them. (The advantages of employing Secret Number Four: Dynamic Manoeuvre in this context are obvious.) Having the best-conceived plan at each level reduces the risk of failure from the outset.

- **Resources**. Are you using the best of what you have in front of you? You can't always go running for more of this or that – what are you not using that is already in front of you? There will never be enough resources to meet every possible requirement. It will rarely be possible to be strong everywhere. Commanders must manage the risks this will inevitably present by making the best use of what they have. This where a full understanding of 'Right Team, Right Stuff' (Secret Number Three) comes into play, and all the conceptual tools described in Secret Number One, Synchronised Thinking, become vital aids to making good decisions, in particular by.

- **Concentrating Force.** What power are you employing? Is that the right form of power? Where else could you use your power, your knowledge, your skills? Forces need to be concentrated at the decisive place and time – rather than dribbling effort everywhere to no great result.

- **Using Economy of Effort.** Where are you putting your effort? Is that the right place? Effort is conserved at times and places where the risks of having less strength can be managed, so that decisive strength can be concentrated elsewhere.

- **Sequencing**. Have you thought smart enough about putting one thing before the other, instead of trying to offer everything? Resources can be applied concurrently, in priority order or in turn to activities – rather than spread too thinly around too many things at once.

- **Maintaining a Reserve.** What reserves do you have? If your main person or piece of kit did not work, what back-up have you? A reserve of resources is essential so that the unexpected can be dealt with, successful enemy actions overcome and the effect of just plain bad luck dealt with.

- **Coordination**. Have you a proper presence? Are you face to face with the people on the ground? How well are you co-ordinating efforts and focusing attention? Once a commander has his instructions in accordance with Mission Command, he is not usually simply cast off and told to report back when he is having a victory breakfast in the enemy's camp. The activities of subordinate commanders will require some element of coordination. For an army, this might mean managing the movement of thousands of vehicles from different units along congested routes whilst being defended against enemy air attack. Once battle has been joined it will be essential that reports on progress are regularly provided up and down the chain of command, so that various activities remain synchronised even when the enemy interferes. It is no good if one brigade in a division-sized attack forges so far ahead that it offers vulnerable flanks for an enemy counter-attack. So successful execution of Mission Command will still require coordination by the superior HQ, which will inevitably result in some freedoms and constraints being applied to the actions of subordinates. It is a question of balance.

MISSION MANAGEMENT

Having reviewed the idea of Mission Command in contemporary military thought, the next step is to translate it into wider use in almost any organisation of more than two people as 'Mission Management'. This is not new to the commercial world; the core ideas have been expounded already by some companies. What we wish to show here is not just what Mission Management means but also how it can be used to best effect as part of the complete Business General package. If you draw on the organisational thinking in the 'Power Pyramid' (Secrets One, Two and Three) and apply Secret Number Four: Dynamic Manoeuvre with the freedoms of Secret Number Five: Mission Management, you will be well placed for success. This systemic approach will be developed further in the final two Secrets.

In business, Mission Management means:

- Specifying the corporate Intent and Concept at board level.
- Giving mission statements for subordinate divisions/business units.
- Cascading Mission Management to all levels.
- Empowering subordinates to decide how to achieve their tasks.
- Implementing a Discussion and Review Cycle.

At board level, there must be clarity about what the organisation is going to achieve and why. This clarity should be the result of the work done to arrive at a corporate strategy: settling on a strategy should mean there is no doubt about the goals of the organisation, why they matter and why they have been chosen in preference to others. (We look more at strategy in Secret Number Six). This is more than a general 'vision' statement;

nobody will argue against the dream that the company is going to be 'the most profitable, happiest and environmentally aware producer of things in history'. That is all ambitious, laudable and hard to argue with, but also free of any sense of substance or articulation of how it will be done.

The definition of what the organisation is going to do and why is called the Intent and should be supplemented by the broad outline of the route to be taken to achieving it (this is called the Concept). These need not be in the same statement, sometimes the Intent can be spelt out separately from the Concept, but it is usually clearer and more succinct to put them together. In setting out what specific major actions are to be taken to deliver the results they want, the board must designate the most vital activity – the corporate Main Effort – to which the lion's share of resources will go if hard spending decisions have to be taken. Taken together, the Intent, Concept and designation of Main Effort give staff at every level the big picture on where they will be going, why, and the general idea of the way. As an example:

Midshire Motor Manufacturers will become the largest European manufacturer of large family cars through developing and selling innovative and attractive new models at competitive prices for the domestic and European markets, and by establishing additional manufacturing capacity in the small commercial vans sector. Investment in new plant and processes, aggressive marketing and new distribution arrangements will contribute to improving market share. As market share increases, profits and share price will be expected to rise, thereby securing future investment and improved return to shareholders. The Main Effort is selling new large family cars in Europe.'

Mission Statements

The Intent and Concept will be supplemented by Mission Statements given to each subordinate element in the organisation. In the case of 'Midshire Motor Manufacturers', if it had three Divisions (Family Cars, Vans, and Corporate Services) each of these would receive its own Mission Statement from the board. The Mission Statement should include the task (the *what*) and the purpose (the *why*). For example:

> *'The Family Cars Division will develop and sell innovative and attractive large family cars at competitive prices for the Domestic and European Markets in order to increase market share and so drive up profits and the share price, securing future investment and improved return to shareholders.'*

For larger and more complex organisations, these Mission Statements can be followed up by a list of specific targets or objectives that must be achieved. These specific objectives can be wide ranging – spanning, say, the requirement to conform to a corporate governance regime, to specific figures for increasing sales and gross revenue, or reducing costs. These can be the same objectives that then feature in individual objectives and appraisals, making collective success synonymous with an individual's success. In so doing, however, it is important to keep to a minimum the degree of constraint on the freedom of action of the recipient. The value in Mission Management lies in giving a subordinate the requirement he must fulfil, and the reasoning behind it, and allowing him the maximum freedom of action in how to deliver the desired result.

It also follows that the Mission Statement is achievable – you do not want the recipient self-destructing with anxiety when presented with it. As described under Mission Command, the Mission must be handed down with enough trust, resources and information, and a suitable co-ordination mechanism to make it work in practice.

Corporate Mission Statements, many of which may include the organisation's statement of its values, can be used more generally to: focus the minds of the people on the overall aim; to remind people of the way in which the organisation wants to go about its business; and as a motivational tool for everyone. They can also be used as an excuse, if one was needed, to have a dialogue about behaviours – plenty of people, men in particular, are uncomfortable talking about relationships and specific behaviour and a mission/value statement gives them a device to do so. Certainly those that use Mission Statements to assert their leadership on the inner workings of the organisation find them useful. For those cynics who think that Mission Statements are merely for external image building, and do nothing with them other than hang them up and then scoff at their futility:

- A study in 2001 of 83 large US and Canadian firms showed that Mission Statements do positively affect financial performance when the statements are matched by a strong commitment to aligning activities to them.
- A survey in 2002 covering the UK, Scandinavia, Africa, and New Zealand found that over 80 per cent of firms had Mission Statements, but only 40 per cent of their managers believed they represented reality because much of it was seen to be PR. The real pressure was to be on target to cut costs, meet sales targets. Customer service aims usually played second fiddle.

Mission Statements should not deter firms from being nimble, agile and able to grow through trial and error. They are not obstacles on the road to success, but are there to be tuned, to be dynamic, to change with new information on the environment as you learn more about your organisation's internal strengths/ weaknesses.

Cascade Mission Management to All Levels

The process that we have described between the board and its principal divisions is replicated down through each division. The leadership of 'Family Cars' will take the Mission Statement provided to it as the start point for writing their own Intent and Concept for the division, which articulates simply and clearly to the whole division what is to be done and why. Similarly, there will be separate divisions or units within 'Family Cars' that each requires its own Mission Statement. This process cascades down through the organisation to the lowest point where it makes sense to do so.

As the process continues downwards the Mission Statement should be expected to become shorter and simpler, to reflect the nature of the work being done – but no one should lose sight of the purpose to which they are contributing. This means that leaders at even the lowest level of management and their teams can see how their work contributes to overall success. It is highly likely that the 'purpose' elements of a Mission Statement (the *why*) will be the same for each element within a Division and so provide an overarching unity, although the tasks will certainly vary. As a check, it should be possible for the CEO of the company to look at the Mission Statements for a unit like research and development or an assembly line and see how they conform to the overall corporate Intent.

Empowered Subordinates Decide How to Achieve their Tasks

The process of cascading missions down to the lowest practical level sets the scene for genuine empowerment. Those in receipt of a Mission Statement know what they have to do and why, and have the trust placed in them to find the best way of doing it with the resources given to them. If they succeed, they will expect to be rewarded. If they fail, they may need more training, more help or replacing. We should expect new or inexperienced leaders to take a little time to find their feet, just as we expect start-up businesses to take a little time to turn a profit.

In the environment of Mission Management we recommend that Business Generals set the conditions for empowering their subordinates:

- Take stock of their organisational capabilities by using the Power Pyramid as a model. This will give them an accurate idea of the relative strengths and weaknesses they have to play with. For example, do they have the right ideas to follow and are they applied consistently across the firm? Is the workforce well motivated and engaged – or does this need attention before the will exists to start a new and demanding period? Are the right skills, the right equipment and the right training regimes in place to turn brilliant ideas into successful goods and services? In other words, the leader should be clear about the organisational power available to him before he embarks on his Mission, and then make the improvements and modifications he needs to get the overall fit right between Mission and organisation.

- In identifying the best way of achieving the Mission with the organisation available, the leader should apply Secret Number Four: Dynamic Manoeuvre. Instead of settling for doing more of the same a bit better, the leader should exploit the trust and scope for initiative placed in him or her to find novel solutions. This is where the leader's creativity and will to succeed can be given full rein. The leaders above, recognising the potential value in Dynamic Manoeuvre, should not only offer encouragement to push out the boundaries but also be prepared to share any risks that this may incur.

Implement a Discussion and Review Cycle

Having issued an Intent, a Concept and Mission Statements, the board should not just head for the golf course and await good news. Nor should management at any level settle for despatching cleverly phrased statements as a substitute for effective leadership. Bold words are the start of a management process – not the end. Board members and the leadership below them should maintain regular personal contact, to ensure that the Intent, Concept and Missions are well understood and to hear how the target will be met in outline.

It is during these discussions that senior leaders will be able to see who is winning and who is losing, who are the movers and shakers, and where can the lessons learned from past experience help to head off an unnecessary mistake. This dialogue helps to build a relationship of mutual trust and confidence, which reinforces the ability of the complete organisation to pull together and encourages people to take the well-managed risks necessary for success. Where it is not working, it is often because of people's inability to communicate well, or their lack of discipline around the process, or people hanging onto power and controlling the work of others too tightly. In such cases, work needs to be done to help these people realise that this isn't going to go away; it is being monitored and helping them see the benefits (and penalties).

There needs to be a formal process of reporting and record-ing progress. Most organisations have systems for gathering and analysing data – particularly financial information – and for bring-ing leaderships together to examine progress. If the Mission Statements are used as the starting point for these discussions, the ensuing dialogue should be well focused and structured in such a way that it is clear how well or otherwise different elements of the firm are contributing to overall success, to meeting the Intent.

Whatever form of discussion or review is established, it is important that they are not used as a back-door route to under-mining the freedoms given to subordinates through Mission Management. Unless a leader is clearly failing, he or she should not be hedged in with compulsory guidance on *how* to meet his or her tasks. Constraints should be limited to the realities of changes in the flow of resources and any key co-ordination meas-ures necessary to synchronise the operation of the organisation as a whole. These will generally be unpopular, especially where a leader is forging ahead of peers and has to be reined back, but senior leadership has to manage overall success as well as encour-age subordinates to be the best they can.

To conclude this Secret, here are some more details to refer to on how to apply the idea of Mission Management. We now move on to look in more detail at the art and science of strategy and planning.

BUILD YOUR ARMOURY
Mission Management

Some tips for Business Generals on 'mission management':

▷ Develop and exercise your emotional intelligence. You need to know your capabilities as a person accurately and honestly and be able to control yourself in all conditions – otherwise you will struggle to lead or manage others in a complex mission.

▷ Work on understanding your personal drivers, your skills, and the effects you have on others, both by design and by accident. Ask yourself why you want to be a leader? Why a Business General? Ask yourself, why should others follow you? The answers should be inspiring to followers!

▷ Develop yourself in a planned way. Go on courses that take you out of your comfort zone, that expand you, and develop you.

▷ Seek and act on honest feedback about you from superiors, subordinates, friends and family.

▷ Get the basic conditions right before launching on a mission using the Power Pyramid. Make a frank assessment of your organisation's capacity for Synchronised Thinking (Secret Number One). Is there a common conceptual approach and understanding to the basic principles of the business, and do people analyse the challenge in a structured way that everyone else can follow? Is there a mechanism for encouraging and rewarding creativity and innovation, as well as sustained hard work? What training is needed to put the way the staff think on a higher plane? In particular, if you are going to apply Mission Management, is the concept well articulated and understood throughout the organisation?

▷ Assess the organisation's 'soul' (Secret Number Two). Are your people motivated, committed, energetic, resilient and reliable? Are the leaders trusted and believed in – do they have genuinely engaged followers or are people coming along just to pay the bills? If there is a shortfall here, how can it be put right?

▷ Assess the organisation's Right Team, Right Stuff (Secret Number Three). Do you have the right people in the right jobs? Have they been given enough training to be trusted? Is the necessary equipment and infrastructure in place, do the office systems work, are the logistics sharp and can people communicate? If not, what do you need to do about it?

▷ Work out your intent and concept. Once you have formed a clear idea of your organisation using the Power Pyramid, you can take a realistic view of what can be accomplished and how to fine tune the organisation to work to optimum effect. A new direction may need new people, more training, fresh investment funds and so forth. The organisation's process for working out a corporate strategy should now be allowed to make clear what options are open to the board. (We go into strategy in Secret Number Six, see page 291) There are bound to be hard choices to be made, but it is up to the board to decide what the goal of the organisation is, why it has been selected, and the route – or strategy for getting there. These are then enshrined in the Intent and Concept.

▷ Be certain that the strategy process is as fully informed, open and well considered as possible. The Intent and Concept are so vital to success that this stage cannot be fudged or ambushed by prejudices.

▷ Make sure the most senior leaders in the organisation have had a personal hand in agreeing the Intent. Ideally, they have written it themselves. This means they are in full agreement with it. It is then not something that can be easily disowned when the going gets tough. Modifications should be just as well thought through and personalised.

▷ Communicate the Intent and Concept. There is no point having a brilliant set of well-conceived and coherent ideas if they are kept secret from the people who must put them into action. Once you are clear about your Intent and Concept, about where you are heading and why it is important, valuable and worthwhile, it has to be communicated effectively. The message must reach a range of audiences: staff, shareholders, sources of finance, the media, and perhaps even Government. Messages will also naturally be targeted at the competition, and this requires especially careful thought.

▷ Communication by leaders must be genuine and convincing. This helps people to identify in their own way how they can contribute to the Mission in a fully effective and engaged manner. The *what* and *why* need to be clear and understood by all parties receiving it.

▷ Prepare yourself to deliver your messages about the what and why. Use a variety of situations and give speeches lasting, say, one minute, 10 minutes and 20 minutes.

▷ Practise your delivery with a tape-recorder and a video. Hone the impact and be as succinct as you can.

▷ Be aware of the effect your words will have. Think about their impact on internal audiences two levels up and two levels down. Check it is consistent and feasible. Be prepared to overcome cynicism and objection – especially where change is implied. Do staff have the resources? Will they be overwhelmed? Is it challenging enough (could they do more)? Will they be under-utilised?

▷ Deliver your key messages, especially the Intent, face to face. Do not use proxies or electronic media if it can be avoided.

▷ Check back. Make sure people have formed the correct understanding of what is required of them.

▷ Monitor the cascade process of Mission Management as it flows through the organisation. Make sure that what emerges from the lowest levels reflects the Intent at board level.

▷ Maintain a two-way street. Create tight feedback cycles between the thinking, the strategy and the action. This will allow your organisation to achieve success in a variety of situations, however novel. Create a process whereby subordinates can ask questions freely and keep leaders informed about how they will accomplish their Mission in theory and what progress they are making in practice. The person who has given the Intent needs to be on top of activities that will deliver it.

▷ Monitor progress. Each level of manager or leader who has issued Mission Statements around the Intent must be aware of progress – or lack of it – two levels up and two levels down. They must be constantly on the ball to know this information at all times.

▷ Keep questioning. Everyone given a Mission should ask themselves: What are our intended results and how will we be measured? What challenges might we face and overcome? What are we assuming? What have we learned from similar situations? How can we take that learning to be successful this time?

This will allow leaders to:

▷ Re-allocate resources and co-ordinate efforts.

▷ Encourage and offer retraining/coaching if people fail.

▷ Be decisive about bringing in new people if failure persists in those who have been given training/guidance.

▷ Build the lessons back into the strategy and the plan, so avoiding future failure and ensuring that the organisation is keeping ahead of events.

Summary of Secret Number Five: Mission Management

- This Secret looks at how best to delegate responsibility to others, without becoming detached from the key decision-making process yourself.
- It is about empowering your people in ways that allow them to make full use of their skills, ideas and energy and to act on their initiative without fear of recrimination.

- This Secret draws on the system known as Mission Command used in the Armed Forces, that enables people to be well informed and have the right level and flow of information to make sound decisions.

- At the heart of Mission Command are the Intent (the Mission and its purpose) and the Concept (an outline of how the Intent will be carried out). These establish the overall guidelines within which subordinates can freely move.

- Mission Command also explains how concentration of force and economy of effort can be combined to make best use of available resources.

- When applied to the business world, Mission Command becomes Mission Management.

Next Secret...

Once the framework is in place to delegate responsibility and empower the staff, the Business General is free to Command the Campaign – the subject of Secret Number Six.

Secret Six
Command the Campaign
The art and science of successful strategy

*'The victorious strategist only seeks battle after the
victory has been won, whereas he who is destined to
defeat first fights and afterwards looks for victory.'*
SUN TZU, THE ART OF WAR

*'Grand strategy must always remember
that peace follows war.'*
BASIL LIDDELL-HART

In this Secret, we will explain how the Business General
can take a new look at strategy. We offer the tools of
Operational Art and Campaign Planning, including Ways, Ends
and Means, Endstate, Operational Pause, Branches and
Sequels, Lines of Activity, and Decisive and Culminating
Points. These are the links between the big idea that comes
from the directors and the detailed activity on the shop floor
and in the marketplace. In our view, this ability – a blend of art
and science – to think through how an organisation will achieve
all its objectives by combining complex activities into a single
campaign plan, can make the difference between achieving an

exhilarating take-off to brilliant success and collapsing into miserable failure.

What's the Point?

Strategy is one of the most over-used words in all types of organisation, pasted liberally over almost all aspects of thinking and planning. Its use ranges from the upper reaches of complex corporate strategy in global companies, to 'strategies' for reducing paper consumption in a single office. Such an imprecise definition is really not helpful in separating out the important types of planning activities that should occur at different levels of thinking in any organisation, from world player in global business to a self-employed sole trader.

The military have wrestled with this problem for centuries, and done so throughout seismic changes in politics, culture, economics and technology – and many other dynamics that affect how force can be threatened or applied. When armies and navies were commanded in battle by a single general or admiral, who personally controlled all the fighting, strategic options were usually more clear-cut.

The leadership of one state would decide that having looked around the world they had identified the need to improve their security and their prospects for being richer (the Objective). Their strategy to do this was to invade their neighbours, so preventing them from being a security risk – as well as to seize their lands. How the general then marched over the border and actually slaughtered the army of the unfortunate state next door was a matter of tactics: the drills skilfully and bravely performed by soldiers and sailors to beat their opponents and so win their slice of the loot.

Modern Strategy

Modern times are more complicated. The world has changed; nations now have a far more global perspective of how their security, politics, economy and culture are interdependent and how much their future depends on co-operation or confrontation with other states. Wars have been fought over vast distances, with battles taking place simultaneously on land, sea and in the air. We saw in Secret Number Five that this expansion in distance and complexity has led to the idea of Mission Command, where commanders are told what result to deliver and then let loose to work out how to achieve it with the resources put at their disposal.

Working out a strategy that will lay out what a state should achieve to stay ahead in these high-tempo, fluid and increasingly interdependent times is an immense problem. Turning those strategic decisions into action is also no easy task. Many critical factors will keep changing beyond the control of any one state or person, so the objectives and the ways of achieving them will also need to be modified. It is very attractive and reassuring to think that in business or in war we can just pause to work out a comprehensive plan and then implement it while all the variables that affect it stand still. In practice, we have to be able to plan and implement with many aspects outside our control and constantly on the move. For example, a CEO may decide that the route to stock market heaven for his firm is the acquisition of a competitor, but if the money and staff capacity does not exist to pull off the bid he is doomed to fail.

The point is that high-level strategy has to be conditioned not only by what *should* be done on the basis of the best analysis of the overall situation, but also by what *can* be done in practical terms. It can also be driven by the necessity of dealing with what others are trying to do to you: business and military affairs are not like shadow boxing – opponents may strike first and draw blood.

Matching Capability and Strategy

In the short term, the strength of low-level capabilities can be a significant brake on what strategic actions can be contemplated, but in the longer term capabilities can be developed specifically to meet the objectives of a well-defined strategy. This is clearly seen today in the remodelling of many western Armed Forces away from the large tank armies built to fight on mainland Europe during the Cold War up to 1989 and towards lighter, more flexible forces able to deploy rapidly around the globe in the early twenty-first century.

It is hard to be clear about what the future will really need, and it is expensive and painful to change organisations, equipment and tactics, but standing still is not an option. A balance has always to be struck between what we would like to be able to do and what we actually can do. Where the need to change an organisation in order to pursue a particular strategy is identified, the leadership has to make those changes happen before setting off down the road. Good intentions alone don't win wars or takeovers. The Power Pyramid in Secrets One, Two and Three, drawn on the military approach to building fighting power, provides a coherent and readily usable way of establishing what organisational strengths and weaknesses exist in your organisation now, and how to identify what needs to be developed to shift the organisation into a condition where it can deliver the aims of evolving strategy.

LEVELS OF STRATEGY

'Strategy without tactics is the slowest route to victory.
Tactics without strategy is the noise before defeat.'
SUN TZU, THE ART OF WAR

It can be helpful to try to view the planning activities in any organisation as layers, as this can make the task more manageable. However, it is important to bear in mind that these layers are closely interconnected and so the distinctions between the layers are, to some degree, artificial. In Government, and in the Government's relationships with the Armed Forces, four broad levels of planning can usefully be adopted. Later on in this chapter we suggest how this could work for business.

Grand or 'National' Strategy

This refers to the level of strategy that applies to Governments and is the set of 'big ideas' that political parties put to the test at national elections. They need to work out the overall direction of the country, and how this is achieved through the main levers of national action: politics, diplomacy, economics, the military, overseas aid, social services, education, and many others. It is also about ensuring that the separate branches of government work together to achieve the overall aim.

Military Strategy

Based on the overall direction set by grand strategy, the Armed Forces must establish how they can play their part. This will be a compromise between what is theoretically achievable and what resources are actually available to make it possible. There may be many things that the Armed Forces could do to contribute to the aims of grand strategy, but they will be in competition with other avenues of Government spending, such as hospitals, schools and roads. Military strategy is the function of the Defence Ministry and is formed by discussion between politicians, civil servants and the heads of the Armed Forces.

> *'The military objective should be governed by the political*
> *objective subject to the basic condition that policy does not*
> *demand what is militarily impossible.'*
>
> BASIL LIDDELL-HART

The Operational Level

It is not usually practical to go straight from the decisions taken by heads of the Armed Forces to planning and leading the detail of an attack on a cave stronghold in Afghanistan. There is an exception to this, which is where the top level of Government at the highest level decides to use Special Forces to take action on a small scale that has obvious importance at the level of grand or Military strategy – such as assassinating the head of a terrorist organisation. But for the most part, there is a need to bridge between the Government's overall aims and the tactics used to achieve them. Try as they might, most politicians are not much use at commanding tank battles from their desks, and generals should stick to crushing enemy forces and not worrying about party politics. It is the senior military commanders actually leading the fighting in the theatre of operations that provide the bridge between strategy and action. They focus on creating and leading a plan of campaign that will result in the achievement of one or more of the aims of military strategy. This is about planning sequences of battles and other activities, not just fighting individual battles.

The Tactical Level

This is about the detailed business of fighting; it is the level at which battles are fought. The commander of an armoured brigade, of, say, 5,000 soldiers and 150 tanks and other armoured vehicles, focuses on how to win this battle and be ready for the next. This demands the orchestration of combat power to win as quickly as possible at least cost. The brigade commander's battle plan will be influenced by higher-level factors such as the need to safeguard power and water services and retain the support of the civilian population, but his core business is to manoeuvre his armoured forces supported by massed firepower to defeat his opponent's military forces. This is a long way from opinion polls and focus groups in capitals in order to agree what Grand Strategy should be.

It may be helpful to illustrate these levels and the link between them with a recent example, based on personal experience. The attack on the World Trade Center and the Pentagon on 11 September 2001 brought about a dramatic change in US Government strategy – the need to take action to secure the homeland. The question was how should this be tackled?

At the level of **grand strategy**, the US considered itself at war with terrorism at home and across the globe. This required measures to strengthen homeland security and to take action against terrorists and their supporters in their strongholds abroad. The **grand strategic** response included aspects of domestic politics, internal security measures, diplomacy, foreign aid and military action. US allies had similar considerations: was the threat directed at them, too, and should they play a part in the US response?

At the level of military strategy, the US began to focus its Armed Forces on identifying where specifically the terrorist threat originated and how best to deal with it. Strategists analysed the sources, potential and actual, of terrorism in the Middle East and Central Asia, and looked at military options such as attacking known targets with precision air-delivered weapons, Special Forces activity on the ground, and improving the training of the Armed Forces in countries deemed to be at risk from terrorist groups. This work also identified the requirement to take military action to unseat the Taliban, the fundamentalist Islamic regime, in power in Afghanistan. The Taliban were known to be harbouring the terrorist group responsible for organising the 11 September attacks.

To do this, a plan of campaign was required at the operational level. This plan had to establish how to defeat the Taliban forces and then establish a new Government. This Government would need to be secure and stable, and to prevent a recurrence of support for terrorism there would have to be progress in improving the dire economic and social conditions in a country shattered by 23 years of civil war and strife It would start with a combat group (in support of the Taliban's Afghan opponents such as the Northern Alliance) with the aim of ousting the Taliban forces, but there would soon be a need for an international peacekeeping force, training teams to build a new police force and army from scratch, and all this synchronised with wider UN-led political and aid efforts to rebuild the institutions of democratic government. The military operational-level plan was the prime responsibility of the US Central Command, supported by representatives from many nations contributing forces and co-ordinating at the highest levels of government and UN agencies.

At the tactical level, command on the ground was divided between two forces. US-led forces concentrated on the destruction of Taliban forces, first driving them from key locations such as the capital Kabul, then winkling out opposition from their networks of caves high in the mountains adjacent to the border with Pakistan. This required new thinking about the detailed conduct of air and ground operations. At much the same time, a UK-led peacekeeping force (the International Security Assistance Force (ISAF) was established in Kabul with troops from some 19 nations. Their task was to provide security to help the newly installed Interim Administration establish itself and allow the new democratic institutions to develop in accordance with the 2001 Bonn Agreement. The author found himself at Christmas 2001 sleeping on the floor of the old stables in the British Embassy compound in Kabul as Chief of Staff of HQ ISAF, laying the foundations for the deployment of a multinational force into an uncertain and challenging situation. The tactical challenge included deploying and sustaining the force by aircraft only (the nearest port was 1,000 miles away), with no local sources of power, water or buildings to call on in sub-zero temperatures, and in the face of very mixed public opinion in Afghanistan (and at home). These are challenges that can really only be addressed on the ground, not managed through a 3,000-mile-long screwdriver twiddled from capitals.

The Strategic Thread

This example illustrates the threads that run from grand strategy down to the tactical level. The logistic challenge of deploying and sustaining ISAF effectively capped the size of the force that could be deployed and increased political nervousness about the risks involved and how they might play on public opinion. The practicalities put a constraint on strategy. Yet the grand strategic imperative to win the war against terrorism meant that taking counsel of these fears and staying at home was not an option.

Although different levels of Government and military leaders took part in the debates at each level (the mix shifting from political dominance at the grand strategy level to military dominance at the tactical level), and the different levels have separate areas of responsibility, there has to be clear linkage between them. This 'strategic thread' applies equally strongly during the planning phase and – just as important – during the conduct of the operation. Military commanders operating under the tenets of Mission Command (see Secret Number Five, page 249) had considerable latitude, but knew well that they had to work within the overall direction of either grand and military strategy. For example, if the decision to launch a high-risk operation had resulted in unacceptably high levels of casualties, then public and political support might begin to evaporate.

An Inclusive Strategy

The example of Afghanistan brings out another key point: the need for strategy to embrace all the factors that will affect the outcome. Military commanders may do their best to create a sense of internal and external security, but this work is wasted if the means are not there to take advantage of the improved situation to build political, economic and social improvements. Real security is as much to do with repairing infrastructure, creating employment, getting schools reopened, improving health care and ensuring women have a full and active involvement in work, society and politics as it has to do with training new police officers and building a new Afghan National Army. Where these things do not occur, both crime and insurrection are inclined to follow – in Afghanistan's case, opium production is even greater since the fall of the Taliban, to the extent that 90 per cent of the heroin on the UK's streets now starts life in a remote Afghan field. This principle of the multiple strands being drawn together to produce a coherent and effective overall plan is one of the central themes to operational art and campaign planning.

COMMANDER'S COMFY CHAIR
Take Stock of Strategy

Take a few hours to think about the following. You might decide that it needs further work – over days/weeks.

What is your organisation's Grand Strategy?

If you asked others, would they say exactly the same?

Where does the 'operational level' sit in your organisation?

Who runs the 'tactical plan' in your team?

Do they know how what they do fits with the overall strategy?

Where is the business really placing its effort?

Does it fit with the strategy?

Where is the business putting too much focus?

Where is the business putting too little focus?

What are the repercussions of that, now and in the future?

What strikes you when comparing how you normally express your strategy with the format described here?

The Business Strategy Experience

There is no shortage of strategy in business. There are, of course, some small organisations that still operate day-to-day/month-to-month. But most businesses of any size have at least sketched out how they want to grow, develop or just stay in business. If we confine the idea of 'strategy' to the need to work out what an organisation should be doing, why it should be doing it and how it should set about it, there is an intuitive sense in most organisations that this really is important.

Literature on strategy ranges from generalist guides to the subject of strategy to very refined and specific methods for analysing and modelling particular sectors or activities. In the right hands these can all make a significant difference to the enduring success of a business or large public service organisation. A great deal of emphasis is, rightly, placed on strategy and strategic thinking in business courses such as a typical MBA. Critics of MBAs say the students do too many case studies, with insufficient information, and while looking for overarching patterns they miss the important details. These are the complexities that really exist – dealing with confusing, shifting, dynamic dramas. Most MBAs take a methodical and coherent approach to the subject of strategy, and include:

- **Starting with defining a 'corporate vision'.** This broadly aligns to the Intent described in Secret Number Five.
- **Doing an 'environmental scan'.** This can be in the form of a **SWOT** and includes detailed analysis of the firm's **S**trengths that need to be leveraged, the **W**eaknesses that need to be addressed, **O**pportunities that exist in the form of ideas/trends to exploit, and **T**hreats, in terms of forces outside of their control that need to be mitigated against plus any internal strife. Another useful process, known as **PEST**, is to examine the data in terms of the following factors: external **P**olitical (border controls, aid, funds, regulators), **E**conomic (exchange rates, rises in Indian and Chinese fortunes, pension crisis with people living longer), **S**ocial (ageing population in Europe and Japan, movement towards single householders) and **T**echnological (on-demand business, immediacy of transactions).

- **Supplementary industry analysis.** This involves using a structured analytical framework to establish data on entry barriers, suppliers, customers, substitute products and industry rivalry.
- **A definition of what the firm should achieve**. This is then refined as far as possible into measurable objectives, financial targets and the corporate responsibility targets allocated to individuals and departments.

Strategy Layers

In general terms, it is usual to distinguish between several layers of strategy in most medium- to large-scale businesses:

- **Corporate level.** The firm looks at director level to decide: what market they are in; what the market is looking for; how to capture the market; how different business units should be co-ordinated; how to develop synergies across business units; and how business units should be governed (that is, through direct corporate intervention – centralisation – or more autonomous decentralisation).
- **Business unit level.** A division, product line or profit centre will develop its own strategy. They are concerned with how to create sustained advantage over rivals, where to focus and differentiate; and how to anticipate and manage changes in demand/supply.
- **Functional or departmental level.** Within a business unit there will be functions and departments, each requiring their own strategy in order to contribute to overall success. This is the level at which business processes and the value chain are developed, always looking to maximise efficiencies.

Is Strategy Still Needed?

These layers will be familiar to many, yet there is some scepticism about whether conventional ideas about strategy work in the high-tempo and dynamic world of contemporary commerce. Twenty-five years ago, strategy was the 'big thing', but now some people ask if it really adds value. The argument is that as the competitive positioning of goods and services can be so transitory, all that is required is an inspired grasp of short-termism. If the world is rocketing around, maybe you can't plan longer than a year ahead and the key is to switch from one brief success to another, regardless of where it comes from?

A survey in 2005 by the Economist Intelligence Unit showed that many executives feel the hours spent on strategy result in little improvement in performance. On the other hand many studies that have looked at the long-term performance of firms have shown that strategic statements can improve performance – if they are communicated well, and well understood and fully aligned with activities.

Strategy is usually taken to mean taking the longer view – protecting the long-term positions of the current business – usually through scale or evolutionary product development. Is this still possible in an age of disruptive technologies that change the game overnight? What about the powerful effects of globalisation, the reliance on capital markets that demand quick and high share-holder returns and discriminate against longer-term projects, even those that offer potentially better returns? In fact, as the dynamics of the modern business world have changed, it means that the need for strategy is probably greater, not less.

In today's conditions, most businesses need to focus on achieving a level of operational excellence that will yield on-target profits (without which the top team know they will get moved on), and also sustain a process of continuous organisational transformation in order to create the capabilities required to win in the next round. Business leaders are looking for improved revenue and profitability through either breakthrough or a constant flow of incremental improvements in what is offered. They search for progress in how it is produced, distributed and to whom; for ways to reduce costs; and how to understand the value they give to each of their customer groups and how they can differentiate over their competitors' offerings.

It is also worth stressing that although most businesses and other organisations can claim to have a 'strategy', many are either badly articulated or not articulated enough, or not backed up with well-aligned resources. In some cases, the 'strategy' is simply a list of desirable outcomes unencumbered by any substance about the route, length or timescale of the journey. In other cases, the board has conceived an excellent strategy, only to neglect to tell anyone other than their immediate circle about it. This may sometimes be necessary in part to protect commercially sensitive information, but more often than not it is more to do with weak internal communications.

The CEO of a financial services firm came up with a clever and revolutionary plan. However, when the board and non-execs were interviewed, there was a huge disparity in what each member thought this plan meant. Many of the board did not understand the strategy and were too scared to say so, lest they bear the wrath of the CEO – who had thrown out 40 per cent of his board in two years. The consequence was that each member was working independently on those parts of the strategy they understood, or liked, or thought they would specifically be measured on. In effect, they were not all pulling in one direction together but hauling and tugging in as many directions as there were board members. Eager to achieve something, keen not to be showed up, they talked the key words in the strategy but actually did something else. This brings us to the heart of this Secret. While working in a complicated, high-tempo and pressurised environment you need to check that everyone understands the mission and is acting towards it. Obvious, but not done rigorously often enough.

Operational Art – The Business Case

We described the four broad levels of planning above: grand strategy, military strategy, operational level and tactical level. A Business General will know the grand strategy, from the tactical level even in a small business, but the distinction will be smaller than if running a global conglomerate with several large brands.

What is Operational Art in Business?

In every organisation, but most particularly large and complicated ones, it is essential that the activities of each department are well co-ordinated and synchronised. Each will contribute to the achievement of an overall strategic aim, and each will incur a cost. The task of the Business General is to blend all these together in the most effective and efficient way. This has to be planned as far out as possible and done well on a day-to-day basis. Operational art is about planning what the detailed objectives of each department should be and how their activities can be orchestrated to hit a common goal. It is about fighting a complete business campaign, rather than just an unplanned series of daily battles.

Operational art is the art and science of campaign planning. In business this usually sits at the level of business unit/director level and is the bridge between the overarching corporate strategy and the tactical level of daily office or factory activity.

The crisis in Kosovo provided a good illustration of operational art in action and can be broken down into the following essential points:

- The General responsible for NATO activities in Kosovo needed a campaign plan that would move in a well-considered and logical way to success.
- This involved working out what needed to be done to achieve success and in what order.
- It required the synchronisation of several 'lines of operation' or activities, such as political activity, intelligence, air power, ground forces, information operations, shipping, logistics and many civil activities (with the UN). It also involved engaging and maintaining the active support of several NATO nations and the countries bordering Serbia.
- These activities would change in importance and emphasis as the campaign unfolded. At the start air power was the major tool. Then ground forces became the decisive element (with air power in close support). Now, perhaps, it is the UN's political leadership that is pre-eminent.
- Each of these activities had its own leadership: the ground forces under a British general worked alongside air forces commanded by a US general. It was essential that all these elements were subordinated to a single NATO joint commander who was responsible for the overall campaign and its co-ordination. Had these elements each run their own autonomous war, or the forces provided by NATO countries tried to fight their own independent battles, the result would have been chaos and disaster.
- It had to be done in circumstances that were undoubtedly stressful and in which the opposition, an extremely agitated

Serbia, could inflict real damage on NATO's effectiveness and reputation. The plan had to survive contact with events, and be modified accordingly.

The key to all this was the 'operational art' of the single NATO joint commander on the ground, the man responsible for directing and fusing all these complicated activities through an imaginative, well-planned and well-led sequence based on a clear analysis of what had to be done.

Campaign Planning Tools

A Campaign Plan is led by the man or woman at the top – the creative spark cannot be delegated although much of the detail will be. This is the documented, authoritative plan explaining what the organisation is to do and broadly how it will do it. The Campaign Plan relies on the commander identifying what will be decisive in delivering the required results and what actions will be necessary to get there. This probably means taking some 'shaping' steps before closing on the decisive act itself. Aligned with the concept of Secret Number Five: Mission Management, the Campaign Plan will tell subordinates *what* they are to do, not *how* they are to do it, and allocate them the resources needed. It will make clear to subordinate and supporting organisations how their activities fit together. In the Armed Forces, for example, it will be clear to the logistics people how they need to support the sea, air and ground forces at each stage. In business it would show where research and development will lead marketing initially, and how finance would support both over time. This synchronisation and simultaneity is an essential part of Campaign Planning; it makes all parts of an organisation work together to create the greatest combined effect. It is about synergy.

Campaign Planning Tools help to structure analysis and provide a common framework within which large teams can contribute to a single solution. These tools help to lead to a Campaign Plan that sets out in a readily understandable way how various activities will contribute to overall success, and this becomes the point of origin for the detailed planning of each single activity. These tools have much in common with the project management systems commonly in use in many organisations. The added factor is that those carrying out the activities have the advantage of using Secret Number One: Synchronised Thinking, Secret Number Two: Soul Matters, providing strong psychological and motivational power, and Secret Number Three: Right Team, Right Stuff, ensuring the physical power that is up for the task. You can see how the blend of the Secrets we have described can make the difference and how they are interrelated: you can't steal parts from an engine and expect it to run like a dream.

Ownership – Make the Plan Yours

This Campaign Plan is not something that can be delegated for others to conjure up. It is driven by the senior commander personally. It is where all his experience, creativity, judgement and intuition are applied. This is his plan, not a train timetable. The commander is able to maximise his chances of success by creating a plan that attacks his opponent harder, faster, at more places, and in greater depth than he can handle. This is not about hoping to win by the smallest possible margin, it is about designing a crushing victory at least cost. The Campaign Plan becomes the medium through which the senior commander explains what he wants done, and why, to his subordinates and to his superiors. It has to be understood by other agencies such as the UN, as well as audiences in the Armed Forces. It is the starting point for discussions about the resources required to make it happen and is used as a yardstick against which to measure success. It could hardly be a more important document, and senior commanders regard it as a personal statement – if it fails, they fail.

> *'It is not genius which reveals to me suddenly and secretly*
> *what I should do in circumstances unexpected by others;*
> *it is thought and meditation.'*
>
> NAPOLEON BONAPARTE

Ends, Ways and Means – Winning at Least Cost

One of the first requirements of a successful leader is to establish and maintain equilibrium between what he wants to do and how he is going to do it. If they are not in rough balance, the result is either failure – the objective is not achieved – or success won at disproportionate cost. There is no point winning a stunning victory by using an entire army to crush a single enemy outpost if the result is that the army is then in the wrong place and worn out to fight the major battle needed next day.

The Business General considers the campaign in terms of Ends, Ways and Means. Make a point of carrying out a rough audit of your firm and its activities using the following framework. If the campaign seems to be in balance it should make for easier sleep. If it doesn't, investigate further and do something about it.

- Ends are the definition of the purpose, the objectives of the organisation and why they matter.
- Ways are the methods and options of achieving those objectives.
- Means are the resources available to make things happen and sustain forward action.

It is intuitively easy to judge whether these are roughly in balance, if you know your people, your market and your product/service. Before committing to a particular course of action, detailed work must be carried out to establish with accuracy and confidence that the Means (resources) exist to act in the Ways (methods) to achieve the required Ends (objective).

Endstate – Know Where You're Going

It follows from the concept of Ends, Ways and Means that before a plan can be constructed it is essential to be absolutely clear about what the precise objective is. Get the Endstate right and the rest will follow. The Endstate is the state of affairs that needs to be achieved at the end of a campaign. For the Armed Forces this is often possible only in very general terms at the start of a campaign. At this early stage the political climate, and the understanding of potential adversaries and their possible alternative courses of action are so vague it is not possible to have total certainty. This can be a bit disquieting. It is not easy to plan to invade another country (often a large-scale and complicated business at which the leadership gets one attempt) if the political level wishes to wait to the last minute to decide whether to do that or something else entirely.

Senior leaders should not be surprised by vacillation and mixed signals – it is a feature of higher-level command. This uncertainty means that there are bound to be contingencies and risks to be managed, but also opportunities to seize. So, leaders must settle on an Endstate against which to plan, and make this as clear as possible to their staff, but they must also expect the Endstate to evolve over time, and must ensure the Campaign Plan evolves with it.

There is a subtle difference between starting out with a hazy

Endstate and allowing it to firm up as events unfold, and setting off with a hazy Endstate because you haven't done your homework – and then simply keep moving the goal posts. The Endstate needs to be well communicated at all levels of an organisation. If it changes, the reason and rationale for this change needs to be equally well communicated. Changes need to be clearly seen as necessary if confidence in the leadership is not to be undermined.

Centre of Gravity – Getting to the Heart of the Matter

Business strategists offer a range of conceptual tools for getting to the root of a problem, understanding what is important and what is not. Approaches like SWOT analysis (Strengths, Weaknesses, Opportunities and Threats) have very wide utility. In the military domain, where it is vital to understand what will most likely lead to the collapse of the opponent, the idea of a Centre of Gravity (CoG) is employed. The NATO definition is:

> *'That characteristic, capability, or locality from which a nation, an alliance, a military force or other grouping derives its freedom of action, physical strength or will to fight.'*

Like many NATO definitions, this one was sweated out to find a form of words that was succinct, accurate and readily understandable to all NATO forces. It may lack a little humour or colour, but if you say CoG to a German officer he will know exactly what it means and probably be able to recite the definition. If you say CoG to a British officer he will know what you mean, in an approximate way, but would be astonished to be asked for the precise definition from memory. However, both officers will know how to use it as a planning tool.

The idea of a Centre of Gravity is most useful at levels of strategy and planning above the purely tactical. It is likely that different, related Centres will exist at each level of planning, and it is essential that the linkages are clearly understood. For a Government contemplating how to bring down the resistance of a neighbouring state, the CoG could be something tangible such as the control of the only water supply – but it will more likely be something intangible like popular support for the Government or the collective willpower of the Cabinet.

The CoG must be the most significant and decisive thing standing between you and the achievement of the Endstate. Think about that as a Business General. What is the most significant and decisive thing standing between you and the achievement of your Endstate? Collect opinions on this from a wide cross-section in the organisation. Once you have identified the CoG at the level of Grand Strategy then the next level down must conform by establishing how to attack it, and all operational-level activity will then be conducted with that in mind. So, if a global pharmaceutical company identified that the CoG at the strategic level was to overcome access barriers to their products to markets outside Europe, the subordinate operating divisions would look to overcome this by, for example, relocating production to the countries operating restrictions and so gain access from the inside.

To be successful in the military there is a clarity, a certainty, a cohesiveness of effort around the plan. How clear and certain are people around you about the levels of strategy, and the reasons behind it? How cohesive is the effort in your team, between teams, between units/countries?

Although the best commanders can often determine the CoG of an adversary through experience, intuition and with only a cursory study of the problem, there are structured ways to help identify it. Ask yourself 'What is it that makes my opponent powerful? What is in the way of my Endstate?' And then look for:

- **Critical Capabilities.** What are the strengths of the opposing forces that can be used to threaten or defeat you? And what are the constraints on your potential to achieving the Endstate? For example, what have your competitors got that gives them more profit, market share, ability to attract talent? Critical Capabilities could be your competitors' new promise to market, the authority of their point of view, their slice of market share or an employment package second to none.

- **Critical Requirements.** What do your opponents need to make their Critical Capabilities work effectively? Another way of looking at this would be the opposing forces that can be used to threaten you. If market share is their key capability, ask yourself what are their key requirements to maintain market share? This could be as tangible as road access, Broadband, supply of raw materials or as intangible as popularity, kudos, a key personality. You need to ask yourself how can you influence these.

- **Critical Vulnerabilities.** Where do your opponents lack a particular Critical Requirement (and thus a weakened set of Capabilities), or where is their Critical Requirement open to attack? Such things could be a service they do not provide, a market they were late getting into, key skill sets their people do not have, state-of-the-art equipment that is prone to failure.

Of course, just as we can look for the Centre of Gravity of an opponent, so must we identify our own CoG and protect it. This demands honest thinking by leaders about where the weaknesses exist in their own organisation and what needs to be done to remedy or protect them from attack. They can safely be assumed to be obvious to an adversary.

The idea of CoG is useful in business. In examining a market, it will be possible to fathom what it is that wins customers: is it novelty, reliability, style, variety, or something else? In launching a hostile take-over, it should be possible to work out what will make the receiving board crumble – what will break their will to resist the bid? In challenging the competition in a market or in a competitive bidding process, what is it that will make the others give way, or the customer roll your way? It is also important to apply all these rules to all aspects of the business, including key suppliers.

Your Competitor's CoG

You will also need to do this exercise from the perspective of your key competitors. Find out their Endstate. Look at the CoG of your business – the most decisive and significant thing in the way of achieving your Endstate – and ask your competitors how they might downgrade your Critical Capabilities, extinguish your Critical Requirements and attack your Critical Vulnerabilities. Make a list of other significant and decisive things in the way of achieving their Endstate – both external and internal – and ask the same questions.

Your Customer's CoG

Now do the exercise on your top three customers. Really get into your customers' shoes and do some added-value work. Discuss with them and define their Endstate (in the case of a business, their precise objective; in the case of consumers, their reasons for doing business with you). Look at their CoG – the most decisive and significant thing in the way of achieving their Endstate. (For a business, this could be a multitude of things. For consumers, all the things that might prevent them choosing and shopping with you.) Ask how others could downgrade their Critical Capabilities (take away their strengths, their buying power). Think through how their Critical Requirements could be extinguished (what do they need in order to do business or to buy from you and how could these be interrupted). Finally, assess their Critical Vulnerabilities and how they could be attacked.

Once the CoG is identified it becomes the focus of the Campaign Plan, all activity must be directed at achieving victory over the CoG, and the validity of anything that doesn't contribute to it must be questioned hard. Pause now to consider Campaign Planning in the context of your own organisation.

COMMANDER'S COMFY CHAIR
Finding Centres of Gravity

Look at your team's/organisation's 'centres of gravity' systematically. You might decide that it needs further work – over days/weeks.

What is the Endstate (your precise main objective)?
What are the Ends (objectives, and why they matter – make corresponding ones for all levels)?
What are the Ways (methods and options for achieving Ends)?
What are the Means (all the resources available to you)?
What is your Centre of Gravity (CoG, the most significant and decisive thing standing in the way of Endstate)?
What are your Critical Capabilities (best assets/strengths/skills)?

What are your Critical Requirements (what you need in order to deliver)?

What are your Critical Vulnerabilities (skill or resource shortages or potential blocks)?

What are the DPs (Decisive Points that must be overcome on the route to the CoG)?

How can you protect your own CoG?

What other vulnerabilities do you have?

Now look at your key suppliers:

What are their CoGs, Critical Capabilities/Requirements/Vulnerabilities? What is their Endstate?

What are their Ends, Ways, Means, CoG?

What are their DPs?

Now do the CoG exercise from the perspective of your key competitors:

What is their Endstate?

How could they downgrade your Critical Capabilities, extinguish your Critical Requirements and attack your Critical Vulnerabilities?

Make a list of other significant and decisive things in the way of achieving their Endstate – both external and internal – and ask the same questions.

Now do the CoG exercise on your top three customers:

What is their Endstate?

What are their Critical Capabilities/Requirements/ Vulnerabilities?

Milestones on the Way to the CoG – Decisive Points

It is often not possible to get to an opponent's CoG directly, in which case you will have to establish the milestones, or Decisive Points (DPs) that must be achieved on the way. The DPs should become clear as you do the exercise just described. A business bare-bones example might be:

- **Endstate.** To be the largest specialist mergers and acquisitions (M and A) strategic consultancy in Europe.
- **Ends**. To have three multinational clients within the first year (to ensure you are in profit in your first year and so keep the group together).
- **Ways**. To approach ex-clients of the firm you now work for, with whom you still have good relations. Network with Chairs.
- **Means**. Three top consultants, one secretary, £150,000 investment, use of converted office from the stables of one of the consultants.
- **CoG**. Convince global firms to give the business to a small consultancy.
- **Critical capabilities**. Three partners with 53 years' experience between them having orchestrated and pulled off some of the world's biggest M and As.
- **Critical requirements**. Relationships with global CEOs, credible presence in the market, access to information, income within the year commensurate with previous six-figure salaries for the three partners.
- **Critical vulnerabilities**. No direct new-business experience (leads have previously been supplied by US division). Working alone (previously had two assistants each). No Excel or PowerPoint experience. Lack of research team (may have

to buy in). No global presence (lack of local knowledge/ culture/languages). Dissenting voice in the team (criticisms expressed by one partner over how you deal with clients).

In this example, the Decisive Points are: signing off with past employer the three clients you want to prospect, finding and negotiating a price on research data, and establishing sufficient skills.

Lines of Activity – How to Synchronise Action

Synchronising Action is a bit like conducting an orchestra – it helps if every instrument is able to play from the same score. Having selected his Centre of Gravity (CoG), and the Decisive Points (DPs) that lead to it, the leader then has to decide which activities will have the necessary effect – that is, the lines of activity that connect to DPs on the path to the CoG. It is likely that more than one activity will be able to influence a single DP, so activities need to be synchronised so that they reinforce rather than cancel each other out.

In the business example just given, early work in securing access to the market with the past employer is an important first step (as your firm doesn't want to be sued). One of the partners, who is closest to the Chair can do this. You then need to work on ensuring the team works as a team. This might involve:

- Boosting morale – organise a social event so that you can get to know each other.
- Synchronising thinking – facilitate discussion on the doctrine, build in time to think and reflect, dialogue on Lessons Identified.
- Finding your data – negotiate a price on getting the research you need.

- Improving skills base – research and debate what technology and skills training are specifically needed and by whom.
- Establish strategic allies – firm up ties with associates from your network abroad.

Lines of Activity

The next stage is to be clear about what Lines of Activity will have a bearing upon your chosen Decisive Points. In the military context there are two broad ways of defining these: by 'environment' – that is sea, land and air, or by 'function' – such as attack, protect, support, inform. In a commercial setting, the 'function' approach is more likely to be useful, and the Campaign Plan will show how different Lines of Activity support each function over time. This general idea is best shown as a diagram:

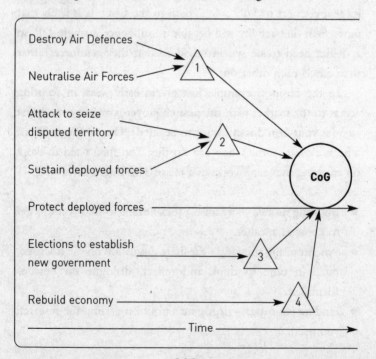

Decisive Points (indicated by triangles):

1 Establish control of the air to ensure freedom of movement.
2 Occupy the territory, expelling enemy forces, and hold.
3 Establish a new and legitimate government.
4 Create sufficient prosperity.

Centre of Gravity: The support and consent of the people.

In this military example, the selected Lines of Activity are listed at the left, and time runs from left to right. It shows where one or more Lines of Activity contribute to a Decisive Point (the triangles), and how Decisive Points contribute to the Centre of Gravity (the support and consent of the people). This example is obviously simplistic, and in practice a Campaign Plan can be much more complex and fully supported by a wealth of detail. For our purposes here it is enough to show the general approach. In fact, at senior leadership levels, refining a complex undertaking down to bare essentials such as this can be a useful mind-clearing exercise, especially under conditions of stress, to ensure that the organisation is focusing on the essentials. Simple diagrams like this are also a good way of conveying a Campaign Plan to a wider audience – such as politicians, the media and stakeholders.

The idea of using Lines of Activity can also be applied in a commercial context. Most organisations already operate in well-defined departments or functions, and even integrated project teams are formed from a mix of people drawn in for their particular expertise. In a business campaign, Lines of Activity could be expressed like this:

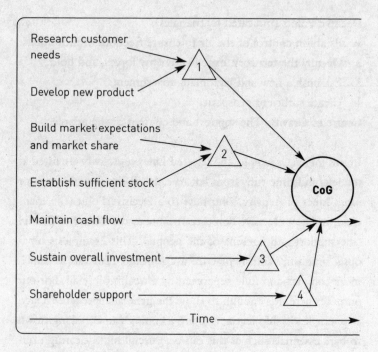

Decisive Points (indicated by triangles):

1   Create new proposition for the market.
2   Sell the proposition successfully at target levels.
3   Maintain the flow of investment funds.
4   Obtain shareholder support for continuing the programme.

Cente of Gravity: Customer commitment to the product and its successor as the market leader.

Synchronisation – Sequencing and Phasing

Implicit in these diagrams is the idea of having to sequence activities. Sequencing may simply be a matter of logic: you can't invade until you have destroyed the enemy's air power, and you can't sell a new product until it has actually been developed sufficiently.

Sequencing may also be a matter of resources. If a military commander has only enough tanks to attack one place at a time and be certain of winning, it would be necessary to take each objective in turn – sequencing available resources. It would be a mistake to try to use too few tanks concurrently at too many places, thereby allowing the enemy to defeat them. If the commander had more tanks it would then be possible to attack more than one objective at a time, which should lead to a quicker and more decisive victory. (In war as in business, quantity has a quality all of its own.)

Where activities fall into a logical or unavoidable sequence, the Campaign Plan can be divided into Phases, with perhaps a chance to stop and review progress and decisions for future activities between Phases. This applies to the business world, such as complex project management. Leaders divide such work into controllable, fundable packages that keep things manageable, measurable and within budget. If the work is also divided into Phases, a review can be made at the end of each one before commitment is secured to the next.

Contingency Planning – Branches and Sequels

> *'If GE's strategy of investment in China is wrong,*
> *it represents a loss of a billion dollars, perhaps a couple*
> *of billion dollars. If it is right, it is the future*
> *of this company for the next century.'*
> JACK WELCH, CEO

Few plans emerge unscathed from contact with real life and real people. This is the case in battle, where the opponent is doing his level best to frustrate your activities, with very high stakes. And it is the same in business. During the progress of a large-scale plan there will inevitably be setbacks, interference and the unforeseen to deal with – and just plain bad luck to take into account. So although we can make a Campaign Plan that shows how various Lines of Activity are harnessed to achieve a particular Decisive Point, we do need to take into account the possibility of alternative outcomes. Business Generals need to make provision for:

- **Branches**. Pre-planned options, set out in as much detail as possible, that cater for different results and give alternative courses of action that can be selected and implemented. They are there to deal with the inevitable uncertainty that accompanies *current* activity in a complex and dynamic environment.
- **Sequels**. Options for the *next* phase of activity. They allow for choices to be made about what happens next, in the light of new or better information.

Remember to work through the detail of all your alternative plans. What future steps must be taken regarding the consequences of each of the branches. What would you do next if all your options failed? Most organisations have plans with 'branches' (options), but how thought through are they, how much detail is really put into the alternative options? How little some organisations think through the *next phase* of even routine activity! As a plan rolls along and has to be modified, it is inevitable that there will be sequels – consequences – to be thought through. If they are planned in advance they are easier to manage; if they are taken only as events unfold the organisation may become committed to endless unnecessary and risky fire-fighting. In the 1990s Shell Oil was remarkably good at thinking through the future using a system that precluded creative thought and then worked it through, but in practice few firms do this sort of thinking well.

Branches and Sequels provide a logical way of thinking through decisions that leaders may have to make – both now and in the future. They offer an important way of managing crises in advance by having thought through, and planned, alternative courses of action. This reduces the chances of being surprised and makes for a faster and more agile response to changes of events. This is firmly the business of senior leaders. While most staff should be getting on with doing the best they can in the activity in hand, the boss must keep his or her eye on the horizon and be alert to the need to make swift and decisive changes to the plan.

In our example of the strategic consultancy:

- **Branch**. Sign off with ex-employer the list of prospects, get the agreement signed. Plan to approach three global clients within two months of research. You may have to moderate the list if barred from all significant players and move down from FTSE 100 and Fortune 50 to FTSE 250 and Fortune 100.
- **Sequel**. Decide on which sector of middle-sized industries to target, as all the big boys are covered with their preferred suppliers.

COMMANDER'S COMFY CHAIR
Managing the Plan

In the light of the answers you arrived at after asking yourself the questions posed in the previous Commander's Comfy Chair, take a few hours to think through the following. You might decide that it needs further work – over days/weeks.

What are the Decisive Points you would have to achieve in order to get to the Centre of Gravity?

What are the 'Lines of Operation' (functions or activities) that can achieve these Decisive Points?

What is the most important thing you must do (your main effort) to succeed in reaching your Endstate?

If you are hazy about what to do, what information do you need to have to be able to complete an outline Campaign Plan?

Have you thought about the sequence of your activities and planned that properly?

How do you ensure that activities in your organisation are well synchronised?

Does everybody understand the importance of this?

Have you considered where your plan needs branches for alternative courses? You might want to do this pictorially.

What if those branches were ripped off – what would you do next?

How are you going to communicate that to the team?

Operational Pause – Essential Quiet Time

In a long campaign, especially if it is hard fought and close, it is neither desirable nor possible to go full tilt all the time. Supplies take longer to move and build up than they do to use, people get tired and need to recuperate, and it can take time to get even close allies to agree on what needs to be done next. In business, although there is an ideal of constant growth, change and dynamic activity, some breaks between surges of activity can be beneficial. We cannot stress this enough. Modern-day executives tend to go from one high-stress drama to the next.

Many employees today feel that they are being driven relentlessly hard – and they are! That is a big mistake. Employers must stop driving themselves and others, and employees need to muster their courage and be assertive about the need for recuperation. You must recognise when you need to take time out so that you can come back with a clearer head, a willing body, and with your keenness and sense of humour reinstalled. The long-hours culture, endless meetings, conference calls at unsocial hours, hundreds of e-mails to respond to within 24 hours ... these things do not allow space for people to take stock or recharge their creative batteries.

In a military context, the idea of an Operational Pause is easy to illustrate. Before the Allies could invade mainland Europe from Britain it was necessary to gather the necessary strength and come up with a winning plan. This took time, around three years after the fall of France, during which the battle in Western Europe was very quiet. But while an Operational Pause took place there, fighting continued through other lines of operation: the battle for control of the Atlantic, and the campaign in North Africa, for example. When preparing for D Day in June 1944, it was then necessary to pause activity in other theatres to focus maximum effort on Normandy. The concept of an Operational Pause reflects two principles of war: concentration of force and economy of effort.

The concept of an Operational Pause is also useful in a business sense. By maintaining good intelligence on competitors a leader can judge when they have saturated the market, spent all their marketing funds, or reached maximum production capacity. By so doing, the Business General can judge when to launch her or his own activity, ideally choosing the moment when the competition is least able to react. This fits well with the Manoeuvrist idea of striking at weakness rather than strength and finding the most effective way of achieving the desired result at least cost (see Secret Number Four: Dynamic Manoeuvre).

Pause on Your Own Terms

Pauses need to occur when you choose and not be inflicted on you by the successful actions of the opposition. This means that Operational Pauses are planned in, with people knowing in advance when they are required to surge and when they need to just tick over. The pauses should be defined in terms of length and purpose: people must know how long they have got to wait or regenerate, why this is so, and how it fits into the overall Campaign Plan. This synchronisation across Lines of Activity is obviously something that has to be done by senior leaders, only they will have the oversight of the operation of the whole plan and the authority to rein in a particular activity in spite of general enthusiasm to forge on regardless.

There is also a useful psychological reason for an Operational Pause. The military have learned the importance of regulating activity to ensure that resources of all types are carefully husbanded and employed to maximum effect. It may be necessary to regulate the tempo of activity between lines of operation by pausing activity in one sector to allow another to catch up and receive more resources. For example, it is no good the logisticians rushing ahead with storage and distribution plans until research and development has worked out what the product will look like and how much space and weight is involved. Similarly, a business leader may decide to get one part of the organisation, say marketing, to ease off while he or she devotes more people, money and attention to getting the production process right. If you need an excuse to take an Operational Pause, pick from the following!

Operational Pauses are useful to:

- Allow time to think.
- Allow time to recuperate, refresh, rebuild.

- Create space – to see something from a different point of view.
- To see the funny side of something, to get things into perspective.
- Recognise there can be benefit in allowing people a short fallow period.
- Allow others to catch up so that activities are synchronised.
- Economise effort and force, to stop burning resources when you don't need to.
- Gather your 'forces' to move on later with decisive capability.
- Stop pretending you are superhuman and to recognise the inefficiencies of pointless tiredness.
- Pause while your opponents exhaust themselves.
- Learn lessons, rebuild morale and restore motivation after a hard encounter.

CULMINATION POINT – KNOW WHEN TO STOP

'However beautiful the strategy,
you should occasionally look at the results.'
WINSTON CHURCHILL

Every commander, and every business leader, embarks on a new venture determined to bring it to a successful conclusion. The anticipated results will be clear from the outset – otherwise there is no point starting out – but nobody can be absolutely sure what the eventual outcome will be. Sometimes the results will be beyond all reasonable expectations, like the Sony Walkman and the Personal Computer, and sometimes the vision just doesn't catch on – like the Sinclair C5 electric 'car'. In war, when actions are so highly charged and the stakes so significant, the results are even more important. The Coalition invasion of Iraq in 2003 was always controversial around the world, and the relief in US and UK governments when Baghdad was seized was considerable – and the subsequent insurgency deeply unwelcome in its ferocity and duration.

One of the most important tasks of a leader, military or civilian, is to judge when to stop. In all military operations there comes a point when further investment in terms of manpower, equipment and supplies becomes unlikely to produce a positive return, indeed it may turn a modest tactical victory into a higher-level defeat by using up the resources needed for the next battle. No matter how much effort was invested in the planning and the execution, no matter how much personal credibility is at stake, the commander must identify when enough is enough and call a halt. This moment is defined in Campaign Plan terms as the 'Culmination Point'. It is the point at which any further effort and investment is going to produce insufficient or even negative gains.

THE END OF THE SECOND WORLD WAR IN EUROPE

The Allies landed in Normandy in June 1944, broke out after some hard fighting and advanced painfully as far as the German border. At the same time the Russian Army bore down on the German Eastern border as it pushed the Germans out of Russia and back towards Berlin. At this time it was clear to many military commanders, German and Allied, that the war would have only one result. The rational decision at the time would have been for the Germans to have asked for the best surrender terms they could get, in order to limit any further losses and damage to their country and also to try and stave off occupation by Russian forces in particular (who were not known at the time for their friendliness or respect for lives and property, reciprocating in full for the German invasion of Russia). The German war effort had certainly culminated.

In these circumstances the Allies made ending the war far more difficult by demanding unconditional surrender, and in any case Hitler and his inner circle were past the point of reason. The result was that fighting continued right up to the fall of Berlin in April 1945, the death of Hitler, and the occupation of what became (temporarily) East Germany by Soviet forces.

Identifying the Culmination Point

As a Business General you need to know that there are two principal difficulties involved in identifying the Culmination Point:

- First, it has to be detected in advance, without all the benefits of clarity that hindsight will confer. It is often very hard to judge when enough is enough until the moment has passed. It requires good information, good analysis and honest judgement – and probably a streak of ruthlessness. Sometimes the people involved in managing a campaign – military or business – are least well placed to see that the game is up. It may be easier viewed from a distance – and this is where Governments and shareholders can play a role.

- Second, quite apart from the practical difficulties, there are emotional challenges to be overcome. After so much hope and effort, with success maybe just around the corner, it is difficult to decide to stop and also tell the staff and others to halt too. After all, they may feel that they are just about to succeed, and if they stop – what was all their work and sacrifice for? These sentiments are common to the military and business arenas.

The challenge can be eased by laying out clearly, before even starting, what the conditions will be for declaring that the campaign has culminated. These conditions are then measured along the way, triggering the necessary response if they are satisfied. This makes culmination less of a surprise, and less difficult to deal with.

Are you sure what you will see, hear, feel when you are successful?

What level of success will be enough? Do you and others have the willpower, the wisdom, the grace to know when to stop – or will greed and adrenalin grip you?

As with the concept of Operational Pause, there is immense value in devoting effort to spotting an opponent's Culmination Point. Think about two main competitors – what are they still attempting but clearly failing to achieve? What have they achieved but are now over-egging? Where are they stuck?

COMMANDER'S COMFY CHAIR
Operational Pauses and Culmination Points

Review the following regarding 'operational pauses and culmination points'. You might decide that these issues need further work – over days/weeks.

Do you and your team need an Operational Pause? Why?

What would be the purpose of an Operational Pause?

What would you be better placed to do after an Operational Pause?

Can you plan where you could make an Operational Pause in the future?

Review your current activities. Have you reached a Culmination

Point? What are you still chasing that isn't getting closer?

What price are you paying for having achieved and not stopped?

Are you simply grasping for more?

Are there other parts of your organisation that have
'culminated'?

Do they realise this?

How will you know whether you are about to reach the
Culmination Point of your main aim? What will you see, hear,
feel?

What is stopping you owning up to a Culmination Point?

Is it a matter of enough honesty, courage, ruthlessness,
practicality, common sense?

It is important to see how this Secret fits in with its predecessors.

- **Secrets Number One, Two and Three**. These described the Power Pyramid, which paints a picture of organisational strengths and weaknesses, in terms of its conceptual/moral/ physical elements. This understanding should underpin all thinking about what strategy to follow – there is no point deciding to do something if the means of achieving it do not exist and cannot be created.

- **Secret Number Four: Dynamic Manoeuvre**. This explained the concept of working and thinking smarter rather than harder. This is applied by leaders in how they conceive their campaign, and by attacking weakness rather than strength – ideally from an unexpected direction. It is also applied by subordinates in the way that they execute their part in the plan.

- **Secret Number Five: Mission Management.** This described a system of delegation and empowerment that fits alongside

Dynamic Manoeuvre, enabling subordinates to exercise maximum initiative in how they achieve their objectives.

- **Secret Number Six: Command the Campaign**. This has now provided the planning framework within which Secrets One to Five can be deployed.

BUILD YOUR ARMOURY
Campaign Planning

Some tips on 'campaign planning':

▷ Decide what levels of strategy you need in your business and make sure that this is clear to all leaders.

▷ Decide who is responsible for the 'Operational Level' between corporate strategy and daily activity. Make them responsible for planning your campaign.

▷ Test employees to see they understand your Endstate (the objectives of your strategy). Are your objectives clearly articulated?

▷ Consider what might lead you to change your Endstate. Make sure you are getting the information you need to monitor this.

▷ Check your strategy has the Ends, Ways and Means in balance.

▷ Articulate the CoG. What is the most significant and decisive thing standing between you and the achievement of the Endstate? Detail it in terms of Critical Capabilities, Critical Requirements and Critical Vulnerabilities. Do this with your own firm, your opponent, your competitors, your suppliers and even your customers. Focus the campaign on achieving victory over the CoG and question the validity of anything that doesn't contribute to it.

▷ Take a good hard look at your Lines of Activity. Identify which ones will bear most upon your chosen Decisive Points (DPs). How are they synchronised? Map them out.

▷ Where do you need to introduce Sequencing and Phasing?

▷ Make sure the necessary Branches and Sequels are really thought through in detail.

▷ Plan for, and take, Operational Pauses.

▷ Know when to stop. Make the conditions of success clear and identify when you need to pull out. Keep your radar on to detect how things are really going far enough in advance.

Summary of Secret Number Six: Command the Campaign

- This Secret is about strategy and planning, and in particular it covers the level of planning that sits between higher level strategy and the daily activities of the workforce.

- This Secret is about the art and science of planning a campaign from beginning to end by using a controlled sequence of complex activities.

- The key components of this Secret are the military techniques of Operational Art and Campaign Planning – which involve establishing the Lines of Activity, Branches, Sequels, and Decisive Points.

- This is conducted via a series of linked activities, rather than taking everything step by step as it comes. It also means being so on top of the challenge that it is easier to see when things are going wrong, or run out of steam, and so decide to change direction or stop before being forced by circumstances to do so.

Next Secret...

We will now go on to look at the final section, Secret Number Seven: Ride the Tiger. This focuses on how to make decisions under pressure and exploit opportunities in a way that is consistent with Dynamic Manoeuvre, Mission Management and Command the Campaign, and apply the polish that makes them all shine – leadership.

Secret Seven
Ride the Tiger
Seize the moment and exploit opportunities

'Battles are lost or won in fifteen minutes.'
NAPOLEON BONAPARTE

This Secret is about decision-making that ensures the best possible start. It is about how to react to change and the need to make changes. And – by way of summing up much of the content of the whole book – it is about the kind of leadership that makes this happen. It looks at how Business Generals must be ready to seize success, no matter what happens to their plan or how things turn out. Among the military adages that have been handed down the ages are 'no plan survives contact with the enemy', and 'when in doubt soldiers should march towards the sound of gunfire'.

So, although we have discussed the conceptual process of strategy and campaign planning and operational art – much of a Business General's success comes from coping with 'hairy' moments as well. That comes down to individual judgement and managing the loneliness of command well. It is an enduring truth that no matter how well a plan is constructed, checked for errors and briefed to everyone who must carry it out, there is every chance that as soon as it is put into action something unexpected will occur to throw it into disarray. What Clausewitz called the 'friction of war' can intercede with catastrophic consequences: '*War is very simple, but in War the simplest things become very difficult.*'

Why Plans Change In War

A military plan – indeed any plan – may have to be changed during its execution for many reasons, for example:

- It is based on false assumptions. (The enemy stands and fights when it was thought he would run off.)
- It contains incomplete, inaccurate or misunderstood information. (Details about enemy capabilities, locations and weapons are found to be wrong.)
- It contains incorrect information about your own capabilities. (It is no good knowing you have 10 fighter aircraft but not knowing that they have no ammunition or fuel left.)
- It goes wrong. (One of your side makes a mess of his part, throwing everything out of synch and producing vulnerabilities the enemy can exploit).
- It is disrupted by factors beyond your control. (Bad weather means aircraft can't fly, tanks get bogged down in mud and ships can't offload supplies.)

Why Plans Change In Business

In business, too, plans change, for all kinds of reasons:

- The objective was misconceived, perhaps owing to an ill-considered view from management.
- A group didn't follow instructions.
- Messages thought to be clear actually left the listener confused.

- New equipment was faulty or incompatible with current equipment.
- Staff lacked the breadth or level of competence needed to put the plan into effect.
- The leadership interfered, thus preventing capable people from getting on with the plan.

How to Make Good Judgements in Adversity

Business Generals need to deal with all this uncertainty, to face up to blunt truths and not pretend that a threat will go away of its own accord. Too many leaders (in all walks of life) think 'managing chaos and uncertainty' means tolerating it, shrugging their shoulders and accepting it as the new status quo.

In responding to a changed situation, a wide spectrum of mistakes are commonly made. For example, in an environment that is inherently dynamic, high-tempo and hostile and where action is required even though information is incomplete, the team may wait too long for data to arrive or for protocol to be followed. Other mistakes include acting on information so scant that the plan is based more on hope and luck than reason. Typically, professionals in giant professional service firms will glimpse an opportunity, but then wait until they have gathered more information and received 'signoff' before they act – and in so doing find they miss the chance to advance.

Grabbing 'The Moment' with Both Hands

An entrepreneurial person can cut through red tape, make decisions faster than the opposition, so that by the time their competitors make a decision, he or she is so far ahead the decision is no longer relevant. Getting and using information in a timely manner is vital – and 'timely manner' does not mean proper and ponderous; sometimes it will be snatch and go. As discussed already, leaders must be mindful of rejecting unpalatable information just because it conflicts with a plan that has taken a great deal of effort to put together, or because they cannot face up to it. Leaders must coach their subordinates to have the moral courage to say what they believe is really happening, and so create the climate whereby the bearer of bad (yet accurate) news is applauded – not punished.

> *'To know what is right and not to do it*
> *is the worst cowardice.'*
> CONFUCIUS, 500BC

Leaders must avoid confusing consensus with certainty. A phenomenon called Groupthink can occur when groups conform to the consensus view, become arrogant and over-optimistic, lack vigilance and take more risks than they would do if they were making the decision alone. The tendency is worse for homogeneous groups, who are well bonded, under stress and have an aggressive boss. Many poor decisions, fiascos and disasters have been put down to the phenomenon of Groupthink. These include the Bay of Pigs disaster (the failed CIA-backed invasion of Cuba to depose the country's president, Fidel Castro), the bombing of Pearl Harbor by the Japanese (which brought the USA into the Second World War) and – according to some officials – the failure by intelligence agencies to correctly identify Iraqi's weapons of mass destruction capability. Business Generals need to stop and check that the Groupthink phenomenon isn't fuelling poor decision making. If everyone is in agreement, someone needs to challenge the assumptions.

> *'If everybody is thinking alike, then somebody isn't thinking.'*
> GENERAL GEORGE S. PATTON

COMMANDER'S COMFY CHAIR
Making Decisions Under Pressure

Take a few hours to think about your ability to 'make decisions under pressure'. You might decide that it needs further work – over days/weeks.

Do you have a common framework for analysing your situation and thinking through new problems?

Do you have plans that are well understood by everyone involved?

Are the plans based on complete information?

What is the tempo in gathering information – and using it?

What proportion of information gathered is used properly?

What are the reasons for that?

Do people understand the *intent* behind their role as well as what they are required to do?

Will your subordinates be honest with you if they see disaster looming?

Would any of your people allow the organisation to fail just to see a leader fall flat on his face?

What happens in a crisis or other chaotic event?

When a crisis is identified, is there a common approach to finding a solution across the organisation?

Are people trained in a system to do this?

If things go wrong – what is the usual aftermath?

If 80 per cent of your people like something and 20 per cent don't – who is listened to and how? (Dissenting voices – if the intention is good – are useful to challenge assumptions. But he who shouts loudest may be a bully who always gets his way.)

Have you taken time out to think about what might change or go
wrong? Have you made plans (at least in outline) to deal with
these eventualities?

Do you have an agreed way of reacting to sudden changes?

Do you have an agreed way of making decisions quickly to
change a plan?

If you were unexpectedly called away or absent, who would take
charge?

Does he or she know this?

Does the rest of the team know this?

Does he or she know where to find the right information to carry
on without you?

KEYS TO GOOD DECISION MAKING

Military and Business Generals share the requirement to do two
key things. First, they must have a system of planning that is
comprehensive, rigorous and accurate, and based on all the information and resources available, in order to produce a plan that is
most likely to succeed. This may need to be more than just a
'strategic fit' (goals fitting resources precisely) as that could be
too limiting. Many businesses have been outwitted by cheekier,
more audacious new competitors whose goals were incorrectly
seen as outrageously over-ambitious. The plan must certainly fit
the strategic *intent* – and this may be heroically ambitious. The
plan still needs to be within what is actually possible, even in a
'can-do' environment. In other words, the plan must not only be
adventurous ('reaching for the stars') but also grounded in the
art of the possible ('keeping your feet on the floor'). This planning system must be user-friendly and easily accessible so that

everybody in the organisation who *needs to* contribute to it *can* contribute and be able to understand the results. It must be usable in different settings, from large and complex undertakings that can be planned at a leisurely pace, to smaller tasks where a more rapid response is needed.

Second, Business Generals must have *an agreed way* of reacting quickly and decisively when circumstances require a change of plan. This will ensure that activity is constantly tuned at all levels to meet the intent. Quick, decisive reaction might be required to seize a golden opportunity that has opened up unexpectedly and may exist for only a short while, or prevent the opposition from exploiting a changed situation. In either case, the aim is to out-think and out-manoeuvre the opposition with a decisiveness and strength that they cannot match.

Once military commanders have worked out in principle what they are going to do they still have to get the detail right, for which a thorough planning process is required. This would once have been no more than an oral 'council of war' at which the senior leaders sat around a camp fire deliberating until they came to a consensus about which enemy force to hurl themselves at first with primal fury. The amount of detail would have been minimal as all instructions had to be carried by word of mouth and co-ordinated on the ground by the Commander-in-Chief through shouts, hand signals and runners with verbal messages.

Even before the nineteenth century, this had evolved into lengthier debate and study, the results of which were turned into instructions written by hand. With rows of scribes or secretaries copying out the details, this was bound to be a slow process, limited in part by the time transmission took by horse and ship – and the hope that the recipient could read the scribble. Modern digital communications using the World Wide Web mean that leaders at opposite sides of the globe can look at the same document or picture at the same time and discuss its implications. So now it is possible for military and commercial planners to examine the same issues at the same time without being in the same place. To do this coherently they need to be following a common planning framework into which they place their contributions. Without this sort of standardisation they may fail to make themselves understood, waste or duplicate effort, or miss something vital.

'The Appreciation' – Harnessing Logical Thought

In the British Armed Forces, the common method of analysing a problem to produce a detailed plan throughout most of the twentieth century was known as an 'Appreciation'. For years this was the centrepiece of all teaching at staff colleges and the document that underpinned all military activity, from small-scale platoon attacks (30 soldiers) to huge events such as D Day, which took over 18 months to plan and involved depositing 150,000 troops with thousands of tanks and other vehicles on the beaches of Normandy in a single day.

Writing an 'Appreciation' was the bane of every staff college student's life, requiring not only slavish adherence to a set format, rigid application of service writing conventions (such as when to underline a full stop in a paragraph title – and when not), a ruthless logic and the management of enormous detail. As an approach to planning, it had many strengths. It relied on a straightforward deductive process: spelling out a factor, such as the nature of the ground or an enemy's capability, and then asking, 'So what?' The deduction that resulted from asking this was used to shape decisions about what to do. It provided a way of delivering a good answer, even when the stakes were high and people were tired, frightened and working against the clock. The process tried to avoid pre-judging the conclusion or being steered towards a favoured outcome from the outset (still known as 'situating the Appreciation'), by considering likely enemy courses of action and at least three of your own viable courses of action.

The Appreciation also had its weaknesses. It could be cumbersome and, even when scaled down to its essentials, was often not ideal for use in the heat of the moment. It could also go to great lengths to labour what was blindingly obvious: sometimes what needed to be done was so clear to an experienced officer that the requirement to spend days committing to paper everything in the known universe about the problem was simply unnecessary. If a leader can see the answer at a glance, why bother writing out an explanation? Sometimes what was really important was lost in a mass of unwieldy and irrelevant detail.

A lot of people who dislike planning – or do not see the point of it – feel this way. Entrepreneurs are often at the creative, instinctual edge and grasping at opportunities. They don't see the point of a load of 'management information'. As plans usually change from when they were first written down, they can seem false from the start and too 'left brained' for creatives. They have a point.

The Appreciation could also fail to take advantage of the intuition and judgement of a commander from the start of the process. As in many walks of life, what was simple and obvious to a senior leader may be complicated and obscure to a novice, so by failing to get the senior officer's view at the start many hours were wasted and many red herrings pursued to death. By relying so heavily on a logical process, even if it took a long time, the Appreciation often discriminated against the value of the intuition and judgement found in experienced leaders and caused opportunities to be missed by taking too long over reaching a decision. Too much western business planning and strategy makes the same mistakes, but there is a whole body of knowledge on planning and decision-making used by the contemporary Armed Forces that offers a new way (and one that is tried and tested, so you can rely on it).

The Ingredients of a Decision-making System.

The purpose of outlining the history of the Appreciation is to highlight what is required from a modern decision-making process, and indeed what the Armed Forces have taken forward into their current system. A good decision-making process requires:

- **A way of thinking through the essentials of the problem before getting immersed in the detail**. This includes getting the senior leadership's views early on. The design of any sort of intervention needs this. If one is designing a piece of kit, a management development programme, new information technology or considering an acquisition – the first step is to find out the essentials of the problem. This is vital. When things go wrong and seem to get compounded, you can usually trace back the cause to a lack of proper information about the problem. If things go wrong and this thinking has been done, it is easy to regroup and recommit.

- **A structured way of examining the relevant factors that will affect the outcome.** This needs to be known to all who might provide some input or be affected by the outcome. Training is imperative to get Synchronised Thinking about the relevant factors and the structure that will be employed. You can't be the only enlightened one here: when enemy fire starts raining down you need to rally the troops to defend or attack – not start educating them in how they might like to see this.

- **The rigour to keep it relative.** You need a method that ensures the process is conducted on a *relative* basis with judgements made on how it relates to the real enemy, and what the enemy might do in response.

- **Choices are presented clearly.** The construction of viable options ensures that the leader isn't stuck thinking that there is just one path to follow. This allows choices to be made between selecting one option or directing a combination of options.

- **A method that leads to decisions in the time available to stay ahead of the opposition.** An elaborate and sophisticated system that might work in the training centre, but is too slow or cumbersome in real life, is pretty useless. The decision-making system must make allowances for how quickly the enemy can get ahead and seize the initiative. So the system must be adaptable for differences in time scales and levels of complexity.

- **The method must be understood at all levels of the organisation affected by it.** This is important so that everybody who needs to can contribute to the work and understand and use the results intelligently. As a Business General you cannot expect success if your team has not been trained in the tools and processes. Investment in training is needed if you have a hope of running a tight ship.

The Armed Forces have adopted all this into the contemporary form of the Appreciation, known as 'The Estimate'. At its start is a process called 'Mission Analysis' that provides a structured way of getting to the essentials of a problem before deciding what detailed work is required. This has very broad application in other organisations, too.

Blending Logic and Intuition

The purpose of the Estimate process is to understand the situation with which you are faced, be clear what you are being asked to do about it, and consider all the relevant factors so that you arrive at the optimum plan. In principle, this is no different from what many people and organisations do already, either by instinct or more formal process. The first step is to conduct a four-stage 'Mission Analysis', which is designed to lead you to a very clear idea about *what* you are to do before trying to work out *how* to do it – which comes later.

MISSION ANALYSIS

Mission Analysis is a four-stage process that should be led by the commander or Business General personally, with key staff present. For example, a general in command of a division could complete the Mission Analysis for a forthcoming operation accompanied by the chief of staff, the chief of logistics, the commander of the artillery and other firepower, and the chief combat engineer. The commercial equivalent of this is the CEO examining an issue in company with senior directors and key executives. The time available to complete the analysis depends on the circumstances. For an event well in the future they may be able to take all the time they wish. For an imminent crisis they may have only a few hours. In the latter circumstances, by sticking to a well-tried and familiar format they can focus on the issues more directly, even when the adrenaline is pumping. The time available is a vital factor, whether you are a general faced with repelling an unexpected enemy attack or a CEO dealing with a hostile take-over bid or other aggressive move by a competitor.

The process can be broken down to four key questions, which can be adjusted in detailed language for different levels and circumstances:

Question 1. What is the situation and what is my part in it?
Question 2. What are the tasks that I must accomplish?
Question 3. What constraints and assumptions exist?
Question 4. Has the situation changed since we started?

Mission Analysis in Business

Mission Analysis can be applied to the commercial and wider arena. Let's take a simple example. A small consultancy turning over, say, £50 million, wants to grow to £100 million in five years (so that the owners can exit through a sale). Our Business General has recently been headhunted to run the London division and has inherited a small team of five. Previously, this team had just two functions: first, supporting the British CEO/founder as he travelled between the eight overseas satellite offices and, second, doing a small amount of consultancy, which took up 40 per cent of their time. The team is now required to get on with growing the business.

Our Business General has no previous management experience other than responsibility for a couple of junior peers, within a huge global firm. She is also inexperienced in selling and in developing new business. In her previous role she simply recruited suppliers, such as this small consultancy. She wants to undertake a Mission Analysis to see the size and nature of this challenge.

The first question she asks herself is: what is the situation and what is my part in it? Her part is clearly to lead this team as they spend all their time now on business capture and in running client-facing projects. She needs to communicate the new aim and the purpose behind it to the team. She needs to engage them all in that aim and help them see their part in it.

The second question she asks herself is: what are the tasks I need to accomplish? She needs to bring in new business and retain current clients. This involves an understanding of what it takes to win business, the process, the lead times, the best marketing route, the best route to market – what is it that other clients are looking for? She may, for instance, decide that they need to increase their networks, to build closer face-to-face relationships. She then has to make sure that her team are clear about what it takes to win business; analyse their current knowledge skills and capabilities; understand what they want from their careers, their level of commitment and what they need. She needs to understand and communicate the owner's role and actions, her own role/actions, and those of the team. She might think, for example, that she needs to ask the CEO to increase share options to all staff of over one year's tenure to increase their motivation.

The third question she asks herself is: what constraints and assumptions am I making? She needs to investigate the motivators and satisfiers of her team. This might be money. Or it might be that they liked doing the previous 'support' work and resent having to give it up. She needs to assess their capabilities and their potential for winning business and managing client projects. If they are not up to it, changes will be necessary.

The fourth question she needs to ask herself is: what has changed since I received this directive from the CEO? The results of this inquiry might lead her to appreciate that morale is low; one of the team is pregnant; the most immediate competitor has just brought a new offer to the market, and the office is due for relocation. Any of these may have a bearing on the plan that she makes.

BUILD YOUR ARMOURY
Business Mission Analysis

The four questions posed in Mission Analysis are also usefully applied in business and other organisations, and are simple to carry over into many activities.

▷ **Question 1.** What is the situation and what is my part in it? This question applies in any setting where you as a Business General recognise that you have an issue to address and need to be clear what your part is in it. In defining what part is to be played, you will know whether you are being required to fulfil a role in a larger scheme, or whether you have the freedom to decide what you want to do. As the business's commanding officer, the Business General will be clear about: the general situation, what the overall plan is intended to achieve ('thinking two levels up'), and your specific role in it. If you are not clear on these points, you must have the moral courage to seek clarification.

▷ **Question 2.** What are the tasks that I must accomplish? The division into specified and implied tasks has broad utility in any setting. There will be things you know you have to do or have been told to do (that is, 'specified tasks'). There will be other things that have to be done by *implication* in order to achieve the specified tasks (the 'implied tasks'). Setting out both types of task in any setting will help to clarify what must be done in total.

▷ **Question 3.** What constraints and assumptions exist? There will always be factors that limit what can be done – the availability of investment funds, research and development priorities, the allocation of staff, cash flow restrictions and many others. By identifying these, the Business General can be clear what restrictions he or she will have to accommodate in forming the plan. Similarly, if assumptions are made they must be registered as such and tested regularly to see if they hold good. Much of business planning is a 'political', negotiated settlement and tends to result in underestimating what the business can deliver in the short term or overestimating what it can do in the long term. Focus on checking that current assumptions reflect past performances. Look closely at the morale and climate of the organisation, and if it is low do something concrete as part of an urgent campaign to address it. Check assumptions about the roles and capability of the talent available, and the level of teamwork.

▷ **Question 4.** Has the situation changed since we started? In many cases, Question 4 is the most useful of all. Leaders will often know very well what situation they are facing, what they want to do about it and what limits there are on their actions. You must be alert to the danger of thinking that your ambitions are self-fulfilling prophecies, immune to the effects of other factors. Asking Question 4 regularly in any environment is an essential way of making sure that Business Generals are not caught out by events as a result of becoming too focused on their own thoughts and insufficiently aware of what is going on around them. It is not only external factors that can thwart the course but also performance dips due to tired, jaded, hindered employees.

How to Make Rapid – Not Rash – Decisions

Many businesses struggle between making bold entrepreneurial leaps (for fear of the cost of failing) and settling for realistic targets (risking that competitors may get ahead). The conundrum is how to set ambitious, audacious and stretching goals in the strategy, while at the same time work out how to meet them with the skills base, equipment and other resources currently available. If this 'strategic fit' is obviously poor, the hapless workforce regards the strategy as 'a farce', 'unfair' or 'just an exercise'.

The question is, how can you be very ambitious on the one hand and practical on the other? Well, the contemporary Armed Forces approach could have the answer. Flowing from the strategic intent, through connected layers of missions and tasks, to the on-the-spot judgements needed as the plan unfolds, the Armed Forces have developed a way to achieve balance and integration between ambitious goals and tight resources. It is a process, a structured method of inquiry that leads to confidence and good judgement.

The need to be able to meet a complicated and high-risk challenge with a robust and successful plan as quickly and accurately as possible is one of the key dilemmas for military leaders. At every turn, a balance has had to be struck between the completeness achieved by thrashing through as much detail as possible and the speed gained by relying on intuition and professional judgement to pick out the right answers. As in any walk of life, intuition and judgement come with experience: a senior military commander or business leader will be more confident about going with his instincts than the young officer in his first battle.

'Seven Questions' of Planning

The success of the Mission Analysis process has been to eliminate a great deal of nugatory work by focusing on the essentials from the start. But Mission Analysis alone, in either a commercial or military setting, does not lead to a detailed plan without some follow-up work. A great deal of military thought has gone into producing a planning framework called 'The Seven Questions' that leads smoothly through a combination of logic and intuition to a more detailed plan. It effectively wraps in the basic ideas of Mission Analysis and carries on through a planning framework. This is especially suitable for smaller organisations and tasks where a full-blown Estimate process is unnecessary and cumbersome. This can also be applied to the business world. At every stage, it seeks to introduce originality and well-judged boldness. Doing the same thing as last time is not usually encouraged.

> *'Prejudice against innovation is a typical characteristic of an Officer Corps which has grown up in a well-tried and proven system.'*
>
> FIELD MARSHAL ERWIN ROMMEL

The 'Seven Questions' are:

- **Question 1: .** What are the enemy doing and why?

  Military. The first step is to establish what the enemy is doing and – just as important – 'why?', because 'why?' will provide clues about how the enemy may react and what he will try to do next.

  Business. In a commercial context, the 'enemy' can be any obstacle or interference on the route to your goal. It can be the fickleness of your customers, a new product by your competitors, the disloyalty of your top talent or unreliable suppliers. If you focus on customers you need to ask 'what do the customers want and why?' What are different groups of customers doing and why? Where am I going to get my next cadre of talent, what is it doing, where is it going and why?

- **Question 2.** What have I been told to do and why?

  Military. A military commander will look at the mission he has been given and make sure he understands why it is important and how it fits into the wider plan. If he has not been given a mission he may work out for himself at this stage what he should do and why.

  Business. A Business General will see what she has been told to do, and how it fits into the overall corporate plan – or work out what she thinks should be done and why. She will look through and beyond the glossy strategy instructions and think through the interdependencies and synergies that she will need and others will need from her.

- **Question 3.** What effects do I want to have on the enemy and what direction must I give to develop my plan?

  Military. The military leader will decide how he will deliver success in his mission by defining it in terms of the 'effects' he needs to achieve. For example, if required to attack Mount Tora Bora, in Afghanistan, he may need to 'fix' the enemy in some places (prevent him from moving or interfering) and he will need to destroy him in others. Having worked this out in general terms, he can get his staff to work out the all-important details needed to make it happen – such as arranging helicopters and air strikes.

  Business. The Business General in our previous example of the small consultancy, would need to work out what effects she needs to have on her team, prospective clients, existing customers, competitors, suppliers, networks and media in order to deliver the results she seeks. Details are then worked out by functional experts. Each role holder exercises the empowerment given to them by the Mission Management approach. Individuals will hold themselves responsible for working out how they will go about meeting their aim, communicate 'two levels up' and 'two levels down', keep information flowing and with thorough, dependable rigour report back to their boss on how they are doing.

- **Question 4.** Where can I best accomplish each action/effect?
Military. The military commander decides where on the ground he wants to achieve the effects he has decided on. He will look for 'manoeuvrist' approaches that will give him the chance of inflicting surprise and striking at the enemy's weaknesses rather than strengths. He will apply the Principles of War to point him in the right direction of where and how to maximise his chances of success.
Business. The Business General will also need to work out the location and timing of her activities, such as which customers to target and what type of marketing campaign to run. She will work through the Principles of Winning to make the shrewd and smart moves.

- **Question 5.** What resources do I need to accomplish each action/effect?
Military. The military commander judges what combat power is needed to accomplish each task. In an attack a ratio of at least 3:1 is usual, although 10:1 works rather better. So, to attack, a company will need three or more companies and support such as artillery and air power.
Business. The Business General faces just as much of a challenge with scarce resources. How much investment in marketing and training, and what kinds of each? How many

people will each task need? Where is the balance to be struck between quick gains and longer term effort that has proper strategic fit?

- **Question 6.** When and where do the actions take place in relation to each other?

  Military. The commander will work out how actions relate to each other. This is partly a question of geography and mostly a question of resources. If resources are plentiful he can do more things at the same time. If resources are thin, activities will have to be done one at a time in a well-orchestrated sequence.

  Business. This can be obvious (completing the research before starting production) or it can be subtle (timing product launches to coincide with seasonal imperatives or to neutralise a competitor's efforts). The key point is that the leader must make sure this is a matter of choice, not accident. The real 'creatives' are those who seize responsibility for an idea and make it happen:

  > '*Action springs not from thought*
  > *but from a readiness for responsibility.*'
  > DIETRICH BONHEOFFER, GERMAN THEOLOGIAN

- **Question 7.** What control measures do I need to impose?

  Military. Control measures can include marking boundaries between units so that they do not blunder into each other as they move across country, carefully organising movement along congested routes, calling for progress reports at specific times, and setting key timings.

  Business. Control measures include cost/margin/yield

management, progress reports, process management, targets and head-count balance.

The 'Seven Questions' in Business

Here is another example of how the 'Seven Questions' can be applied in business. Let us assume that your boss is the owner of a business turning over £7 million and that his new goal (Endstate) is to increase factory turnover by 40 per cent in two years.

- **Question 1.** What is the enemy doing and why?

Who you want to choose as the enemy depends on your goal. In this example, what are the top three most significant obstacles to increasing factory turnover by 40 per cent? Work each response in terms of the seven questions, starting with the most significant. Let's imagine the most significant was the ability to secure an acquisition while maintaining equilibrium at the original site; the sort of questions that would require answers are: How secure is the acquisition looking? Are the sellers in discussion with anyone else? What process are they using? What is their history of integrity? What is the depth of our relationship with them? What is the optimum funding?

Due diligence – who will do it, how shall we introduce it?

- **Question 2.** What have you been told to do and why?

You need to understand why your boss wants to increase turnover by 40 per cent. Is it to dominate the market or to sell out? In the example of the acquisition, you need to find options for how the due diligence could be achieved, based on factors such as style, cost, risk management ethos, and experience in your market. Do you need to join the owner and develop relationships with the other firm's equivalent of yourself?

How would you go about that? You have been told to 'get the structure of the firm right and decide what assets you have'. You decide to analyse the tasks to be done, compare them with the capabilities of the people in the business, redesign some job roles, negotiate with the existing team how their jobs could change and discuss succession.

- **Question 3.** What effect do you want to make on the enemy? You need to impress on the seller that you are serious so that no other bidder comes in. You need to keep it confidential so that the 'big boy' sharks don't have the information they need in order to move in with a better offer. You need to find appropriate professional advice so that you don't overcommit before you are ready.

- **Question 4.** Where and how can you accomplish each task? You need to invest in training and organise shadowing, secondments and mentoring to improve skills and give confidence to staff at all levels as they approach the acquisition. You need media-handling advice because the acquisition will attract publicity. You need advice on the options for raising the necessary finance. You need to get close to their business and understand their equipment, their assets, their client base, their accounts, their ethos and culture, and climate and skills – what is their power base?

- **Question 5.** What resources are available?
You cannot use existing staff only, as they don't have the experience for an acquisition, so you'll need to use your network to find advice on public relations, law, mergers and acquisitions, tax and pensions – all at a higher level than you have currently. You won't be able to continue to rely on the managing director's secretary

and wife doing all the human resources work. You will need an HR professional.

- **Question 6.** When and where do all the actions take place? The timetable for the acquisition needs careful thought so that key events occur in the right sequence. The timing of factors such as raising the money, informing the workforce and informing the market is vitally important.

- **Question 7.** What controls and measures do you need? There are obvious measures, such as not ignoring what is going on at the original site while forming the new plans. Once real information from due diligence has been had, the current financial director will have to work out new cost/margin/yield ratios and you can have discussions about what to do with the extra space in the second factory. The key Decision Points for the acquisition need to be identified so that each stage proceeds from a solid foundation. Monitor the stress levels of senior staff – they are taking on what could be a double workload.

The Devil in the Detail

Applying the Seven Questions approach in any setting, military or commercial, requires training and practice. It is important that it is not only the chiefs who know how to use it but also the staff who must crack the necessary supporting detail – that means collective training again! The key advantage of the system is that it is very user-friendly and intuitive – it is easy to see how one stage leads to the next. At the end of the process there should be no doubt in anyone's mind about the plan in outline, and what detail must be worked up to make it happen.

There is an important point here: every leader must avoid

being satisfied that he has led the production of a brilliant concept and then march off to the golf course to await a call announcing total victory. Getting to this stage is about 10 per cent of the problem. Making it happen is the other 90 per cent. This requires, first, that leaders are alert to the very real problems that points of minor detail can cause in their plan, such as failing to order enough bolts when trying to build a bridge. The other side of this is that leaders may well have to encourage staff who see insurmountable difficulties in minor things – they may need leadership and encouragement to get through the challenge. The second requirement is for leaders to lead. Having created a brilliant plan, the leader needs to make it happen:

> *'When placed in command – take charge.'*
> GENERAL NORMAN SCHWARZKOPF, US ARMY, GULF WAR 1991

That brings us to the concluding section of this Secret – the vital question of leadership and how it makes the difference between seizing and missing opportunities, between success and failure.

LEADERSHIP WITH POWER AND HUMILITY

> *'We are not in a position in which we have nothing to work with. We already have capacities, talents, missions, callings.'*
> ABRAHAM MASLOW, PSYCHOLOGIST AND MOTIVATION EXPERT TO THE ARMED FORCES

The whole of this book has been about aspects of leadership, from questions about the best way to understand an organisation, to ideas about how to achieve empowerment, creativity, good strategy and successful plans. In business as in military affairs, it is not enough just to run down a checklist or template of best practice in a mechanical way in order to get great results:

it requires leadership to inspire people, to get the will, dedication and effort from every member of the organisation, that builds the best chance of victory in any competitive sphere. This is the part that involves character and character development.

Like a good wine or an attractive picture, most people will agree when they see good leadership, even if attempts to define it exactly provoke more heat than light. Part of the challenge in defining leadership is in dealing with the two very different role requirements that leaders face: the situation and level of engagement of their people and the situation and level of engagement at which the leader must operate. There is a common thread between what a shift supervisor and a main board director must do to lead successfully, but there are also substantial variations in the scale, scope, time and consequences of the decisions that each must take. The same is true of a lieutenant commanding his platoon of 30 men in the jungle, all within earshot, and the four-star general commanding coalition forces of perhaps 150,000 men spread over more than a continent.

Military leadership on the battlefield is enacted in the most challenging environment of all human endeavours. It is bound to be hard to get people to do something that runs contrary to all their natural instincts of self-preservation and yet must be done with the greatest physical and spiritual force that they can muster. Yet time after time, soldiers have got up behind their leader and charged the enemy machine guns, aircrew have flown through seemingly impenetrable barrages to get to their target, and sailors have turned towards the enemy's bigger and more powerful battleships to sink them. We have touched on why this is so in Secret Number Two: Soul Matters, but there is no doubt that it is often the personal effect that the man or woman in charge has on the people around them that is the difference between success and failure.

Many ex-military people talk nostalgically of the deep friendships made, the thrill of the adventure, the pride in the team's contribution, the sheer fun of operations. How many business people talk in such a way of their past work? Why is it that the military do? The men and women that do so much in battle are just people, who make other organisations work. Training plays a part, of course, and so do circumstances, but it would be wrong to think of servicemen and servicewomen as somehow intrinsically different from the rest of society.

For the purposes of *The 7 Secrets of Leadership Success*, we will now touch on the aspects of leadership that appear to us to be the most relevant to the employment of the ideas promoted in this book. This will not be an exhaustive list: it may only add to the wider debate about how to get the kind of successful leadership that has lasted for centuries and will probably continue for many more.

Successful leadership is a combination of:

- Who you are, and who you are being.
- What you know.
- What you give.
- What you want to achieve.

Although there are some constants, things that are the same for every leader at every level, the *exact* nature of this combination will need to change to reflect the many different circumstances in which leadership is required. For some, 'what you know' may be the defining leadership characteristic; for others, 'who you are' or 'what you want to achieve' will be the key. In some cases it will all come down to 'what you give'. The trick is to examine your own situation honestly and clearly in order to think through the best mix – and how it may need to change over time.

Who You Are, and Who You Are Being

The UK's Royal Military Academy Sandhurst (RMAS) is now the only route to a regular service commission in the British Army, just as the Royal Navy and the Royal Air Force have their equivalents at Dartmouth and Cranwell respectively. Selection for a place is rigorous and competitive: there is an entry requirement that has to be met, and this bar is not lowered in response to variables such as a drop in applicants or a higher demand for officers. This quality threshold is partly set by tangible criteria – such as a basic level of physical fitness and proven academic performance. Valid and reliable psychometrics for assessing character are employed (the Armed Forces were among the first organisations to use them). More important in all this is the assessment of character – not some Edwardian concept of 'proper' competence with cutlery, polo ponies, and the foxtrot, but how an individual will fare as a junior leader in combat. The selectors have to establish the degree to which an aspiring officer is capable of leading, deciding and inspiring under pressure.

This is all about 'who you are', and summed up by the RMAS motto of 'serve to lead'. 'Who you are' means leaders looking deep inside themselves to understand their true strengths and weaknesses, real ambitions and fears, and having done that then working on developing the vital personal qualities of leadership they will need. 'Who you are being' means following through so that your personal leadership reflects those qualities in action. There is no room for lip service to slogans here: leaders must be unequivocal examples of values in action. There are some vital elements that contribute in particular to making up a Business General: it is much more than using the tools and processes – for Business Generals it is about 'who you are' and 'who you are being'. When looking for talent, the best advice is to define your entry criteria carefully and do not drop the bar if the right people do not come forward – just look elsewhere, continue to present yourself differently and keep going. The qualities required are:

- Selfless commitment
- Integrity
- Dedication to your people
- Moral courage
- Resilience
- Knowledge

Business Generals and Selfless Commitment

The first requirement of the military leader is to place his own personal interests second to those of his team; this is the vital element in answering 'who you are'. It is not unique to the Armed Forces: Jim Collins' (the leading management professor and author) work on 'Level 5' leadership was based on research conducted over five years. He found empirical evidence that the firms who moved from good to great had humble, self-effacing, if strong-willed leaders. This strikes many as odd since historically, in western cultures at least, high-profile leaders are perceived to be charismatic, selfish and egocentric people:

> *'He was like a cock who thought the sun
> had risen to hear him crow.'*
> GEORGE ELIOT

We looked at many aspects of this when we examined character in Secret Number Two: Soul Matters. The relationship between character, leadership and the soul of an organisation is inseparable and profound. The Armed Forces recruit and develop people with selfless commitment as a core quality; the result is officers and soldiers that live this way instinctively and expect it from others. There are formal sanctions for failing to match the behaviour required, but many people would find the opprobrium of their peers far more painful. The greatest motivator in the military seems to be fear of letting comrades down.

The same could not be said of all or even most businesses. Look around you: if there are plenty of bosses who are selfish, who lack the character of selfless commitment, the ability to inspire you and others they meet, the ability to generate a positive will to commit, you will ultimately suffer the pain and the deterioration of a team with its soul and character drained out of it.

When you think of a general, you don't think of a shy or weak-willed person, and for good reason – such people are not selected. Commanding officers in the Armed Forces generally conform to a paradoxical model of thinking, behaving and acting. They must have the strong will needed to succeed, ruthlessness in reasonable measure and yet also a genuine humility that puts the needs and goals of the mission and the team before their own. It is by getting this balance right that people are chosen for advancement – and not by simply trampling on those they command. It does not imply any shortfall at all in drive, will to win or enthusiasm:

> *'Nothing great was ever achieved without enthusiasm.'*
> RALPH WALDO EMERSON

If you meet aggressive people who trample on you, bully you into submitting to their way of looking at things, then resist, stand firm and do yourself, them and the organisation a favour by letting them know their opinion is nobody's but their own. Your voice counts – as do the voices of others. Aggressive behaviour indicates that that person is following a personal rather than a team agenda.

Their task, and you can help them, is to look at where they can learn, where they can serve. Critics, you may have noticed, often stop short of being helpful – they can't go the next step and be constructive. Criticising is easy and cheap: it's those who can be honest, insightful and constructive that you want to listen to.

Arrogant, big-mouthed big-heads are often insecure and have developed elaborate and dysfunctional ways of hiding their vulnerability. A lot of senior managers are potentially like this, and a lot of them inflict mass destruction on their own teams as the price of their achievements – so it is worth understanding them and knowing how to deal with them. The Business General *must* deal with them.

The Armed Forces have learned that the hard way. Across history, many bullying, ignorant, fundamentally conservative, and rather stupid leaders led their forces to defeat and destruction. Through an iterative process of reinvention the Armed Forces have found superb ways to identify and develop the right leaders – and cull the liabilities.

The most confident and aggressive leaders are often hiding something – but not always. In psychological terms you can have high ego-strength (and this is entirely positive) and yet not be egocentric. You can be very confident and humble at the same time, pleased to talk about your capabilities but also to offer up what you are not good at just as readily. Those with positive ego-strength look to enquire rather than blame when things go wrong, so it is easy to spot the difference between those who appear strong, but are just shouting over their own inadequacies and fears. Those with high ego-strength seek feedback, ask how they contributed, what helped, what hindered.

Luckily, those with 'me-me-me' ambitions are easy to spot: this sort of attitude can't be disguised: it seeps through their choice of words. They tend to go for easy wins and rarely take on the most challenging people, instinctively going for those who are vulnerable. Unfortunately, unless checked, they usually get their way through persistent aggression. The consequence of 'me-me-me' is that it rots the fabric of teamwork. Team members quickly sense that it is every person for himself – time to sharpen up those elbows and power a way through the ordinary mortals. It also deters the less assertive from giving what they have to offer.

Good manners and consideration play a part in being a Business General. Show your people you know and care about them in symbolic acts of kindness. In the military, these exist in small things, such as ensuring the soldiers have been fed before taking food oneself, and in larger matters such as not asking the soldiers to do something the officer would not do himself. This is why casualty rates for junior officers tend to be higher than average in battle – this is the price of leading the way.

> *'In a quiet surreptitious way I am*
> *feeling very pleased with myself.'*
> IRIS MURDOCH, THE SEA THE SEA

Business Generals and Integrity

An inseparable element of selfless commitment is **integrity**, which we also looked at in Secret Number Two. For any organisation to function well enough, let alone excel, it is imperative that the leadership is seen to operate with unequivocal integrity. This has many dimensions, but common commercial features that specifically affect leadership are:

- **Integrity in technical matters.** This ensures that financial figures and other market- or shareholder-sensitive information are a true reflection of reality. Employees, shareholders, suppliers, customers and competitors interact on the basis of honesty (even, perhaps especially, in conditions of failure) and where lapses are encountered it is absolutely right that the full force of the law is applied – without this the basic fabric of commercial life will be eroded.

- **Integrity in hiring and firing.** This means that the right people are hired, rewarded and promoted for the right reasons, and those who fail or err are warned and, if necessary, removed. There is plenty of legislation covering these issues in most countries, but quite apart from the law the climate of integrity in which an organisation conducts itself is fundamental to its long-term health and success. Getting the right people 'on the bus' and the wrong people off it is a Business General's duty – treating people with dignity, respect and value while doing so is a sign of their integrity.

- **Integrity in acknowledging success and failure.** Business Generals should share equally in the results their organisations achieve, neither seeking to assume all the glory for winning nor absolving themselves for failures. The tendency for the rewards of success to stick at the top and the opprobrium for failure to tumble quickly downwards is an example of failure of integrity. This is not at odds with the pursuit of personal gain, but the leader will achieve recognition for what his or her team succeeds in – sharing in their disappointments as well as their victories. This is not an idea well rooted in some commercial concerns, where the senior leadership appear to prosper no matter how much disaster overtakes the organisation for which they are responsible. There are other commercial models that recognise the community of interest between leader and led: the John Lewis and Arup architects' 'partnership' systems that reward pooled effort are examples. These systems allow a greater integrity in the business because people are not greedy, selfish or scared, grasping at short-term wins to keep their jobs. Instead, the right decisions can be made, even if short-term disequilibrium is caused, because the right result will emerge in due and proper time. Expediency and greed are killers of integrity.

Business Generals and Dedication to Their People

The third aspect of 'who you are' is about people. Modern, charismatic military commanders tend to form a relationship with their subordinates at all levels that recognises that the commander sees them as individual people – with the same dreams and fears – and not as numbers. This does not, of course, mean that the leader has met every single one of them, that is clearly impossible, but it does mean that by a combination of policy, actions and image the leader has the best interests of the personnel at heart. Nor does it mean that difficult decisions are shirked: if it is necessary to send soldiers on hard tasks with a high probability of no return, it will be done – but they will sense that the imperative was there and the price was kept as low as possible. This is the sort of common spirit needed especially in modern campaigns such as Iraq, where the fighting has to be sustained for a protracted period and with fatalities as an inevitable, inescapable and regular feature of a hard job.

The reverse is almost always negative: people feel alienated, abused and vulnerable very quickly if they sense they are just cannon fodder, likely to be dropped into a pointless, badly conceived battle without a second thought. In conditions such as that, the number of people likely to do any serious fighting will be very small – most will find a reason to be out of harm's way as much as possible. They stay below the parapet, not offering ideas or actions that might put themselves at risk or make others think they are expendable. Ultimately, of course, the bright and brave leave. As a Business General you have a responsibility to find out if any managers who report to you treat their teams as numbers – and the only way you'll ever know is to get close to their subordinates and listen to them. If you find that this is the case, you need to confront the manager and give them a chance to change, and if they don't change, they need to be got rid of. It is as simple as that.

Engaging the Staff

In some commercial organisations, there is a record of leaders being too busy to spend quality time, one on one, with their teams other than in the annual appraisal or annual away-day. They simply focus on achieving their own 'deliverables', and their boss. To make up for this inattention, something like an annual 'away-day' is held, a little like an errant husband turning up with flowers for the much-abused wife on their anniversary. This may be better than nothing, but it is much more likely to work if events like away-days and staff parties are the climax of a continual programme of engagement rather than an apology for its absence. The military experience is that time spent by leaders chewing the fat with their subordinates in an open, unrushed and genuine way reaps huge dividends when the chips are down and extraordinary courage and effort is needed.

Business Generals and Moral Courage

Courage exists in both a physical sense and as moral courage. The requirement for physical courage in the Armed Forces does not need elaboration, nor does the physical courage needed to command a lifeboat, lead a mountain rescue team, or direct fire crews. Moral courage is harder to define and frequently more important. Moral courage means that the leader does not shrink from doing the right thing and taking the right decisions, even if this means confrontation, disappointment, tears or anger from any quarter.

As we described in Secret Number Two, the exercise of moral courage is essential to the Soul of any organisation. It is also the soul of leadership. By exercising moral courage, by managing your own emotional response to attack or risk, and rising above your own fears or others' fears, you acknowledge your own soul. One of the surprises in the research for this book, for Deborah, was how earnestly the tough, serious, male environment of the military take soul and, for Richard, the surprise was how scared and scathing of soul were even the softest and fluffiest of people managers out there in business. What is true is that you need courage to talk and deal with soul.

Business Generals and Resilience

With courage comes the mental and emotional resilience that is an essential part of any Business General's armoury. In any walk of life, leaders cannot expect every day to be filled with flowers, profit and free cappuccino. The 'hard knocks of command' in the Armed Forces arrive in many forms to ambush a leader who probably thought everything was going swimmingly well. These knocks may come from suddenly having to deal with wholly unacceptable conduct in a unit that generally prides itself on high standards of discipline. They may come from not being chosen for a leading operational role, or having to implement orders to downsize or relocate. They certainly come from setbacks that are a feature of the battlefield: operations may not succeed, casualties are taken or the enemy successfully attacks out of the blue.

One of the key indicators of a successful leader is the one who rises to the challenge of a reversal of fortune and galvanises his team back into early, rapid and effective action to restore the situation, at the same time as being honest and open about how the setback occurred. This resilience may be called upon not just once, but many times before things are made to get better.

How Is Resilience Developed?

Some people may be genetically predisposed to bounce back from life's ups and downs. You can spot that in some children. For some, 'early life encounters' sets up a series of expectations, rewards or punishments that either fortify resilience or make it fragile and brittle. Early parental attention, care, love, sensible admiration and encouragement all help – but, of course, not everyone has that.

While early life experiences do set up a pattern, character is not set or solid, there are no predestined outcomes or certainties – there are deflection points at the crossroads on our life paths that can change our character. Many people wonder if character can be developed. We believe it can. Resilience has been developed in athletes who need to perform under the scrutiny of the media and of the millions watching them as they try to achieve the dream of a gold medal that they have carried with them since they were children. The pressure of having to perform, there, then, with the prize of glory and financial reward hanging in the balance, has led sports psychologists to study the subject of resilience and how to build it.

Building Resilience

Resilient leaders can build resilient organisations. Brittle, moody, fragile leaders have little likelihood of doing this.

Resilience is important to build in your place of work as it allows people to respond enthusiastically and flexibly to challenges. There are ways in which resilience can be developed, for example:

- Development of a healthy ego-strength and emotional intelligence are essential. This means knowing yourself, feeling good about yourself and managing your moods through personal development, group work, counselling and coaching.
- Managing your perceptions and focus. This means knowing how to focus on the important things and clear the mind of the unimportant (which has an impact on confidence and mood), using mental management techniques such as neuro-linguistic programming (NLP), hypnosis, visualisation and positive affirmations ('I am a composed and considerate leader'; 'I have a right to my own opinion').
- Using positive self-talk (and turning down the volume or ridiculing the sound of one's negative self-talk). This is particularly useful if geared to calming self-talk ('breathe in slowly, relax, lower your voice') and coping self-talk ('you've done this before, you can do it now'; 'remember what your coach/mentor/Mum/Grandpa said at times like this').
- Social events and, if necessary, relationship management exercises. Those with good social contact are more resilient, and family and close friends are an invaluable source of resilience.
- Anger management classes – if needed.
- Gradually breaking down fear and building up confidence through simulations and drill training – having the courage to step into the fray, to commit, and to do so naturally.
- Having fun/celebrations after training so that you begin to enjoy and thrive in the fact that once the commitment has

been taken, joining in the fray is part of the team experience and becomes enjoyable.

- Access to inspirational talks on purpose, commitment and contribution.
- Having a mentor or coach with the specific purpose of building resilience.
- Coping with setbacks, which, properly handled, can build up your resilience (this includes drawing on life's experiences, supported by friends, family or a mentor to talk through and give perspective/balance/help).
- Assertiveness training helps – finding the balance between losing your temper and being walked over, holding your own in the face of aggression.
- Exercise is known to regulate mood and help mental endurance.
- Good diet – limiting your intake of alcohol and sugar, and having plenty of fresh fruit and vegetables, and water.

Business Generals and Knowledge

Modern military commanders receive more formal training than many other professions. Most British officers today are graduates, less those who rise through the ranks – many of whom also complete a degree in mid-career in their own time. Officers also receive a full year's training in leadership. It is not in luxurious surroundings, not full of intellectuals and not just an exercise in thought. It is deliberately tough. Officer training covers the thinking, soul and practicalities of leadership, followed by the technical training appropriate to their speciality – all before being let loose on sailors, soldiers and airmen for the first time.

This balance is important: there is no point investing in giving someone who just does not have the resilience for command in war the 'technical' knowledge he would need in that position. Equally, the most stalwart, charismatic and tough natural leader can be an absolute menace in command if he or she is clueless about tactics or logistics. The same is true elsewhere: leaders need to know enough about the role that they have been assigned to, to put their character and other attributes to good use.

Your 'Need to Knows'

As a Business General you need to know the full and accurate details of the capacity, strengths and weaknesses of the organisation you lead. We have described the Power Pyramid in Secrets One, Two and Three as a model congruent with the tools and processes here. You may have to live with alternative models in your firm. That is fine. But the key is to be clear about the 'fit' between an organisation and its purpose in all the circumstances in which it finds itself and may find itself. Only then can it be tuned as necessary for maximum effect.

As a Business General you need to know the environment in which the organisation must work, covering all the factors that may affect success or failure. The leader must look outwards just as much as inwards, and this requirement increases with seniority: shift leaders may need only a narrow view of how their team can be affected by wider factors in the organisation and beyond, whereas the CEO may spend a majority of time monitoring and managing the effects of variables outside his or her direct control – such as competitors, regulators, government lobbying, currency fluctuations and suppliers.

As a Business General you need to know how to conduct the business of the organisation. Just as an admiral needs to be skilled in the handling of ships, submarines and aircraft in the maritime environment, so a managing director needs to know how his or her business works. This means knowing enough about the technical aspects of how business is done: production, investment, distribution, accounting, for example. For senior leaders, some of this may have been acquired through 'coalface experience', some of it is likely to have been acquired through training such as MBA courses, and some of it by consulting – and trusting relevant experts. For the Armed Forces, the investment in doctrine and training described in Secret Number One: Synchronised Thinking lays the foundations of how business is done.

As a Business General you need to know what success is and how to make it happen. This is hard to define exactly, but organisations expect their leaders to be able to do more than report succinctly that everything is ticking over nicely – they want leaders who have defined the meaning of success and know how to achieve it. An element of this is 'technical' stuff – how processes can be changed to get better results, for example. The most significant part of this, however, is the vital creative spark – that brilliant eye for seeing or creating opportunities and then grabbing the organisation by the lapels to propel it forward and seize them. (We have advocated approaches that foster this appetite for success in Secret Number Four: Dynamic Manoeuvre, Secret Number Five: Mission Management, and Secret Number Six: Command the Campaign.)

As a Business General you need to know how to learn from experience. A significant part of 'what you know' is making sure that success is repeated and failure is not. As already explained, the Armed Forces invest a great deal in formal 'Lessons Identified' processes as a routine part of running current operations (see Secret Number One, page 9).

Focus on What You Give and What You Want to Achieve

> '*Leadership is the art of getting someone else to do*
> *something you want done because he wants to do it.*'
>
> US GENERAL AND PRESIDENT DWIGHT D. EISENHOWER

The balance between 'who you are' and 'what you know' is important, but all the good work done in getting that balance just right can be lost if a leader does not actually go on and lead. To sit in an ivory tower knowing all, seeing all, yet doing nothing constructive with all that wisdom is doomed to failure. People expect their leaders to lead and will judge them by what they give to the organisation and what they want to achieve. This is called 'giving to the organisation'. By 'giving to the organisation', the Business General translates that plan into a form that is easily understood, usually through a combination of written and oral expression. The manner of this will depend partly on the size, structure and culture of the organisation and partly on the character of the leader. For example, in an ice-cool, hip-to-the-point-of-fainting-with-excitement sort of firm the plan will need to be conveyed clearly and sexily to inspire the staff. In a more conservative organisation, a more traditional form of written and verbal briefing may apply. In either case, slogans are not enough: the leader must get the substance of the message across so that people know full well what is required of them and how important it is. As in Secret Number Five: Mission Management, people must get the Intent as well as the action required of them.

Having told people what the plan is, the Business General has to 'make it happen'. He or she does this by getting into the minds of subordinates, informing but also inspiring, supervising, advising and calling to account.

'Opportunities multiply as they are seized.'
SUN TZU, THE ART OF WAR

'Making it happen' requires:

- Good-quality, timely and accurate information with which to review the situation and monitor progress.

- A good personal relationship with key subordinates, based on trust and honesty, where success is rewarded and failure is checked and rectified – with dismissal used only as a last resort.

- A good relationship with superiors and outside organisations, such as banks and the media that may affect the success of the plan. The more senior the leader, the more time may be taken up by these external organisations, but never to the point of entirely excluding in-house attention.

- A good relationship with everyone in the organisation, based on personal presentation, conduct and reputation. People at the lowest level should regard the leader of the organisation with respect and admiration, and so willingly commit themselves to 'the plan'. Leaders who are feared, loathed or disliked for lack of personal credibility will suffer from much-reduced effectiveness.

The point made above about the nature and quality of relationships indicates the significance of leaders making a conscious judgement about the style they bring to command. This is very obviously seen in high-level military leaders such as the British Field Marshal Bernard Montgomery: his ability to touch the souls of soldiers at all levels and make them believe they were winners was legendary. He backed this up with superb, meticulous planning for set-piece battles – and undermined it by his astonishingly arrogant handling of other British generals and US

Allied commanders. But he knew how to get an effective message across – and modern military leaders on the global stage such as the US General Tommy Franks who led the forces in the second Gulf War are just as charismatic and effective.

> *'The will to do, the soul to dare.'*
> SIR WALTER SCOTT, THE LADY OF THE LAKE

Some commanders, such as the Second World War US Army General George Patton, are simply built for war and much less adept in peacetime. General Patton was a brilliant commander of armoured forces and drove his men forward relentlessly, perhaps from time to time at greater cost than might have been the case, but there is no doubting his effectiveness in hard times. He would have been a complete menace in a less tenacious military environment, and a wholesale disaster in leadership roles in civilian life.

Some other leaders have struggled to illuminate the world with their brilliance because of their lack of colour and magnetism when the situation called for vibrant leadership. How many people do you know that have brains to spare, but no real training or facility for taking charge?

So, leaders must examine not just *what* they want to do, but also *how* they communicate and do it. Great thinking and commitment can be undermined just as much by over-assertiveness and bluster as it can by reticence. The question is what will work best for your organisation, and do you know how you come across anyway? How do you grab your organisation to make it go where you want it to?

COMMANDER'S COMFY CHAIR

Grabbing Your Organisation

Take a few hours to think about the following questions. You might decide that further work is required – over days/weeks.

Have you really thought through what you want your organisation to achieve?

How does this fit with your own life and goals?

Have you told your organisation what you want to achieve?

Did they take it in?

Did they believe you?

Have you checked?

Have you told your family what you want to achieve?

Will they support you?

Who do you most admire as a leader in your sector and why?

Have you thought about how you come across as a leader to your organisation?

Have you asked?

How can you be sure the answers were truthful?

When you look at yourself as a leader, from inside and out, do you like what you see?

What three things could you improve upon as a leader and why?

What are your three strongest points as a leader and why?

How much effort do you put into developing the leadership of your subordinates?

Could they manage in your unexpected absence?

Summary of Secret Number Seven: Ride the Tiger

- This Secret is about how Business Generals can exploit opportunities as they appear – in other words: seize the moment.

- In business – as in warfare – there will be problematic times and it is important to know how to deal with them. Rather than fear the unknown these situations can be seen as golden opportunities to be turned to your advantage.
- This means preparing your organisation so that you can make good decisions, even under pressure, and so react to events more quickly and more accurately than your competitors.

In Conclusion...

This completes *The 7 Secrets of Leadership Success*. Becoming a successful Business General requires that you have thought about what you want to achieve and – just as important – *how* you will impose your dreams on the organisation. This is about the characteristics you exhibit, as well as plans and procedures. Vision, imagination and drive need to be applied with an accurate understanding of how to bring people along. Successful Business Generals do not drag their followers like hostages into a dimly illuminated future. Knowing what you want to achieve is essential, but how you 'give' to your organisation will determine whether you get there or not.

Many of the ideas presented in this book have required deep concentration. Your pay-off is that having made that effort you now understand the thinking and can adapt it intelligently to make it fit your organisation. Once you understand the principles that apply and how the tools fit together, you can work creatively with the material. We wish you well and we make

THE 7 SECRETS OF LEADERSHIP SUCCESS

you an offer: let us know how you are doing – and where you could do with more information or support – via our website: www.thebusinessgeneral.com

This was never a book to skip through and treat lightly – there is your career at stake. As you go forward now, there is a balance to make about what you pick up and use, and how to adapt it. Your success will be determined by the character you show in doing this – your integrity, your commitment, your self-discipline and your resilience – as much as by the techniques you have learned.

Good luck!

Addendum

Since this book first came out in 2006 we have had the opportunity to speak to a range of audiences, civilian and military, about the key themes. The reaction has been interesting and challenging and the passage of world events over the same period has unsurprisingly influenced how people relate to what we have to say.

Amongst the military and ex-military there has been widespread enthusiasm for what the book conveys. For many, it has confirmed their instincts that the way contemporary Armed Forces manage their organisations, conceive strategies, plan complex operations, empower junior commanders to deliver well-specified objectives and much else bedsides is extremely valuable in a wider business setting. Many former Armed Force personnel in the UK enter civilian life with a certain amount of trepidation and wonder how they will fare. We are delighted where they have found the book a useful handrail as they engage in commerce, wider public service, or charitable work for the first time. We always hoped that it would make the learning and experience of modern Armed Forces more accessible, and if that includes assisting former soldiers, sailors, airmen and marines to assert their full potential outside the Armed Forces we are delighted. In some cases, we have even been told that a few still serving find the book a more understandable way of learning about and applying the techniques we cover in their military roles than the standard Service texts!

Of course, it takes two to tango: it is important to us that people with no knowledge of Armed Forces find the book helpful and accessible. This has actually proved harder than we had expected, and from an unexpected quarter. It surprised us that at every talk we gave to civilian audiences, the first or second question was always something like, 'Yes, but surely you just get things done in the Armed Forces because you are a strict hierarchy and people simply do as they are told?'

When we probed this further we found that most people have had so little contact with their Armed Forces today that they tried to interpret what we had to say through the prism of a very few common stereotypes. These were often found to be the General Melchett character from the TV series *Blackadder Goes Forth*, Captain Mainwaring in the BBC's long-running *Dad's Army*, and a medley of characters from the better known war films of the last 30 years or so such as *Saving Private Ryan* and *The Longest Day*. In other cases, the audience dwelt on the mythology surrounding major historical events that have involved armed conflict, such as the two world wars of the last century. The familiar 'lions led by donkeys' theme of the First World War, and the Herculean struggles of the first four years of the Second World War came to mind.

This is not surprising given the absence of first hand experiences to draw on, but it is disappointing if people elect to stick with what they think they know rather than open their minds to the bigger picture. We would often argue with the accuracy of these popular myths, but the point is that they *are* myths, otherwise the modern Armed Forces would never make it out of camp, let alone abroad on operations. Human nature is at play, of course, but we have never denied that there have been spectacular military failures across the course of history or that a few serving soldiers have not been exemplars of the contemporary doctrine; sadly there are cases of bullying but they are rare and are certainly not endorsed by senior commanding officers. What we do say is that the advice in this book is the product of centuries of the military looking at what works and what doesn't in conditions of high stress, uncertainty, chaos and ambiguity, so here is the chance to benefit from a truly dynamic learning process. Organisations across the world have suffered from the recession and are in need, more than ever, of a system of leadership development, planning and communication that works in times of change. We are suggesting that the methods inside this book are absolutely appropriate for business and charitable organisations post 2009.

The myth of the soldier operating as some sort of automaton has also been diminished by the greater coverage given recently to Servicemen and women engaged in current operations in Iraq and, especially, Afghanistan. A huge recent growth in public interest in the UK in the wellbeing and effectiveness of their soldiers in particular has been generated by politicians, senior military leaders and Service charities, including new charities such as Help for Heroes, which works closely with the popular media. This has been a very welcome change. Nowadays, it is becoming commonplace for battalions returning from Afghanistan to march through their local towns to a warm reception. These people in uniform are no different in principle from those applauding on the pavement. They are trained and experienced in hardship on operations but they are human beings who live, love and occasionally die in battle all the same. They are no more likely to succeed in difficult, frightening and complex situations simply by obeying than in any other walk of life.

Our hope is that anyone who has seen contemporay documentary material, or even short news clips, will be able to judge that military organisations achieve their results in trying circumstances because they build great teams of committed people, pulling in the same direction and bound together by trust and mutual respect. As we explain in Secret Two: Soul Matters, it is moral courage and self-discipline that count, not blind obedience. The poor economic climate means business leaderships across many industries have lost credibility and trust. The leaders need to work to regain the respect that is needed in order to align employees behind their mission and goals. Within this book, there are answers and solutions to those needs. The 7 Secrets illustrate just how to rebuild trust, create and communicate goals and missions, ensure that the communication has been understood and align focus of effort. They call upon the leader to show their character, use self-discipline and literally serve for the common good. A firm can steal a march on their competition and regain their reputation, their pride and their resilience with the guidance inside this book.

The other principal event relevant to us since the book was first published has been the way people perceive the situation in both Iraq and Afghanistan. When we wrote the book, Iraq was in turmoil and Afghanistan was just drawing into the wider public's consciousness. Since then, Iraq has made great strides towards a brighter future: there is an Iraqi Government in charge, Iraqi security forces have the lead and US forces have reduced in size and are reconfiguring to a short-term supporting role. There are still many problems to be dealt with, but Iraq is now a much more hopeful place.

We would argue that the methods applied by the senior military leadership in Iraq (US, British, Iraqi and others) have been pivotal in bringing about this improved state of affairs. They draw on the same methods outlined in this book, reinforced by massive commitment of will, professional skill and resources to see things through. The principles and techniques described in Secret One: Synchronised Thinking, Two: Soul Matters and Three: Right Team, Right Stuff can all be found in the way US and Iraqi forces have built organisations to see off insurgency and terrorism to the point where Iraq can start to focus on other things, even if residual terrorism is still being diminished. The elements of Secret Four: Dynamic Manoeuvre and the empowerment of Five: Mission Management have also been at the heart of how the Coalition has been able to bear down on the enemies of the new Iraq. There should be no surprise in this: these tools have been employed and refined in countless campaigns and provide a common basis for understanding for officers and soldiers around the globe. Still, it is reassuring to see the tools employed so successfully – and we hope this will add similar confidence to the reader.

For an example of the vast complexity of contemporary military operations, there is no better than modern-day Afghanistan. The legion challenges in supporting the Afghan people to build effective government, establish a functioning lawful economy, throw off the shackles of a hugely wealthy narco-economy, create a new army and police force, establish better relations with all neighbouring countries, as well as defeat the Taliban insurgency and weaken Al Qaeda, all combine in one of the greatest tests of leadership of our time. Distilling and resolving complexity into a campaign plan, applying 'operational art' and synchronising activities in areas as diverse as security operations and fiscal policy demand the sort of techniques described in Secret Six: Command the Campaign. We hope that in recognising this, our readers will be encouraged to look at how their own business careers can be enhanced by employing these methods themselves.

The search for new thinking and methods in commercial life has been sharpened by the onset of a major recession – gone, at least for now, are the conditions of plenty that probably allowed many organisations to coast along, and it is certainly the case that many businesses are searching for a new model to fit new circumstances. Governance and democracy is going to ask more from our leaders. MBA graduates from the Ivy League of universities have led firms into disrepute and collapse – business school alumni are recognising that the programmes they went on are not equipping them for the challenges they face. Good judgement is vital in leaders taking us beyond 2009 and the Mission Analysis process within this book alone would improve decision making in quick or strategic decisions. The 7 Secrets combined together build the foundation for strengthening the moral character of leaders and equipping them with tools and techniques to manage and lead through fast-changing and highly challenging situations.

We would assert that readers faced with these new straitened circumstances should take a hard look at how they organise and operate, and what are the essential things they need to do to be successful. They are faced with similar complexity, uncertainty and risk as the military commander in Afghanistan – albeit with probably less personal or political exposure. So it is worth dipping into these pages to see if a similar scale and complexity of challenge can be met successfully with similar tools. We believe we can encourage businesses with their back to the wall to find something in this book that puts them on the road to a more prosperous future. Whether this is finding the moral courage to take and impose hard decisions, see the value in investing in training, helping engage all employees behind the company mission statement, empowering people to decide 'the how' of every 'what', or exploiting all their talents, this is a book that is intended to help in the bad times as well as the good. We wish you well in winning.

Index

INDEX

About the Authors

Deborah Tom is a Chartered Occupational Psychologist, Fellow of the RSA, Certified Management Consultant and Member of the Worshipful Company of Management Consultants. She has been Managing Director for nearly 20 years of www.human-systems.biz, a management consultancy that has won awards for work on strategy, employee engagement, developing capability and culture.

Her clients include many of the FTSE 100 and Fortune 50 – IBM, KPMG, PwC, Cable and Wireless, British Medical Association, British Airways, Yo, myhotel, SunMicrosystems, BAE Systems and the BBC. She is the author of *Find the Balance* for BBC Books and is doing a doctorate in the Components of Successful Leadership.

Major General Richard Barrons CBE is a serving Army officer. He has broad experience on operational duty. He was Chief of Staff of 5,000 soldiers drawn from 19 nations for the International Security Assistance Force in Afghanistan and Chief of Staff of a multinational division of Coalition Forces in Southern Iraq; a commander in Northern Ireland and Chief of Staff of a Brigade of 5,000 soldiers in Bosnia and Commanding Officer of an artillery regiment in Kosovo.

He was Military Assistant to Chief of the General Staff, contributing to the 1997 Strategic Defence Review in the Ministry of Defence. Working closely with governments, the UN and EU, he has contributed to finding joint, multinational solutions in the midst of complex emergencies. He has a Masters in Defence Administration and has attended the UK's Higher Command and Staff Course.

The authors can be contacted via their website:
www.thebusinessgeneral.com

If you are interested in the learnings
from this book please visit the website
www.thebusinessgeneral.com
or email info@thebusinessgeneral.com